Memories
of an
SOE Historian

Memories
of an
SOE Historian

M.R.D. Foot

Pen & Sword
MILITARY

First published in Great Britain in 2008 by
Pen & Sword Military
An imprint of
Pen & Sword Books Ltd
47 Church Street
Barnsley
South Yorkshire
S70 2AS

Copyright © M.R.D. Foot

ISBN 978 1 84415 849 2

Typeset in 10pt Palatino by Mac Style, Nafferton, East Yorkshire
Printed and bound in the UK
By Biddles

Pen & Sword Books Ltd incorporates the Imprints of Pen & Sword
Aviation,
Pen & Sword Maritime, Pen & Sword Military, Wharncliffe Local History,
Pen & Sword Select, Pen & Sword Military Classics, Leo Cooper,
Remember When, Seaforth Publishing and Frontline Publishing

For a complete list of Pen & Sword titles please contact
PEN & SWORD BOOKS LIMITED
47 Church Street, Barnsley, South Yorkshire, S70 2AS, England
E-mail: enquiries@pen-and-sword.co.uk
Website: www.pen-and-sword.co.uk

For MRIS
in memory of
RMF and cmf

Contents

CHAPTER 1

Ancestry

Günter Grass was quite right to say, in *The Tin Drum*, that 'no one ought to tell the story of his life who hasn't the patience to say a word or two about at least half of his grandparents before plunging into his own existence'. So I begin with Frances Sophie Daniell, who later became my grandmother. She got engaged to be married in 1891. She wrote to her mother's brother, the formidable John Arbuthnot Fisher – known to the Navy as Jackie – who was already a junior Naval Lord, to invite him to the wedding. She was sure that he would like her future husband, who though only twenty-five was already adjutant of his regiment.

Out of his reply there fell a ten-pound note, which caused a sensation at the breakfast table of her father, a clergyman in Southsea. She danced round the table waving it, until her mother told her to sit down and go back to the envelope – surely Jack had written a note as well?

Indeed he had. She was to get herself something nice to wear at her wedding with the enclosed, and as she was being such a damned fool as to marry a soldier, she need never expect to hear again from her affectionate Uncle Jack. Nor did she. She wrote when each of her children was born, inviting him to the christening; no reply. My grandfather wrote, when she died of the second baby, inviting him to the funeral; no reply.

Frances came from an East Anglian family of Daniells, gentry and scholars. My aunt liked to trace them back to Angers in the eleventh century. I hope Frances was related to the great lawyer and historian F W Maitland, whose mother was Emma Daniell, but have not yet clinched the connection.

Our branch of the Foot or Foote family – the final e is optional, one of my father's first cousins used it – traces back to John Foot, son of Simon Foot, born in Truro in the 1660s, and one of the thousands of Cornishmen worried about Bishop Trelawny who marched on London during the Seven Bishops' crisis of 1687. A Canadian cousin has a photograph of a Tudor house in Truro, which bears the family coat of arms. A succession of

Foots, forenamed John and Simon in turn, reached back at least to the mid-sixteenth century, Cornish minor gentry.

The London of 1687 soon proved too hot to hold this John Foot, who had to skip to Holland, whence he came back with King William III, near whose elbow he waded through the Boyne in 1690 as an ensign in Moore's regiment of infantry. (By a piece of family vanity, he was remembered as having been a cornet in Moore's regiment of cavalry, which did not exist.) The king thought well enough of him to give him a small estate at the southern tip of Co Carlow, called Rosbercon, where he settled. His son Jeffery married Jane, niece of Robert Lundy, who had taken the other side in King William's war and tried to betray Londonderry to King James II. Having had an ancestor on each side in that struggle has perhaps been a help, generations later, when trying to get a clear view of the Irish question.

John Foot was first cousin once removed to Samuel Foote the dramatist, acquaintance of Dr Johnson, a spectacular though not always respectable figure on the London stage and buried in Westminster Abbey – before that became a real distinction. John's descendant Lundy Foot sold snuff in Dublin – Mr Grattan was a devoted customer – and figures in the Oxford English Dictionary, under 'lundifoot', the name of his best snuff, as well as in *Ulysses*, when the Viceroy's procession goes past his shop (on which I once set eye) near Essex Bridge. He lived at Holly Park, Dublin, now a convent, in a style fit for an alderman.

When he was not quite three, he was seen at a ball in Trim dancing a few steps with his grandmother's grandmother, who was then a hundred and twelve, and lived five years more – an Irish story, not necessarily false. For one of his sons, Randal, he bought a commission in a cavalry regiment. As Randal's father was in retail trade, his brother officers cut him; he always seemed to be orderly officer, or to have other tiresome tasks loaded on him. He noticed that on guest nights in the mess anybody might, over the port, send his own snuffbox round the table. One night, he sent round the table a double-sided snuffbox, in one half of it his father's best snuff, in the other a pair of balls for duelling pistols. Everyone took snuff with him, thus establishing that he was a gentleman after all. He went out eventually to Australia. I like to think of him as ancestor of the two Australian Foott brothers who won Victoria Crosses in my own lifetime – perhaps more family vanity.

This Lundy's grandson, also Lundy Foot, son and father of clergymen, was rector of Long Bredy in Dorset for over thirty years, an archdeacon and a canon of Salisbury. One of his younger sons, by his second wife Harriett Cunningham, was my great-grandfather. Harriett was a daughter of J W Cunningham, once fifth wrangler at Cambridge, later a figure in the Clapham sect, and for fifty years vicar of Harrow. He makes a brief appearance in the *Dictionary of National Biography*, inserted by his dutiful nephew-in-law, the editor. Peel, Palmerston, and Aberdeen, all Harrow men later Prime Ministers, must have known him, but none of them put him up for a bishopric. One of Harriett's sisters married Sir James Fitzjames Stephen the judge, son of Mr Over-Secretary Stephen of the colonial office and brother of Sir Leslie Stephen the founder-editor of DNB, so Harriett was an aunt-in-law of Virginia Woolf as well as a connexion of Thackeray, though I do not think my branch of the family took in the fact. I certainly did not, till I was past eighty. Nor did I realise till I read Hermione Lee's life of Virginia Woolf that one of Fitzjames Stephen's daughters, Barbara, married a nephew of Florence Nightingale, another connexion of which to be proud.

My future grandfather was the third of the six sons of the Reverend Cunningham Noel Foot, who was a younger son of Lundy Foot of Long Bredy and became rector of Dogmersfield in northern Hampshire. Now Dogmersfield was a plum, like Hawarden: one of the few parishes in the Church of England that had a sizeable stipend attached to it, something like £3,000 a year, an unusually large sum for the 1860s, several times the average. This plum may have fallen to him by a stroke of luck, for he was up at Trinity, Cambridge, where he took a bachelor's degree in divinity, with young Mildmay, the local squire who inherited the living and was my grandfather's godfather.

Edwin, the eldest of the six sons, ran away on his twenty-first birthday. He returned thirty years later, bronzed, with a grown-up daughter; he had retired on his pension. Who had pensioned him? The Lion of Judah and Emperor of Abyssinia, whose chief forester he had been for many years. He wrote a grammar of the Galla language, reprinted by Oxford University Press in the 1970s. He settled at Wimborne Minster in Dorset, remarried (his first wife, whom none of the rest of the family met, was dead), and died early in 1940. His cottage was destroyed by a chance incendiary bomb jettisoned by a fleeing German bomber later that year. I turned out to be among his legatees when his widow died at the end of the war. My share in the estate came to a thousand pounds, which I put into a house purchase, a few pieces of furniture, and £150 in cash (which I blued on a life subscription to the London Library – where it now will not cover half a single year's membership, so it was a lucky investment).

The second brother, Cunningham, went into the Navy. He was a term-mate in *Britannia* with Prince George, the future King George V, long before it was clear that the prince (Wales's second son) was going to become king. I knew Cunningham when I was at Winchester; he lived within bicycling distance at Wickham. By then his wife was dead. They had had no children, and he rather enjoyed having me to talk to. He did a lot to clarify the way I expressed myself on paper. He claimed to have been one of the midshipmen present at a navigation class in the North Sea, at which the instructor said to another – trying unsuccessfully to establish the ship's position – 'Young man, take off your hat. You are standing in York Minster.' This may only be one of the stories sailors enjoy telling each other.

By 1916 Cunningham had risen to be a Captain and to command a pre-Dreadnought battleship, still kept in commission by the Navy in a squadron of sister ships in the Thames estuary. They weighed anchor to take part in the battle of Jutland, but it was over before they got there. At the end of the war he retired from the sea, with a CBE, and settled near Dinan in Brittany with his wife, who was a descendant of Bligh who survived the mutiny in the *Bounty* in 1789, and has been turned by Hollywood into a villain (he had been in his day the next most popular captain to Nelson in the Navy). Cunningham's generation moved up the Navy List automatically, as naval officers had done for centuries, so that he died a full admiral in 1940. One of his forenames was de Clare, to celebrate what his parents believed to be his descent from the earls of Clare who included Strongbow, who first asked the Irish question in 1169, and William Marshall who made King John sign Magna Carta. I am now sorry I never got him to trace out the descent for me.

Even royal descent, on the wrong side of the blanket, has been claimed for the family. Benjamin Fayle (*floruit* in the late eighteenth century), whose granddaughter Sophia married C N Foot is supposed to have married a by-blow of George II. There is in the family a good mid-eighteenth-century chair, upholstered in dark red plush with a fleur-de-lys motif, handed on for several generations as 'the King's chair'. A stronger piece of evidence is that my father and the Duke of Gloucester who was brother to George VI looked very much alike *circa* 1946. I leave this point inconclusive.

Sophia Fayle's sister Isabella married an Indian army officer called Freddie Bagshaw, who fought in the second Sikh war, and was shot dead on the day the mutiny of 1857 broke out at Jullundur. His wife had just been confined, and came out of labour to find her stillborn son one side of her and her husband's body on the other. She survived to recount this to my father long afterwards.

There were three younger Foot brothers, siblings of my grandfather: Alfred who never married, Charles who went into business in Sheffield, and St John who went away to Canada and set up an early motor car business. Edwin, Charles and St John all also have living descendants.

My grandfather, Richard Mildmay Foot (RMF), was born at Dogmersfield in October 1865, just in Lord Palmerston's lifetime. He went to Westward Ho!, Price's new public school on the Devon coast near Bideford, where he met and befriended the young Kipling, a couple of months younger than himself; he was I believe the original of Dick Tertius, a minor character in *Stalky & Co*. He and Kipling exchanged Christmas cards often thereafter, but were never (so far as I know) close friends, though they both became freemasons. He can be seen, wearing a prominent Albert watch-chain, in a well known photograph of the schoolboy Kipling among his companions. RMF went on to Sandhurst, where he was a term-mate of Haig, and passed out moderately. He became an officer in the Inniskilling Fusiliers, an Ulster county regiment (the 27th Foot) with a fine fighting record in the past, immortalised by Kipling in his soldier stories as the Black Tyrone. He was with it on the last occasion when the British Army fought in red coats, at a battle on the Umvolosi River in the now almost forgotten second Zulu war of 1888. Of the two British battalions present, the Inniskillings wore blue, but the Royal Scots wore red.

The Inniskillings had arrived late for the battle of Waterloo. They did not arrive as late as Lord Portarlington, whose private arrangements kept him off the battlefield until seven in the evening – he arrived just in time to have his horse shot under him in one of the last charges of the day – but they arrived late. Indeed, their colonel was still at sea, with all the majors and several other officers who were good at whist, enjoying a leisurely journey home from the United States, where they had helped to burn the President's house (which had to be repainted White) when the British captured Washington. They handed the bulk of the regiment over to the senior captain, Hare, who was made acting major for the journey, and was in command on the afternoon of 18 June 1815 when they marched on to the ridge beyond Waterloo, and were ordered to hold its centre. Next morning they were still there, in an eyewitness's words 'lying dead in square'. This spectacle is said to have triggered off Wellington's well-known remark that, next to a battle lost, the most melancholy sight he knew was of a battle won. Of the seventeen officers present, all were knocked down except Hare and one other, and the two still upright were both wounded, but they held their square. Three in five of their men were killed or severely wounded, but they too held their square. During the battle, a neighbouring regiment sent word across – plenty of subalterns to spare, would the 27th care to borrow some? Hare replied that the sergeants rather enjoyed commanding the companies, and he was loth to deprive them of the privilege.

One of the regiment's drummer-boys, aged twelve, survived the battle, and lived on into his own nineties; the regiment kept him, as a sort of human mascot. Not long before he died he gave his Waterloo medal to the adjutant's daughter, then a little girl of two. This was my father's only sibling, Lindsey, who left the medal to me (it was stolen from me during a house move). This means the battle of Waterloo is only two very long lifetimes away – a point drummed in to me by a *Times* obituary on 7 November 2002, of Eugenie Fraser, *née* Scholts, who was dandled on the knee of an old lady who could remember having seen Napoleon's army retreating from Moscow in 1812.

My father, Richard Cunningham Foot (Dickie to the family, Daddy to me) was born at Dover in November 1892. The regiment then moved to Ireland – it is a myth that Irish regiments were never stationed on Irish soil – and his sister Lindsey Kathleen was born at Kinsale in 1894. But her mother never recovered, and died a few months later at Rincurran in Co Cork, leaving my grandfather with two small children to bring up as best he could. He stayed with the regiment, having no other source of income, and the children had largely to be left to nursemaids. Their upbringing was strict. At breakfast, for example, one could have butter or marmalade on one's toast, to have both at once was greedy. Dickie once decided he would not eat his porridge at breakfast. He got nothing else for breakfast, and had the porridge put in front of him at lunch, at tea, at supper, at breakfast next day, and so on till it grew a mould and he was at last allowed something else to eat. Lindsey, when aged about twelve, got up every morning to be dressed with a holly sprig in the neck of her blouse, to teach her to keep her head upright; which indeed she did, for she always carried herself superbly, showing off a fine Roman nose, for which the gene must be lurking in the family somewhere – though, like the gene for my mother's fine shade of auburn hair, it has not yet shown up again.

RMF had a few friends outside the regiment, including the Cooper family, whose recent ancestor had made a great deal of money, over a million pounds – then a colossal sum – out of Cooper's Sheep Dip in Australia, where it saved sheep from ravaging attacks by ticks. This family settled in England, and had two large country houses: the grander at Shenstone Court near Lichfield, later a madhouse, the other at Ashlyns near Berkhampstead in Hertfordshire, now vanished. Richard, its head, became a baronet in 1905.

My grandfather happened to be staying at Ashlyns in the autumn of 1899, on leave, when he got a telegram from his successor as adjutant: the regiment had just received a warning order to proceed overseas to South Africa, where trouble was impending with the Boers. My grandfather made his apologies to his hostess, and asked if he might see a railway timetable. The womenfolk fussed over him: who was going to look after him? They supposed he had a batman – was he any good? My grandfather indicated, no. Well, would he like to take one of their footmen? My grandfather had rather taken to Herbert – did he mean Ashlyns Herbert, or Shenstone Herbert? Ashlyns Herbert was sent for, and asked whether he would like to go with Captain Foot to fight in South Africa? He would like to very much, and was sworn in to the Inniskillings a few hours later. This was Herbert Camfield, my grandfather's constant companion for the rest of his life. He was a tall, quiet, gentle man, who became a dissenting lay preacher, infinitely patient with children – though married by the time I knew him, he had none of his own – and always conscious of his place below the salt.

The 27th were in Hart's Irish brigade, and soon in action on the advance to relieve Ladysmith. On 27 February 1900, in the final battle of this campaign at Pieter's Hill, my grandfather was wounded in the head, and left isolated in front of the battalion. Some nearby Boers called on him to surrender. He gave the correct reply, 'I'll die first', or so the newspaper legend soon had it. His own diary says that he called out an ancient Ulster slogan, 'No surrender' Either way, he survived, and with a corporal's help managed after dark to roll over and over, away down the hill, rejoining the Irish lines next morning with seven companions, all wounded.

The incident caught the fancy of a war correspondent, and the story was telegraphed home. It earned RMF a full-page illustration in *The Sphere*, then a large-format illustrated weekly. He and his brother officers thought this rather bad form, as one's name was never supposed to appear in the papers at all, except for birth, marriage and death, but nothing could be done about it. (The picture reappeared, without his name attached to it, in a recent volume of Inniskilling diaries.) The tale stayed buried in the files, and then emerged again; most of his short obituaries when he died in 1933 were headlined 'Boer War Hero'. The high command was also impressed. He was offered the choice of a DSO or a brevet majority. As the brevet would be paid, he accepted that, not knowing that the 27th's field officer casualties were so heavy that in three weeks' time he was promoted major anyway. Later, he reckoned that he had made a mistake, because a DSO against his name would have helped to distinguish him from most of his fellows, and might – had he stayed in the regular army – have led on to a command of importance.

When he had recovered from his wound, he was transferred to army administration, with which he saw out the war. Towards the end of it, he fell under the spell of the eldest Cooper daughter, christened Lucy Anne but always known as Dolly, who had gone out to Cape Town in search of a husband; they were married there in May 1902. The villagers of Shenstone presented her, as the squire's eldest daughter, with a silver salver on the occasion of her marriage, a custom that seems to have died out. She did not care for garrison life, and a few years later persuaded RMF, as there were still too many majors senior to him in the regiment for him to have any chance of commanding it, that he would do better to resign and live on her money, as he did. They settled at White Hill, Berkhampstead, where Herbert Camfield became their butler.

Soon thereafter, my grandfather got a persuasive personal letter from R. B. Haldane, the new Secretary of State for War. The various reserve forces were about to be amalgamated into a new second-line force, to be called the Territorial Force. RMF was exactly the sort of man to form one of its new units; would he do so? He thus became the founder lieutenant-colonel of the 4th East Anglian Field Brigade, Royal Field Artillery (TF), from 1907 to May 1914, when for the second time he retired. On retirement, his fellow officers presented him with a silver salver, of a design by Hester Bateman, with his coat of arms on the front and all their names on the back – another custom that seems to have died out.

He lived the life of a country gentleman, and sent his children to decent schools. Dickie went to Hillside, Godalming, where he met several Huxleys and Gielguds, and then on to Winchester, where he spent four energetic years, winning in his last half the school's French prize. A. P. Herbert,

Stafford Cripps, Oswald Mosley, Charles Portal, and A. J. Toynbee were among his schoolfellows, though he knew none of them well. Rockley Wilson who taught him French was still teaching French over twenty-five years later, as Clement Vavasour Durell who had taught him maths was still teaching maths. Lindsey went to Wycombe Abbey, where – grander than her brother – she became head girl.

My grandfather had one sister, Catharine, who married a Dr Grove, and died young, leaving a boy, Peter, on whom she asked my grandfather to keep an eye. Peter went (at my grandfather's expense) to Cambridge, to read engineering, but this left no money, as Dolly was disinclined to provide it, for my father to go to Oxford or Cambridge. He went instead to the School of Mines in South Kensington, commuting in daily by train from Berkhampstead. He spent four years there, playing rugger (Harlequins, wing three-quarter) and enjoying himself, while also working hard. In 1912 his father said to him that he did not like the look of the newspapers; he thought there would soon be another Great War. Had Dickie not better join his TF unit? He did, and Second Lieutenant R. C. Foot's is one of the names on the back of the Bateman salver.

Dickie never forgot being sent down a mine near St Just, in Cornwall, and along a gallery in it till he could hear waves breaking just above his head. He may not have needed this exercise much, having been struck by some lines he had to utter while acting Julius Caesar in a school play at Hillside, and often quoted later:

Of all the wonders that I yet have heard
It seems to me most strange that men should fear;
Seeing that death, a necessary end,
Will come when it will come.

When it came to his finals, he and a few friends discovered that their last paper was to be a chemistry practical, from two to four in the afternoon. They decided to celebrate by taking some girls out on the river at Maidenhead. For that, and the restaurant they meant to dine in, white tie and tails were in those days indispensable. Where were they going to change, if they caught the 4.30 from Paddington, a twenty-minute walk across the park from the School? There would be no time to change at the School, no facilities on the train, and no gentleman dreamed of entering a public lavatory. They looked closely at the university's rules for academic dress, and turned up to take their chemistry practical in white tie and tails. They were all rusticated for impertinence, which meant that they had to take their degrees all over again in September. But this was in June 1914; by September they were all in uniform. My father was the only survivor.

He went out, with a territorial division, to relieve regular troops in Egypt, and was sent for by the senior Royal Artillery officer there. He was a gunner, therefore he knew about survey? Yes he did, because he had studied it at the School of Mines. So he was sent off into the Sinai desert, with a bombardier and a theodolite and a small camel corps escort (the general predicted, correctly, that he would have no trouble with the Turks), and came back a month later with his survey of the peninsula complete. A great many years later, when he was living in Australia on his final career as an export-import merchant, an Israeli customer with whom he had made friends by letter came to visit him, bringing with him the maps on which he had fought the Six Days' War of 1967. My father was delighted to find that the senior on the list of surveys on which the maps were founded was 'Foot, 1915'. After his death, I tried to trace his original map through the woman who had just taken charge of the army's mapping department. She could not find it. We supposed it to have been burned during the great flap in Cairo in July 1942, when the staff believed Rommel was about to arrive. Auchinleck the commander-in-chief had steadier nerves. Rommel was repulsed at First Alamein, and then beaten back by Alexander, Montgomery and the Eighth Army at Second Alamein in the autumn.

My father was promoted major as a reward for his survey, and posted to the Western Front. There he commanded D battery of 4.5-inch howitzers in 310 Brigade, Royal Field Artillery, in Braithwaite's 62nd Division, for the rest of the war. The task of these howitzer batteries was to provide close-range support for the infantry in front of them, both in barrages to check enemy attacks and in counter-battery fire against enemy field guns that were causing our infantry discomfort. In his seventies he wrote an account of his war, which I have lodged at the Imperial War Museum and hope one day to publish.

He remembered an evening when he went forward, as his own observation officer, to an infantry brigade he had not visited before. He found its headquarters, not the usual thousand yards or so behind the front line, but right in it, in a dug-out. They were New Zealanders, and the brigade commander, about his own age, was already wearing a DSO. He was invited to stay to dinner, after which the brigadier-general told his brigade major to wake him in half an hour, dropped his head on his hands, and instantly fell fast asleep. He woke at a touch on his elbow, and invited my father to come for a walk with him. His idea of a walk was to go through both sets of wire, and lie close under the German parapet for a few minutes, trying to pick up some intelligence of interest. This was Freyberg, later VC, of whom Dickie wrote afterwards that 'in battle he had no peer'.

He left out of his memoirs a story I once heard him tell. In 1916 he was riding over French downland, some way behind the lines, with an acquaintance. A magpie got up, and Dickie, from force of long habit, saluted it. His companion protested – surely one should only salute the King's or an Ally's uniform? My father replied that magpies were Hecate's birds, and it brought bad luck to ignore them. A moment later, their paths diverged, and a moment later still, a stray shell arrived out of nowhere and burst beside the other's horse, killing it and wounding him. Dickie galloped over to pick him up, and heard him murmur before he passed out, 'I shall never fail to salute a magpie again.'

On leave in London in 1916, Dickie went to the Gaiety Theatre in the Strand, and was bowled over by the looks of one of the girls in the chorus. During the interval, instead of going to the bar he slipped out and bought a bunch of flowers, waited for her at the stage door after the performance, and, a few months later, married her.

Of my mother's family I know all but nothing, and she forbade her children ever to make any inquiries about it, saying only that she had had a very unhappy childhood. She only ever produced one relative, her older half-sister Allie (Alice Maud Riddiford), an absolute dear who died, aged sixty, in 1934. My mother's stage name was Nina Raymond, which she gave as her maiden name on her passport. Allie's father, as I know from Allie's death certificate, was called John Raymond Riddiford, and had been a village policeman at Merstham in Surrey. By the time my parents were married, he had gone to Canada, and was variously described by my father as 'of Toronto', 'of Quebec', or 'of Montreal'. Again, I leave this inconclusive.

The Foot family, collectively, told my father that, yes, they would receive his new wife, but on the understanding that she gave up her profession on marriage. She complied. But Allie, I noticed long afterwards, never appeared at White Hill.

Nina had done something of distinction before she met Dickie: before the war, she had been one of the first, perhaps the very first, of Englishwomen ever to go up in an aeroplane. She absolutely detested it, and took care never to step into one again. Her friends in the Gaiety chorus – one of whom married a marquis – teased her with netting nobody grander than an army major, but she and my father were, to start with, entirely devoted to each other. They were married on 29 May 1917, on my father's next spell of leave from France. During their honeymoon, he took her down to Winchester, where she had never been, and they called on James Fort, his old housemaster. Fort produced a house photograph, taken in June 1910. Of the forty men on it, four at that moment were still on their feet, and the war had another eighteen months to run. While my father commanded D/310, a total of seventeen officers served in it, never more than five at a time, so rapid was the rate of casualty and rotation. He used his engineering knowledge to buttress his guns properly with sandbags, whenever he could, and recalled an occasion when the battery site came under continuous accurate counter-battery fire by a German medium battery, for twelve hours on end, with an hour's break for a meal in the middle. He had one gun out of action for half an hour, and one man hurt, so effective were his defences.

Once he was badly gassed: mustard gas blinded him. Yet eight days later, he was back in action with his battery. I can thus denounce as false that world-famous picture by Sargent, now in the Imperial War Museum, of a long line of blindfolded men, waiting their turn for hospital while soldiers play football in the background. Most of that line would have been back in action within ten days, as well.

On one most uncomfortable morning, D/310 was lined up beside two other howitzer batteries for a special shoot, but supplied with defective ammunition. Two guns had shells that burst in the muzzle, killing some of their crews – neither in Dickie's own battery, but everyone was waiting for it to happen again, not good for any sort of morale. As they were withdrawing to their more usual position, they ran into a Lancer sergeant carrying a pennon, followed by a very senior officer, whom my father saluted before recognising him as Haig. Haig remembered the name of Foot, and then remembered to have met Dickie before, at White Hill; was sympathetic to the tale of faulty ammunition, and made a note, then said 'Who's that?', gesturing to a body on a limber. Dickie explained that he had lost a subaltern that morning to a chance shell splinter, and had not yet had time to bury him. Haig asked for the lad's address, and wrote a suitable letter to his parents: not the received view of Haig, but true.

My grandfather was also at war and was again wounded, by a chance shell that hit a cottage in which he had paused for a rest while on one of his interminable rounds of inspection. He had of course been dug out – recalled to the army – in August 1914, and spent two years in England preparing two Territorial divisions in turn to go forward to fight. In one of them, the 47th (London) Division, he became a byword for precision and form-filling, evidently feeling (he was the division's chief administrator) that amateur soldiers could only be got to fight correctly if they did everything by the book. He got to France in time for the Somme, and by the end of the war had reached brigadier-general, as Field-Marshal Plumer's chief administrator. Plumer and Jacob, under whom he also served, both thought highly of him. Camfield had again gone with him as his batman. When his corps ammunition dump caught fire RMF secured the DSO that he had foregone in South Africa. Instead of staying at his desk he went down and supervised firefighting on the spot, with ammunition going off all round him. His skills as an administrative and supply officer were well regarded; he was also appointed CMG and CB.

Dickie too was decorated, though not so lavishly. He received an MC for his work in softening up the approaches to the Hindenburg Line. At the end of the war he was also awarded a Star of Roumania, which he always described as a failed bar to his MC. Lindsey had not been idle either. She was out in France as well, as a VAD nurse, from the spring of 1915. My mother had a less combative war, but hardly an enjoyable one. She never forgot how disagreeable the Gotha daylight bombing raids on London had been. She and Allie shared a flat in Maida Vale; she got a major's married allowance to live on. At the end of the war, she took a short lease on a little house in Herne Hill, where Dickie soon joined her. Once he described to me exactly where it was, but I have retained no detail.

CHAPTER 2

Childhood

When the Great War ended, my father with his incomplete university degree was in the very first batch to be demobilised from the army. (My grandfather took faint umbrage; he was let out a couple of months later, on grounds of advanced age.) The School of Mines congratulated Dickie and gave him a BSc without further ado, as he had got first-class marks. He went straight home and set about begetting me on my mother, only turning to look for work when he knew she was pregnant. By then London was full of majors with MCs seeking jobs. He had to apply for fifty-nine before he got one, as assistant engineer to Peek Frean the biscuit manufacturers in Bermondsey. Within seven years he had become their general manager.

I was born in London on Sunday, 14 December 1919, but did not flourish. I weighed less when I was six months old than when I was born. Every Sunday morning my father used to weigh me, on the kitchen scales. The results were so depressing that my mother would burst into tears, leaving him to stalk off to church alone. She tried breast-feeding me; I threw it up. She tried many recommended kinds of baby milk; I treated them all with equal scorn. Just enough got down me to keep me alive, but I must have been a puling, ill-tempered brat, and a distress to both my parents. All three of us went to stay for a few days with the Coopers, who had moved a few miles from Ashlyns to Felden Lodge (also now tumbled down), near Boxmoor. The nanny at Felden sympathized with my mother, and suggested it might be worth while offering me a rusk. She was right, and at last I began to put on weight. I have never yet grown bulky, and trust – in an England now overshadowed by obesity – that I never shall.

For several years, it suited my parents to leave me for long spells at my grandparents' house, White Hill, close to the ruins of Berkhampstead Castle where the newly married Black Prince once lived. White Hill's freehold belonged to the Coopers, to whom it reverted when both my grandparents were dead. (The place was then bought up by a speculative builder, who made sure the house burned down, felled all the trees, put up seventeen houses on the site, and died.) They were too busy to have much time to spare for me. So far as anybody brought me up in detail, it was the butler, Mr Camfield (as I was told always to call him) who did. He in turn always called me Master Michael. Sometimes I was allowed to watch him clean the silver, which he kept in a walk-in safe almost as tall as himself, in the pantry wall. He taught me simple rules which I remember daily about handling silver, such as never putting forks and spoons into the same bowl, lest the tines of the forks scratch the bowls of the spoons. A great many years later, when I said a word (I hope gently) about finding spoons and forks together in a bowl of suds, my wife Mirjam cried 'Shall I ever be free of Mr Camfield's ghost?'

White Hill was a long, three-storied house, built about 1840. Years afterwards, I saw Darwin's Down House, which had a similar feel and was about the same size. Its largest room included a billiard table, later passed over by my grandfather to his brother-in-law, the second baronet, who had settled up the hill at another Shenstone Court, where Dolly's three Cooper nephews played on it. Behind the billiard table was a big glass-fronted Sheraton bookcase, which eventually came to me. Once I took the airgun out of the gun cupboard a few paces away, found a slug for it, and in a thoughtless moment loaded and fired it, at a cardboard box. Of course the slug shot through the box and broke a pane of glass at the bottom of the bookcase. My furious grandmother would never have it repaired, so that the cracked pane should be a standing reproach to me, as it was for years. When the bookcase was moved into my house the removal men supposed they had broken it themselves, and sent a boy to repair it. Eventually, again, I converted the gun cupboard into a bookcase. It now has poetry in the top half and maps in the cupboard below, which used to hold trout flies and ammunition. I sold the guns, getting little for them, except for the revolver, which I kept until government went mad about hand guns, when I passed it over to the Imperial War Museum. They were delighted to have it, believing it to be a very early model. If they took off the trigger guard I had had fitted, they would have been undeceived.

My father had brought back from the Western Front a couple of brass eighteen-pounder shell cases, kept one for a gong and gave the other to White Hill, where it hung in the hall over an old black oaken chest of drawers reputed to have belonged to John Foot (which is still in the family). Several times a day, Camfield would strike this gong with a mallet, to summon us to meals, and half an hour before dinner to warn the grown-ups to change. My grandmother always changed her clothes for the evening meal, long after the menfolk in her household had given up appearing in dinner jackets – as everybody who was anybody normally did in the 1920s. (I recently met the grandson of the third earl of Selborne, who assured me that his grandfather always put on a black tie for dinner, at least up to the end of the 1960s.)

There were quite a dozen servants at White Hill. Brown the groom, a small brown-faced man who had spent all his life close to horses, sometimes had a stable boy as well, to help him muck out. John Brown the chauffeur, much younger and brisker, preferred to do everything himself. He had two motor cars to look after, and in the twenties, my grandfather still carried the family crest, a martlet, discreetly on the door of one of them – a left-over from the days when one kept one's crest on the door of one's carriage. Collins the gardener had Wilmore who had served in the 27th to help him, and sometimes a boy as well. Every spring, Camfield would take the .22" rifle out of the gun cupboard, and bombard the rooks' nests in the beeches beside the drive. A long hornbeam hedge ran beside the railway cutting beyond the garden; the whole house, built on chalk, shook gently when an express passed through. My grandfather always pruned the roses himself, and taught me how to do it, but Collins was otherwise left to garden as he chose. One of his specialities was grapes – succulent large black grapes, grown on vines in a hothouse. That ceased quietly during the depression of the 1930s. Mrs Collins, a splendid woman, looked after dogs, chickens and dairy, sometimes helped by her daughter Grace. The Collinses lived in the lodge, by the steep front drive gate. Off the back drive, there was a big wooden shed in one end of which my grandfather had a dark-room, in which he tried to develop his own photographs – this was well before everybody took photographs round to a local shop to be developed and printed. He even made a few experiments with film, with a hand-held camera. The rest of the shed was a carpenter's shop, in which John Brown the chauffeur taught me a little about carpentry, a skill at which I have remained resolutely ten-thumbed, unlike my father, who had learned to be a sound carpenter under Laverty at Winchester.

Indoors, Mrs Thorne cooked, and had a scullery maid. I recall a series of transient teenage scullery maids, all seeming rather harassed. My grandmother's own maid was Mary, who had been out to India, and there was at least one other housemaid, called Minnie. From the late twenties, my grandparents also had a secretary, Edith Timson, who had neat handwriting and an orderly mind. She lived out, as the Camfields and both Browns did, but worked in the inner hall, where she kept all the breeding records for the dogs and the cattle. After my grandfather's death, she became a secretary-companion to Dolly, and lived in. All these people were more or less devoted to the General, as they called my grandfather. There was nothing servile or undignified about their attitude to him, or to any of us. His own strength of character and gentleness probably helped; no one was less like the choleric retired general of cartoons. When the rest of the family lunched out, I used to take my midday meal in the servants' hall, sitting beside Mr Camfield at the head of the table, and formed the idea that the servants at White Hill were in what the Navy would have called a happy ship. As a small boy, I took for granted I was going to be a naval officer when I grew up – it seemed the only proper career.

Even before I could walk properly, I was rootling about one afternoon underneath a sofa at White Hill, found a big roundish metal object, put it on my head, and crawled out – to be greeted by shouts from the men of 'Take it off!' and screams from the women, because I had put on a German army helmet brought back by my grandfather from the Passchendaele battlefield.

My grandfather was Somebody in Hertfordshire: a deputy lieutenant, a justice of the peace, a director of the largest local firm. As a governor of Berkhampstead School, he helped to appoint Graham and Hugh Greene's father as headmaster. It was his job to sit in court in the town hall every few weeks, to be seen at church every Sunday, to be there if anyone wanted his advice. One of those who took his advice was G.M. Trevelyan, then a neighbour busy on his *England in the Reign of Queen Anne*, which ran to three volumes and covered Marlborough's wars. RMF reminded him of various military details which Trevelyan had forgotten after his war service with an ambulance unit in Italy, or never known, on the condition, unbroken till now, that there was no public acknowledgement. A less respectable historical neighbour was Arthur Bryant, who lived not far away but was never invited to White Hill at all. I never knew why, but felt a touch of grand-parental approval when it fell to me to expose in *The Times* in 2001 how barbarously badly he had edited the Alanbrooke diaries.

The family kept up some degree of state at White Hill. One didn't run or shout indoors, one wasn't late for meals, one never appeared on the ground floor in one's night clothes. The servants looked after keeping up the fires, preparing and serving the food, washing up the dishes, making the beds, and there was a strong general sense of decorum.

For a few years my grandfather tried farming, at Great Gaddesden, did not care for it, and gave it up. Dolly took it up instead, at Hamberlins Farm, Northchurch. She bred Redpoll cattle, and went in for clean milk, sold as 'Tuberculin Tested'. Always a tiresomely inquisitive child, I asked what that meant? 'It means that in every cubic centimetre of the milk I sell, there are not more than 80,000 tuberculosis bacilli.' This made me no more fond of milk.

There were masses of dogs at White Hill. My grandfather bred Irish setters, calling his breed Beorcham (pronounced Berkem), after one of Berkhampstead's many early names. They did promisingly in field trials, and one of them – Beorcham Blazes – though not much use in the field was so beautiful that he won Cruft's prize for the handsomest dog in the show. There were some English setters as well, and several spaniels. Dolly had three Cairn terriers at her heels indoors (where none of my grandfather's dogs were allowed, save one ancient spaniel), and also bred greyhounds. Once I counted them up: there were 103 dogs all told.

When I was about seven, I asked my mother when it was that I had had a nursery wallpaper, mainly grey, with vertical columns of little pink roses on it. I was then able to describe it in some detail, and still retain a very faint recollection of it. She gave me an odd look, and told me that was the room I had been born in; and the family left the house when I was six weeks old. I suppose it was the first object on which my eyes ever focussed, which was why it stuck so fast in my memory. We moved from Penistone Road in Streatham, where I was born – then an intensely respectable suburb – to a tiny house in Stamford Road, Norbury.

By contrast with White Hill, with its many servants, we had a single general maid, who lived in, called Alice Lovejoy. She was a through-and-through Cockney in speech; my father made sure that I did not copy any of her vowel sounds. She was also delightfully child-friendly, though she had no children of her own. She was a devoted reader of the Sunday *News of the World*, at which I was never allowed to look, and during the week of the *Daily Mirror*, in which we both enjoyed the Pip, Squeak & Wilfred strip cartoons. My father took *The Times* to work with him, and read *The Observer* on Sundays. He had one oddity: he could not abide wasps. The presence of even one might drive him to a fury. This, in any English summer, might prove uncomfortable for his family, and was certainly uncomfortable for the wasps. So steady were his hand and eye, even when roused, that I once saw him cut a wasp in half as it flew, with a table knife.

Alice took me to see the eclipse of the sun in 1927, which we watched through fragments of smoked glass from the bridge over the railway line by Norbury station. (I expect my father had taken my mother up on to Peek, Frean's factory roof at Bermondsey.) Alice boasted that she had seen Halley's comet when it had appeared before the Great War, adding, reprovingly, 'you'll never see it' – taking for granted that I would be killed in the next war. She was quite right about the comet, but for the wrong reason. I never did see it directly, for when it reappeared, I tried but failed to pick it out in a night sky too full of London glare, and could only look at it on television.

Occasional relatives looked in to see us, including my great-uncle Alfred, the first man (Father Christmases in shops apart) I had met who wore a beard. To make sure it was real, I gave it a tug; he left me nothing in his will. I suppose I must have met my father's grandparents, Cunningham Noel Foot and his wife Sophia, who had been born a Fayle (and was another niece of a First Naval Lord, Richards, who enforced Mr Gladstone's resignation in 1894), but cannot remember them. They died – he was eighty-nine – when I was small. Allie came to stay quite often. Once she mentioned an advantage of rotten boroughs, not now much remembered, which she knew about from having been brought up at Merstham, at the gates of Gatton, one of the rottenest of all. It was recalled in the village, she said, how useful it had been to have had a tame MP, for whenever a bright young man wanted a post in customs, or any other nomination for which an MP's word would be a help, his parents could usually get the great house to do something about it. Allie often brought her dog with her, a large woolly English sheepdog called Rags, bigger than me when I first met her, with whom I became firm friends. Ever since I have been a dog-lover rather than a cat-lover, though fate has thrown me into a dogless household with cats in it, with whom I manage to get on.

An old lady in Stamford Road once fell ill, and the whole street was covered in straw, to deaden the noise of horseshoes, for several days. Among the vehicles often in the street was a horse-drawn flat cart, bearing blocks of ice, from which each household could, for a few pence, have a hunk chopped off with a hand axe. In the 1920s, the refrigerators that are now commonplace had yet to cross the

Atlantic. Again, most houses held a piece of green cardboard marked 'C P', but nothing to do with the communist party. If one put it in the window, Carter Paterson's cart – also horse-drawn – would stop, and the carter would collect a parcel for anywhere in England. This made a convenient alternative to the parcel post. Carter Paterson faded out, now replaced by the modern express services, usually faster and always much more expensive.

My father had some books about the house – no inordinate number – among them, the 1922 edition of *The Times* atlas, which fascinated me. I pored over it, stretched out on the dining-room floor, on wet days, not only teaching myself geography, but picking up fragments of what is now called sociology as well, from the tables of comparative races and religions. It is now disbound, but I cannot bear to throw it away, for I suppose that among those pages such capacities as I have as a scholar first stirred. I had appeared to be reading before I was three. Dickie had stayed loyal to the Territorial Army, and when his batman came to clean his TA uniform, I went and sat beside him to watch, spread out the Pip, Squeak & Wilfred album on my knee, and read it out to him. In fact I suppose I was reciting it, having got it by heart by dint of having it read to me so often, thus knowing which words went with which pictures. I was certainly reading well before I went to a little day school in London Road when I was five or six, though I cannot claim to have been as learned as John Stuart Mill, who before he was eight (when he started Latin) had read all Aesop, all Herodotus, all Xenophon, and some 'easy' dialogues by Plato, all in Greek. At that school I can remember having a pencil gently but firmly removed from my left hand, with the injunction that one wrote right-handed. Similarly, I can remember at home being made to use a spoon in my right hand, and a fork in my left – being naturally left-handed, I had wanted to do the opposite. I still use my left rather than my right hand for such tasks as hammering or chopping, and wear my wristwatch on my right and less used wrist.

At this day-school, we had a little rudimentary instruction in Christianity. We used to sing Mrs Alexander's hymn, 'All things bright and beautiful', published in the same year as the Communist Manifesto, and always included the verse nowadays corrected out of it, which was then thought a blinding glimpse of the obvious :

The rich man in his castle,
The poor man at his gate,

God made them, high or lowly,
And ordered their estate.

At about this time, I knocked my upper arm against something, and the bruise instead of going down turned into a cyst. Our GP didn't like the look of it, and sent for an anaesthetist. I was laid on the kitchen table and given chloroform. Just as I was passing out, I heard the doctor say, 'Oh Mrs Foot, have you got a nice large sharp knife?' The result was not as bad as I had feared, and the arm soon cleared up entirely.

My father's territorial unit, which he commanded, was the 63rd Field Brigade RFA, at Brixton, also then a well-regarded suburb, with which he once in the late 1920s won the King's Prize for accurate shooting. Now and again I was allowed to go with him to his headquarters, where I learned that one must never walk through a line of guns – you walk round it instead – one of those immutables dinned into me permanently, like:

Never, never let your gun
Pointed be at any one;
That the gun unloaded be
Matters not the least to me.

One of the delights of life at Norbury was that Dickie had a Renault car, in which he would drive us out now and again to walk in Ashdown Forest. There I can remember seeing teams – like Kipling's Cattiwow – managing huge tree trunks with sagacious horses, and delighted in walking on pine-needles in Winnie the Pooh country. Indeed, Dickie was acquainted with A.A. Milne – they had met during the war – and once drove me over to Milne's house at Richmond to take tea with Christopher Robin, who was about my own age. Christopher Robin showed me his teddy bear, assuring me that it was the original Winnie the Pooh, a fact I passed on long afterwards to my incredulous children. Later still I read in the autobiography of E.H. Shepard, who made the drawings for the original editions of *Winnie the Pooh* and *The House at Pooh Corner*, that he had used as the model for Pooh his own child's teddy bear, not Christopher Robin's, – a nice point in historical authenticity. The two bears looked, I suppose, pretty well the same.

Round White Hill there were half a dozen gentry families within what my grandmother called calling distance. Nearest was Granville Ram, the

Treasury solicitor, at Berkhampstead Place on the hilltop west of the castle. His wife Elisabeth had a beautiful voice, but died young. I liked going to the Haslams at Rossway, for their hall had a splendid stand of assegais round a Zulu shield, which I was not allowed to touch but could admire. The largest great house anywhere near, Ashridge, which had been the seat of the great Duke of Bridgewater, had already become the Conservative Party's Bonar Law college. Once or twice I went there, to see the spectacular stone staircase (by George IV's architect Wyattville, Pevsner now tells me, though I supposed it to be fifteenth-century), and knew slightly a school contemporary called Hoskins, whose father General Hoskins was in charge.

The Chetwynd-Stapyltons were another local family with whom White Hill was on visiting terms. There were two sons about my own age (both were later at Winchester with me), and a good-looking blonde daughter, Helen. My grandmother forbade me to try to cultivate Helen's acquaintance, on the ground that she was 'fast'. Helen subsequently married the queen's private secretary, Lord Stamfordham's grandson, and died Lady Adeane. Do I mean that my grandmother was unnecessarily strict? Indeed I do. Her household was also, quite often, intensely boring for a small boy. Once I had learned to read, I could retire into a book, though I was long not allowed to read anything on Sundays except the Bible, the prayer book, or sermons, nor was I allowed to play on that day with any toy. When I attended mealtimes with the grown-ups, I was encouraged to eat rather than to talk. 'Children should be seen but not heard' was an only too familiar motto. (My children do not believe this.)

In the summers, we often went away for a short spell at the seaside. Another early memory – I was then three – is of the feel beneath my bare toes of a blue concrete floor in a bungalow at Selsey. When I saw, long afterwards, a Paul Nash picture of a fragment of walling at the edge of the beach at Sandgate in Kent, I could remember the feel of such a curve of concrete against my infant hand. Once we stayed in a household, belonging I think to friends of Allie's, who were such strict puritans that they had God's eye painted on the wall of every room, to remind everyone that they could never be out of His sight. Being pernickety as well as inquisitive, and having been taught already that God was immutable (though at that age I can hardly have known the word), I went round from room to room. The grown-ups were quite right, God's eye was precisely the same colour everywhere, a rather harsh shade of greenish blue. I never saw an eye in anyone's face that was quite that colour, until May 1944 when military accident threw me nose-to-nose with General Montgomery. As we were both on parade, nothing could be said.

The head of the Cooper family, my step-great-uncle Dick, had by the time I knew him given up much in the way of work, though he remained chairman of Cooper, McDougall and Robertson, a large firm providing fertilisers to farmers, of which my grandfather was a director. Dick Cooper had had a dozen years in the House of Commons, as MP for Walsall, at first as a protectionist Tory, then as one of the two MPs of the National Democratic Party – Henry Page Croft was the other – who stood in 1918 on a platform consisting of a single line: 'We are opposed to the sale of honours.' He assured me that he understood the English working classes far better than I ever would, because as an MP for an industrial area he had met so many of them. He spent a lot of time attempting elaborate jigsaw puzzles; it was a house rule that one could only speak to him after one had fitted a piece into the current puzzle. His wife, Aunt Sally, was a great delight, and is still warmly remembered. She had stood for election in Walsall when he resigned, but without success – women MPs were then great rarities – and was far too well mannered ever to talk politics. Her nephew Jack Pagden, about my age but several inches taller, was another of the figures of whom I saw quite a lot at White Hill. Like my other two step-cousins, Robin and Maurice, of whom more in a moment, he seemed always to be preferred over me. I liked him more than I liked the other two, and still feel sorry to have drifted (by my own fault) out of touch with him.

I did not see much of my Fry cousins. Auntie Fry, as I was to call their mother Alice (my Daniell grandmother's sister), I recall as intimidatingly large, always dressed in black. Her son Charles, the black sheep of Batsfords the publishers, was luckily not interested in me (Dickie could not stand him). Charles's eldest sister Peggy married the son and namesake of John Knox Laughton, the naval historian, and lost her husband to a mosquito bite. Years later she remarried, to an eminent soldier, who died of the bite of a wasp. In an age of antibiotics, we forget too easily how frail human life has recently been, and remains.

Every Sunday, at Berkhampstead church, there was an old lady in black, Alma Smith-Dorrien, born on the day of the battle and named after it. Her brother Sir Horace, by the 1920s a field marshal, was a friend of RMF, and once when I was about ten I had a brief talk with him when he called at White Hill. My grandfather had impressed on me already how infinitely senior to a mere brigadier-general a field marshal was, and I was suitably struck. He had told me also that Smith-Dorrien had served in the Zulu War of 1879, about which I knew a little already. When I asked him how on earth he had survived Isandhlwana, he replied modestly that he had had a very good horse. Years afterwards, in his memoirs, I discovered that he had described it in a letter to his family a few days after the battle as a broken-down old nag, that had just got him part of the way away. I now realise he must have survived because (as he was then a transport officer) he was wearing a blue tunic, and the Zulus were concentrating on red. His throwaway remark to me is an example of the rule of the old officer class, which laid down that even if one had done something rather brave, one must never on any account boast.

Dolly had two younger sisters, Edith who married Colonel Robin Negus a Somersetshire magnate and had one son, also Robin, on whom Dolly doted, and May who married Kenward Barker and had four children, two boys and two girls. All these children were older than me, Maurice Barker only by a couple of years; all were constantly held up to me as models I should follow, but whom I must never expect to equal, let alone surpass. The Barkers lived at Watchbury, a big house by Barford in Warwickshire. I can still remember the tremor that ran through me when the nanny there said, 'Come to bed now, Master Michael, *or Boney will get you.*' Some years passed before I separated the real Napoleon Buonaparté from the terror of my infancy.

Usually we went to White Hill for Christmas. The house had a fine mahogany banister, between the hall and the first floor, with delicately curved balusters. Every Christmas, Camfield wreathed holly through the balusters, all the way up. My grandparents stoically ate a huge Christmas meal at midday on Christmas day, and then went up the hill to Shenstone Court to eat another, identical meal that same evening. My grandfather usually went out with the Old Berkeley on Boxing Day to give his liver a shake-up. Once, at Christmas 1924, Shenstone Court decided to have its main meal at midday instead of in the evening. There were about sixty guests. When it came to pudding time, the curtains were drawn, and all the lights went out. I was alarmed, and clutched my mother's hand; we were all then served Christmas pudding, blazing with brandy, by its own light.

My mother was pregnant again at the time, though I do not recall that her self-centred little boy noticed. She produced me a sister – my only sibling – on Easter Sunday, 12 April 1925. My father, a strong male chauvinist, had hoped for another son, whom he would have called Patrick. A play had been running in London, called *Paddy, or the Next Best Thing*, and he wanted the baby called Paddy. At the font, the priest refused to use so unchristian a name, and she was christened Patricia Avril, but was always called Paddy as a child. I fear I was not a good brother to her. At five and a half years older, I was too much her senior to think like her, and used to bully her for being slower than I was to take things in. She has, bless her, never complained – at any rate, to me.

Occasionally we stayed in the depths of the Sussex Weald, at Buxted, in a thatched cottage where Allie lived. One splendid summer Dickie built a small dam on the streamlet at the bottom of the garden, and thus created a little pool in which Paddy and I could paddle. This was a very different sort of country life from that at White Hill, and much more fun for children. In those pre-disney days, before Mickey Mouse had grown to his world-wide fame, I was a fan of another cartoon character, Felix the cat. So were Peek, Freans: for some months their lorries carried large Felix dolls, quite three feet high, on their fronts. Dickie brought one home when they stopped using them, for me to play with, but it terrified Paddy, and had to be put down.

At one thing she was much better than I: she adored riding. I hated it. I was expected to ride – it was an automatic accomplishment for a gentleman – and it was Brown's duty to teach me how. He and I rode all over Berkhampstead Common, except for the parts covered by a golf course, or by the trench lines dug for training during the Great War (which were out of bounds to me, as well as to the ponies), and I enjoyed its mixture of bracken, gorse, and grassy rides, as well as glimpses of Frithesden Beeches, a spectacular gathering of tall grey trunks in a dell. Dinah, a fourteen-hand black pony, was bought to carry me. As soon as Paddy was old enough to ride, she rode on Dinah and I was mounted on Rachel, a smaller and livelier chestnut. Occasionally, Rachel and I went out cubbing, with Brown on Dolly's mare Jacqueline in charge of us; that I quite enjoyed. Billy, the eldest Cooper boy, was master of the Hertfordshire, the nearest pack of foxhounds. My grandfather wore pink when out with the Hertfordshire, gold when out with the Old Berkeley the nearest hunt to the west. Everybody round me took it for granted that foxhunting was a proper way for men and women to spend their time, and I was brought up to remember that nobody's land was private if hounds in pursuit of a fox ran on to it. Modern anti-hunt campaigners have forgotten what a tremendous force for lowering class barriers fox-hunting used to be.

My earliest inklings about the constitution, gathered from talk round the table at White Hill, were that – under the King – the world was ruled, at sea, by Captains of His Majesty's Ships, whose powers were unlimited, and on land, by Masters of Foxhounds, whose word equally was never to be gainsaid. I learned more later.

Once, when there was a dinner party at White Hill – I must have been seven or eight at the time – I managed to hide under the dining table, and stayed there, still and silent, trying to make sense of the talk around me. Over the port, someone ventured that there was one sin worse than murder – shooting a fox. My grandfather suggested one sin worse even than that – wearing a made-up bow tie. Made-up bow ties are now on sale all over the West End, but that too has changed. Alice Fairfax-Lucy, sister of Alastair and daughter of John Buchan – Alastair was my contemporary at Oxford – was not allowed in the 1930s to walk through the Burlington Arcade without a chaperone.

My aunt Lindsey had married, in December 1919, Gervas Huxley (first cousin of Aldous and Julian), who had been at Hill Side with my father. Gervas became secretary of the now forgotten Empire Marketing Board, and provided for my nursery a big map showing the empire and its prominent place in the world. They had no children, and divorced in 1930. (Gervas's second wife was Elspeth, granddaughter of Lord Richard Grosvenor, who as Elspeth Huxley became a notable writer.) Lindsey became treasurer of the Women's Institutes, having inherited her father's sense of order.

Let me try to recapture what would nowadays be called the mindset of the men at whose knees I was brought up in the twenties – the attitudes and the half-understood recent history. The superiority of Great Britain over all other nations was axiomatic, so was the supremacy of the King-Emperor over all other monarchs, so was the grandeur of the British over all other Empires, not even the Roman excepted, past and present. All foreigners were distrusted, and a leading unspoken assumption was that the French were even less to be trusted than the Germans. The Germans had gone to war with us in 1914 – the intellectuals' doubts about German war guilt had not then spread far outside academe – because they were jealous of our 'place in the sun', and wanted to elbow us out of it. Defeat in battle and later economic ruin should have brought them manners. But the French to whose help we had hurried in 1914 had *mutinied* three years later, and we had had to engage in the slaughterhouse of Passchendaele to keep the

Germans from wiping them out. Bolsheviks were of course simply beyond the pale.

Once at White Hill I asked whether it was true that there was a Secret Service. I got a peremptory reply (I believe from Gervas): of course there was, but it was secret, so the question was never to be raised again. It was run by an admiral – the Navy was not called the Silent Service for nothing. It was for me to learn to shoot straight, to ride straight to hounds, and not to pester my elders with impertinent questions. There were also whole ranges of subjects never to be discussed in the presence of ladies, or talked of in front of the children, or of the servants, and once or twice I heard a forgetful visitor back from overseas use the phrase 'not in front of the natives'. Modern conversational freedom was undreamed of.

Ladies were expected to ride, but were not expected to shoot; gentlemen were. Here I enjoyed myself. My grandfather was an excellent shot – he took me out shooting with him a lot about 1929–32, mostly walking up partridges, and I cannot remember him firing a shot that missed. After his death, Dolly sometimes had shooting parties, at which in my later teens I was expected to play host (she never went out with the guns, though she often went out with hounds). I started to shoot myself in my middle teens, under the guidance of Duncan Lindsay my grandparents' gamekeeper, a quiet, delightful Scotsman from Arran who lived at Dagnall beyond Ashridge. Though never as good a shot as my grandfather or my father, I was more than competent, using my grandfather's Powell twelve-bores.

One shooting party, at Rossway on a dismal wet autumn afternoon, I cannot forget. Camfield had put us up some grouse sandwiches, which we assembled to eat in the lee of a haystack. One of the guests slipped a corner of his sandwich to somebody else's spaniel, a gross breach of decorum, because it spoiled the dog's nose for game. The spaniel's owner upbraided him fiercely when he muttered something about being fond of dogs. 'Gad, sir, you might just as well kiss my wife and tell me you're fond of women.'

* * *

When I was eight and a half, I was sent away to boarding school. I was to have gone to Leighton Park near Reading, where Robin Negus was, but the nasty hacking cough that plagued my childhood persuaded the family to send me instead to The Wick at Hove, in the belief that sea air would do my lungs good. I still remember the third of May, 1928, when I joined The Wick, the first time in my life that I had ever spent a night away from everybody whom I had ever known before. I didn't cry – I knew already that one didn't, but I cannot pretend to have enjoyed it.

The headmaster, Guy Seely Leach, was a nephew of the Jack Seely who became Lord Mottistone, and brought us up on his uncle's book, *Fear, and be Slain* – with disconcerting results. During the next world war, boys from the Wick suffered the average British casualty rate for the previous world war, in which Leach had served (he had won an MC in the Rifle Brigade): one in eight were killed. (This was not a peculiarity of The Wick. Nine of my seventy-four fellow scholars at Winchester in 1933 were also killed, about the same proportion.) Leach had been in College at Winchester, and his professional ambition was to send more boys there; he succeeded about once every five years. A.R.W. Low (whom I never met), later Lord Aldington, had his name on the honours board, well before my time. Dmitri Tornow got into College the summer I reached The Wick. but hardly counted, as he was a war scholar. The same was true of J.S.T. Gibson, who got in in 1929.

When I was about eleven my father said to me, 'You aren't Nelson, are you?' I had to agree. He maintained that if I persisted in going into the navy I would be axed before I was forty – as indeed all of my acquaintance who went into the navy, and survived the next world war, were. He then indicated that Leach reckoned he had found in me some traces of a future scholar, and suggested I thought about that as a career instead.

Leach had done some mountain climbing, and photographing, in the Alps, as well as having an interest in Renaissance art and a past acquaintanceship with Cecil Sharp, the collector of folk-song. He was enough of an all-rounder to make a good prep school headmaster. He was also an Anglican lay reader, and had had built, alongside the rather ramshackle school buildings of The Wick – just south of St Anne's Well Gardens, which were out of bounds – a chapel, in which we had brief daily services, and evensong every Sunday. On Sunday mornings we walked, in crocodile, to one of the local churches for mattins. I thus got used to the rhythms of the 1662 prayer book, which often echoed those of Cranmer's, and the authorized version of the Bible was familiar too, because we studied it regularly in class – this was called Divinity – in a cut-down version suitable for the eyes of the innocent. We became familiar with the stories in Genesis, and with the ups and downs of the prophets and kings of ancient Judah and Israel. This was all part of

Leach's constant aim, to bring us up to be Christian gentlemen, even if we did not become scholars of Winchester.

I would, I fear, at Greyfriars have been denounced as a swot. I won the form prize, six times over, in each of The Wick's six classes. One master, E.H. Blakeney who went on to be a cathedral organist, first gave me the idea that I might be able to write. He too had been through the Great War as an infantry officer, and had emerged with the scar of a bayonet thrust through the palm of his hand – about which he could never be persuaded to talk. Nobody taught us chess, but we played a lot of draughts, and several other board games, particularly 'L'attaque' and 'Dover patrol'. That last game suited Leach's navalist turn; he brought us up to admire Boy Cornwell, who had won a posthumous VC at Jutland for standing by his gun, though mortally wounded, because he had no orders to go to the sick bay and get looked after (no wonder, as all the rest of his gun's crew had been killed by the shell that wounded him).

In the school reading-room there were several volumes of the *Illustrated London News*, which covered 1914–18. From these I picked up the outline history of the Great War, as the British propaganda machine saw it, and some knowledge of the main battles and commanders. There was also a school library, including Rider Haggard, a lot of Conan Doyle, several escape stories of the A.J. Evans *Escaping Club* type, and John Buchan's adventure stories (not only those about Richard Hannay, but such tales as *Prester John* or *John Macnab*). I also read Kipling, whom none of my contemporaries would touch. White Hill held most of his books, and Dolly used to give me a volume by him (in the cheapest edition) every birthday and every Christmas.

Leach brought in occasional lecturers, one of whom, Woolley the archaeologist, gave a talk about his findings at Ur of the Chaldees. This gave me a cultural shock that still reverberates. He showed a slide of a golden head, every hair carved separately, dating from the third millenium before Christ. He said he had asked the Goldsmiths and Silversmiths (later Garrard), the Regent Street jewellers, to copy it for him; they replied that the workmanship was too delicate, they couldn't do it. Here was a short proof that progress is not necessarily forwards.

One had of course from time to time to go to the dentist, never much fun. Nina took me, most holidays, to Mr Downs in Welbeck Street, whose attentions I could endure the more easily because he had spent the war in the Navy, and had been present at Jutland in HMS *Warspite*. That much I could get out of him, but he would never talk about it, beyond saying it had been noisy and uncomfortable; besides, he had been below all through the action. Long afterwards I discovered he had been in the ship's band, and was therefore engaged when in action in fire control; still then a secret subject, about which he was not allowed to talk. There must have been hundreds of sailors silent like him, predecessors of the decipher teams who never gossipped after the next world war.

There were about forty boys at a time at The Wick, including several pairs of brothers. One of these pairs included a Barber, later Chancellor of the Exchequer, who died a peer; another, the Bridges, both reached distinction, one as a judge and the other as a dean. Lakin ii, whom I liked, went on to Christ Church and a military cross in the next world war, and then settled in France. Stancliffe became Dean of Winchester and his son is now a bishop.

During my first term at The Wick the family moved house, from Norbury to West Kensington. Dickie took a small flat opposite Olympia, into which we – including Alice – just fitted. Indeed, for a while we fitted in one extra, Freda Dysli, a delightful Swiss-German girl who wanted to learn English and shared a bedroom with Paddy, leaving me to sleep on a put-u-up sofa in the day nursery. Freda, Paddy and I all got on well, but I now realise I missed a chance to pick up some German.

At The Wick there was a swimming bath, in which I learned – rather reluctantly – to swim, under the eye of Chief Petty Officer Payne who was the school's physical training instructor. He doubled this role with part-time service as a coast defence gunner, and took a few of us once to see his battery of CD guns, on the beach by Shoreham. These provided, I suppose, the ghost of an excuse for Goering's air operations against Brighton and Hove during the 'Baedeker raids' of 1942–3.

A lot of school time went on sport. Cricket I didn't greatly care for playing, but long followed the first-class matches in the newspapers, and went now and again to watch Sussex play at Hove. I have seen Bradman bat, admired Ames, and once saw Ranjitsinji make one of the leg glances that he invented. While Dickie was in Australia he went to Bradman's shop and bought me a bat, which the great man autographed; this of course gave me some degree of kudos. Eventually the bat cracked, and I sent it for repair. The repair man bound it up beautifully, but to compensate for the weight of the binding shaved a bit off the other end of the bat – including all but the first D of the signature. My interest in cricket dwindled sharply thereafter.

My grandfather had an extra aura of superiority for me since he ranked as a first-class cricketer, though he seldom played any longer. He belonged to I Zingari, a club of gentleman amateurs founded in the late nineteenth century, which had done wonders to preserve and stimulate village cricket, all over England, and by courtesy was still ranked with the first-class counties in the 1920s.

At The Wick we learned a little English history, a little mathematics, a little French, and a lot of Latin and Greek, though no science, as such. But I remember being taught, as a scientific fact, buttressed by thousands of observations from the decks of sailing ships and steamships alike, that when the sun sets in a calm sea it emits a bright green flash; as well as being told that it was well known that any attempt to draw electric power from tidal action would slow down the earth's rotation.

Leach thought highly enough of my chances to send me in for the Winchester scholarship in 1932. His school was in quarantine for chicken-pox, so I had to be sequestered in Hyde Abbey – King Alfred's burial-place – under the eye of another master, Allum (who never taught me anything but how to shoot with a .22" rifle, which he managed well). Allum and I were waiting about, in a corner of Chamber Court, for College Hall to empty after lunch so that I could go in for a 2.00pm paper. Down the stairs there came a tall white-haired man with a slighter, balder, beaky-nosed one, at sight of whom Allum stiffened, and murmured reverently 'That's Grey'. So I set eyes, the year before he died, on Lord Grey of Fallodon who had been Asquith's foreign secretary when the Great War broke out, and has often been blamed for having helped to cause what he did his utmost to avert. He was arm-in-arm with H.A.L. Fisher, then warden of New College, for both sat on Winchester's governing body.

The examiners (who included H.W.B. Joseph) did not share Leach's opinion of me. I was placed on College roll, but seventeenth, and next half they only admitted twelve. My father, then away in Australia, was delighted. He had sat the same examination himself in 1906, and had been placed eighteenth. Next year I tried again, and this time was placed sixth.

* * *

I enjoyed Winchester. It stretched me intellectually, and got me used to living in the company of brains a good deal sharper than my own. I also learned, better than I had learned at The Wick, how to live peaceably in company with others, though it was probably also in College that I picked up a habit which has long plagued those nearest to me, of being argumentative about any new proposed course of action. It was a joy that the buildings were many of them so beautiful. College men lived in William of Wykeham's flint and stone quadrangle of the late fourteenth century, suitably re-plumbed, and some of the surroundings were idyllic. Christopher Hawkes's *Winchester*, full of splendid Country Life photographs, had just come out. Most of us bought it and enjoyed it; I re-read it aged eighty, still with pleasure.

We all knew that Wykeham had founded the college, jointly with his New College at Oxford, to train men to become priests. Its full title was the College of the Blessed Virgin Mary of Winchester near Winchester – Collegium Beatae Virginis Mariae Wintoniensis prope Wintoniam. There was – is – a statue of the Virgin over Middle Gate, to which every passer-by was – is? – expected to raise his hat. Every morning, the whole school attended mattins; every evening, in every house there were house prayers; on Sundays, there was early service for the confirmed, and the whole school attended evensong as well as mattins and house prayers. Once a month, evensong was in Cathedral, among the tombs of Anglo-Saxon kings. The impact of this on my own contemporaries was odd: most of us either turned agnostic, as I did, or went over to Rome. Five men in College with me took orders, of whom only two, Dr James Stuart and Canon Cheslyn Jones, rose to any eminence in the church. None of us became bishops.

For one's first fortnight at Winchester, one was responsible for nothing – it was the task of someone from a previous year to look after one, send one to the right classroom with the right books, and all that. I was luckily in the charge of Peter de Wesselow, a descendant of General Craufurd, at once informative and helpful, and learned the school's numerous 'notions' fast. One of these was that there were no boys at Winchester. We were all, from the start, called men. Moreover – a delightful change from The Wick, a prudish school – there was in College a cult of nakedness. First thing every morning, everyone walked naked into a bathroom for a cold splash. (In the summer, one could bathe in Gunner's Hole, a fenced-off stretch of the Itchen where the whole school bathed naked, hundreds of us together, on summer afternoons.) Though I call it a bathroom, there were no baths – we splashed and bathed in flat metal tubs, called bidets, about eight inches deep and a yard across. Scholars wore odd clothes: dark striped trousers, a black sleeved waistcoat, and over that a knee-length black gown with leg-of-mutton sleeves. Within a week, this seemed perfectly normal wear, just as within two or three nights I got used to sleeping through College clock that struck every quarter of an hour.

More senior men in College in my time included John Humphrey, Prefect of Hall, who turned left early, made DNB in the end, and was a leading immunologist in the sixties and seventies; B.B. King who was at Bletchley and talked about it, when it went public, to Ronald Lewin; Christopher Foxley-Norris who flew in the Battle of Britain and went on to be a knighted air chief marshal; John Willett who broadened the mind of the *Times Literary Supplement*; Charles Gordon, knighted like Norris, who was clerk to the House of Lords; Richard Blackwell who won a DSC during the war and later ran the family bookshop in Oxford; Tim Bennett, who earned a naval DSO before he was killed in an accident; and Peter Scott-Malden who flew a glider to Arnhem and had to act as Urquhart's intelligence officer, because the divisional IO's glider had not arrived. Years afterwards, he still could not bear to talk about it.

Fifteen men were on my roll. Five of us became professors. Henry Brandon outsoared us all, and became a law lord, picking up an MC in Madagascar on the way. Three of us were killed in the war. John Armitage, wounded and captured in the western desert as an anti-tank troop commander, died in enemy hands. Roddy Gow, an airborne gunner captain, did not survive Arnhem; and Frank Thompson, poet and son of a poet, captured in uniform on an SOE mission, was murdered by the police in Bulgaria, and became a Bulgarian national hero. Peter's brother David Scott-Malden flew a Spitfire in the Battle of Britain, commanded the Norwegian Spitfire wing in the Dieppe raid, stayed in the air force, and died an air vice marshal with a DSO as well as a DFC. (At his funeral in 2000, as the coffin was carried out of the church a Spitfire appeared in the sky to give a farewell salute.) John Dancy was headmaster successively of Lancing and of Marlborough. Marcus Dick became a fellow of Balliol, then a professor of philosophy, and died quite young. Geoffrey Parkinson disappeared from his friends' acquaintance during the war, presumably – like King, he had been a pupil of Hugh Alexander's – to Bletchley; he has never resurfaced, except as a distant address. Hilton Stowell also went away to America. Seymour Schlesinger changed his name to Spencer and became a mad-doctor. Peter Spicer who spent the war in the navy inherited a baronetcy, but did not use the title; James Stewart found himself a career at the United Nations. David Johnson fought at Imphal, and then became a legal adviser in the foreign office before going to a chair of law in Australia.

Of them all, I was closest friends with John Hasted, with whom I used to toll cloisters – walk and talk round the 14th century cloisters south of chapel – most evenings. He was a scientist. He was also the grandson of a field marshal, Barrett, the only senior officer to leave Mesopotamia with his reputation undamaged. His father commanded a battalion of the Durham Light Infantry, and claimed to be among the inventors of battledress. John later became professor of chemistry at Birkbeck. He was intensely musical, and did much to foster folk music. Though we seldom met after I left the school, I always felt close to him, and was moved to the verge of tears when he died in May 2002.

He was perhaps the last survivor of a brand of political sympathizer unintelligible to the post-cold-war era: he was, like Frank Thompson who made him one, a libertarian bolshevik. Knowing nothing then, and very unwilling to believe anything later, about Stalin's Gulag, they honestly believed that Leninist principles were going to be able to build a new heaven on earth. They were captivated by Stalin's 1936 constitution for the USSR, and missed the little clause in it that gave all power to the party in moments of crisis – the clause on which the subsequent atrocities were built. They were, in short, complete political *ingénus*, crazed with the spell of far Muscovia, but, in their own eyes at least, they were perfectly honest. Robert Conquest, whose *Great Terror* did so much to explain to the English-reading political classes what Stalinism meant, was a year or two senior to us in the school (he was not in College), going through his own libertarian bolshevik spell at the time. He saw the darkness before most of us.

Among College men junior to me were two future heads of university colleges, Warnock and Lighthill; two leading scientists, Murdoch Mitchison, Naomi's son, and the still more formidable Freeman Dyson; and Christopher Longuet-Higgins, as well as Richard Pendered whom Alexander recruited to Bletchley, where he helped sink *Scharnhorst*, and David Malan who – I discovered over fifty years later – had been a bomb-designing expert in SOE.

At other schools, if one can believe the novels, junior boys often had to make tea for senior ones. By an opposite arrangement, the prefects in College used to make toast for everybody else, at a large fire in the centre of College Hall, lit every year, as Wykeham's statutes had laid down, on the feast of SS Simon & Jude, 28 October. There were eighteen prefects among seventy-odd scholars, so the supply of toast was plentiful, and the custom gave scholars an early intimation of the need not to be entirely selfish. The whole ethos of the school was founded on a pair of phrases in St Luke: from those to whom much is given, much shall be required.

In school, I was first put under H.A. Jackson, housemaster of Dickie's old house, who detested both Germans (whose prisoner he had been) and College men, in Middle Part III (the same level in the school as Willie Whitelaw, who stood by Mrs Thatcher and died a viscount, and who was then not in his first half but his last.) During my first half, Hugh Seton-Watson who was Bib. Prae. went out of his way to show me how to use a library, and how to pursue a learned reference, a fragment of elementary instruction that has stayed with me for good, and for which I have always been grateful. Next year, Bib. Prae. (library perfect) was B.B. King, who took Parkinson and myself as his writers – that is, it was our job to keep Moberly Library tidy, put borrowers' books away, chase up late returns and so on. This gave me, again, some useful elementary knowledge, and also brought me into touch with Walter Oakeshott the librarian. I was thus one of the first to hear that Oakeshott had discovered, at the bottom of a chest in Muniment Room, a manuscript of Malory's *Morte d'Arthur* – the very manuscript, Lotte Hellinga proved years afterwards, from which Caxton had set the first printed version of the text. I read the text (in Everyman's edition, which I still have, rebound by Mirjam), when it was set for the Gillespie English literature prize, named after a contemporary of Dickie's killed in the Great War, and have treasured it ever since.

As I had been elected as a classics scholar, everyone took for granted that I should persevere with the classics, except myself. After two years' wrestling, rather ineffectually, with them, I combined with David Johnson to insist that we be allowed to follow an example recently set by John Aris, Andrew Ensor and Terence Lecky, and move from the classical ladder (called 'a') to the 'b' ladder which dealt in languages and history. We five were the first College men, war scholars apart, whom anyone could remember having done so – one was supposed not to leave the 'a' ladder in College unless one was a scientist or a mathematician, or a war scholar, let in to College because one's father had been killed in the Great War, and possibly not up to the travails of real hard work.

The change was a delight for me, because it exposed me to three men who gave proper nourishment to my brain, and persuaded me I might have a mind of my own, not simply the mind of a copyist. The finest of these, for my purposes, was Donald McLachlan, who had come to teach at Winchester for a change, after an exhausting spell on *The Times*. He had been *The Times*'s man in Warsaw, and happened to be standing in for the usual man in Berlin (who was on a skiing holiday) the night the Reichstag burned down. McLachlan's dispatch on this was so crisp and so vivid that the manager realised he was wasted in Warsaw, and brought him back to Printing House Square to write leaders. He got bored with this, and tried schoolmastering instead, to his pupils' great advantage.

He was a devout agnostic, but the school required each class to spend two hours a week on divine studies. He got round this neatly, by taking us through English versions of the simpler dialogues of Plato, or more daringly through a study of Voltaire. He also taught us how to read a daily newspaper, using the knowledge he had picked up in Printing House Square, and kept us up to date on international developments, which were already grisly: this was the era of the Abyssinian war and the Spanish civil war, with the probability of a further world war looming larger every week. There were maps, with the fronts pinned up to date daily, on our classroom wall. Once he arranged to take several of us round the House of Commons, one fairly quiet afternoon when nothing much was going on, where I was able to set eyes on several notables whom I recognised from their newspaper photographs, and even heard a few words from the most notorious of them, David Lloyd George. He also took us to Printing House Square to see how *The Times* was printed. There I glimpsed a full-page obituary of Kipling, never used because he died so close to George V that the king crowded the obituary spaces out. (Max Beerbohm remarked that Mrs Kipling thought it in bad taste of the king to die so soon after her husband.)

Specialising in history, I went for tutorials – just as if already up at Oxbridge – with the great H.E. Walker, correctly called "that prince of schoolmasters" when he died. By some accident he had missed a first at Cambridge, and so did not teach at a university. He had wonderful gifts of quiet exposition, both in lectures and in conversation *tête-à-tête*, and a firm grasp of historical method which he was happy to impart. He had been a gunner officer through the Great War, in heavy artillery, a calmer warrior's life than Dickie's. And for my last five halves I was taught by Budge Firth, one of the school chaplains, who preached delightful sermons and had a most civilised mind. His rotund figure made it hard to believe that he had once taken ten wickets in Eton Match, and his benevolent air made it hard to believe that he had fought, at the tail end of the Great War, in the Household Brigade. He was proud just to have been born in the reign of Queen Victoria.

He was not as afraid of recent history as many of his contemporaries. In my first half under him, in the summer of 1936, we read R.C.K. Ensor's *England 1870–1914*, the just-published latest volume of the Oxford History of England, of which the indexer, Ensor's son Andrew, was present in the class. An early lesson for me on the unreliability of official sources came when Firth laid down something about British policy during the Boer war, and Michael Brodrick chipped in, 'But sir, my father [who died Earl of Midleton] was in the cabinet at the time and has always told me the contrary'.

The headmaster for my first year – I revered, but can hardly claim to have met him – was the great A.T.P. Williams, who moved on to be in turn Dean of Christ Church and Bishop of Winchester. He was followed by Spencer Leeson, a less impressive figure, but brainy. He had been in the naval intelligence division during the Great War, and was said to complete the Torquemada crossword in *The Observer* between Sunday morning breakfast at nine and mattins at half-past ten. Ensor and I, sitting side by side, developed a gesture of turning to each other with our eyebrows raised, every time we thought Leeson had made a mistake in the Napoleonic history he was discussing. Williams and Leeson were in holy orders; this, up to then, had been taken for granted. Winchester's first lay headmaster, after my time there, was Walter Oakeshott, who took over from Leeson when Leeson decided he must have some parish experience, and went off to be rector of St Mary's, Southampton (he died Bishop of Peterborough). Oakeshott had shared with R.M.Y. Gleadowe the teaching of art history; Gleadowe tried, without much success, to teach me how to draw. It was Gleadowe, who also had a past in the naval intelligence division, who was later employed by George VI to design the Sword of Stalingrad, and was paid over a hundred guineas for doing so (I stumbled once on the file in the record office at Kew).

As well as history, I learned French and German, quite well. A little elementary physics and chemistry did not carry me far. For mathematics, of which again a little was compulsory, I was sent to C.V. Durell who had taught Dickie, but was long past his best. His assistant was Hugh Alexander, who took all the really bright mathematicians, and also taught chess as a special subject – he was chess champion of England at the time. None of us knew that he was also a leading cryptographer, destined to be one of the brightest stars at Bletchley Park in the impending world war.

I had a brief, intense spell of enthusiasm for the Church of England, into which I was confirmed by the saintly Garbett, bishop of Winchester, late in

1935. The spell did not last; reasonable doubts kept getting in the way of preachers' certainties, as they still do. Chapel remained compulsory. One unforgettable event was going to Cathedral for an armistice day service. Just before eleven, two cavalry trumpeters sounded the Last Post from the far east end, and after the two minutes' silence fifty more trumpeters sounded the Reveille from the west door.

At The Wick, I had written a little verse for the school magazine. In College I persevered with verse-writing on my own in English as well as the compulsory Latin, and began to think I might have some poetry in me. Indeed in my last summer half (called Cloister Time) I won a gold medal for English verse, for which I should certainly have been beaten by Frank Thompson, who was a real poet, had he not won the same prize himself the previous year, and so been disqualified.

There was an active debating society, in which I occasionally spoke, often devoted to current affairs, in which (under McLachlan's influence) I was beginning to take an interest. Each chamber in College – we lived in groups of fifteen or so of various ages, called chambers – regularly took *The Times*, at which the prefects had first go, but anyone who cared could spend half an hour or so a day on it if he wanted, as I quite often did. College was good at encouraging one to look after one's own time. It also introduced me to classical music. Most chambers had a gramophone, on which one could hear (with frequent changes of record) Beethoven's symphonies and piano concertos and similar fare.

Occasionally, the whole school was lectured by some notable – Lord Ronaldshay, for instance (later Marquess of Zetland), who had governed a province in India, and talked *de haut en bas* to us, as he must have talked in India to natives. His social superiority was undoubted, but there did not seem to be a great deal of brain. Much more interesting was General A.P. Wavell, who had once been in College, and gave us a talk early in 1937 about the Russian army after attending its manoeuvres. He mentioned the use they had made of small teams of parachutists, dropping well behind enemy lines to disrupt headquarters and communications. I said to myself then that if another great war broke out, as already seemed quite likely, that was the sort of warfare I would like to get into.

I rather enjoyed the OTC, which was all but compulsory – those who had serious objections to military training could join Pinsent's Boy Scout troop instead. It was commanded by Walter Cowland, aided by Robin Ridgway and Ronald Hamilton, who taught modern languages, and Emmett a science don ('Mr Emmett/Was heard to mutter "Demmit!/Would the Brigade of Guards have got/Into such a knot?"'). We were drilled with short model Lee-Enfield rifles, with which we also went to shoot at Chilcomb range. Better than drill every Wednesday, and much better than cleaning our brass buttons, were the occasional field days, when we could practise infantry tactics in the open. Anyone who was the least good at soldiering could pass Certificate A, which meant that one was qualified to command an infantry platoon. Chilcomb, like hundreds of other villages, had on its village green a captured German cannon, brought back from the western front to help form a war memorial. Early in the next world war, all those guns were unobtrusively withdrawn, to be melted down and turned into better guns to fight the same enemy, who had turned worse.

I have never been at all good at singing. This was perhaps one reason why (to my private annoyance) I was never invited to join SROGUS, the Shakespeare Reading and Orpheus Glee Society, which met once or twice a term, usually to read a Shakespeare play. I made up for not being in SROGUS by making myself useful in the archaeological society, of which I became secretary. Early in my time in the school, Stuart and King (a long way my seniors) took me out to help them dig what turned out to be a La Tène II village on the slope south of St Catherine's Hill, now swept away by a motorway, so that I had a fragment of actual working practice. We found nothing more striking than a few bits of broken saucer and pot. Though I sang badly, I sang with enjoyment. College singings were fun, with songs now regarded as hopelessly old-fashioned such as 'Hearts of Oak', and so were occasional informal German singings in Hall, usually with Smith-Masters at the piano, which did no harm to our German grammar or pronunciation. More seriously, Harry Altham, housemaster of A House, collected Chinese porcelain. I have never forgotten being shown by him one evening some Sung saucers, perfectly plain, yet perfectly exquisite in form: an early lesson in quality. This was the same H.S. Altham who had come back from the Western Front with a major's DSO, and remained a pillar of amateur English cricket.

I saw a great deal more of College men than of commoners – this arose naturally from where we lived; but made a few friends among the commoners, especially Michael Brodrick, Andrew Boyd and Charles von Blumenthal, whose great-grandfather had been chief of staff to the Crown Prince of Prussia during the Franco-Prussian war. He came back from the summer holidays of 1935 looking particularly bronzed. I asked him where he had been. His family had had a great stroke of luck; they had found a sandy Mediterranean beach with hardly anybody else there, all through August, at a little village I would never have heard of called St Tropez.

Other commoners in the school with me, whom I hardly knew, included Jellicoe's son, Haig's nephew, Kitchener's nephew and heir, a grandson of Asquith's, Hugh Beach, a future master-general of the ordnance, Sinclair and Davies-Scourfield the escapers, a Clementi and a Mavrogordato. Dickie once claimed to me that, one half, he had known the whole school by sight and by name; I was not quite as well informed as he had been. Cricket I was allowed to give up in my third year – a relief. Winchester football I rather liked, and was quite good at, as I was able to shout loud while running fast: it was a rough, unscientific game, fun to play. I still often wear in cold weather the long thick woollen scarf (called, in all innocence, a pussy) which I was awarded as a member of College XV.

Out of the blue, Dickie gave me a portable typewriter, on the condition – which I kept – that I learned to use it properly, and did not simply use two fingers. To show off, I used it to write to Dolly, and can still recall the rocket she gave me by return of post for daring to use a machine to write to a lady. Nowadays I quite often have to, rather than expose ladies to a decrepit handwriting, but the lesson in manners stuck. The typewriter was borrowed by John Willett for a magical production of Twelfth Night in modern dress, which he put on as a College play; Feste appeared in the opening scene, typing on it, as Olivia's secretary. It was enormous fun to watch.

By an arrangement not then usual, for my last two years at Winchester I paid my own school bills, out of a bank account Dickie had started for me on the condition that it was never overdrawn. I was getting the best education to be had in the country, and as a scholar on Wykeham's endowment I paid £10 a term for board, tuition and lodging combined.

How on earth was this possible? Because Wykeham had endowed both his colleges heavily with land, and the governing body of Winchester had later made one most lucky investment. About a century and a quarter after the foundation, in the early 1500s, they got a letter from Wykeham's successor as Chancellor of England, instructing them to sell him some meadow land at Esher, opposite Hampton. They replied, politely, that they did not sell land. If, his secretary riposted, they persisted in their contumacy, the chancellor would make sure that nobody from either college got any church preferment he could block; so they sold. Esher palace, which Wolsey meant to rival Hampton Court from which the king had ousted him, now consists of a brick Tudor gateway and some mounds in the grass. But the governing body, having secured a fair price in cash, decided that the founder had been right about meadow land, and bought some more – which turned into the site of Southampton docks. No ship subsequently docked there without paying the college a fee.

Fate caught up, as it usually does. In 1947 docks were nationalised. Winchester got compensation – again a fair sum, but this time not in cash. The school was paid in treasury bonds, bearing two per cent per annum, with a clause typed in at the bottom of each bond, 'This bond is inalienable.'

When I was about sixteen, and staying as usual at White Hill for part of the summer holidays, Dolly invited some friends round for sherry, which we drank on the lawn. Noticing me tucking into it, she took me on one side afterwards. If I would promise her, then and there, not again to touch alcohol, or to smoke tobacco, till I was twenty-one, she would give me *a hundred pounds* as a twenty-first birthday present. The bribe seemed colossal. I accepted, and kept my word.

About then, she and some women friends of her own age were deploring the weakness of the current Conservative government, and wishing the men in it were more formidable. Why not, I ventured, invite Churchill to join it? They all shuddered at the thought. *'He's clever'*, explained why he was inadmissible. Only after her death, when Middlemass and Barnes published their life of Baldwin, including a photograph of her marked 'unknown', did I discover that the journeys Dolly often made to Aix-en-Provence coincided with the Baldwins' holidays there: she was their bridge partner. This was not of course a subject fit for discussion with me.

One spring (1937, I think), she took me on a tour of English cathedrals. We saw Gloucester, Worcester and Hereford, passing the vale of Evesham in full cherry blossom on the way, and then went on to Lichfield, where she had been brought up. She took me to lunch with an old admirer, in a lovely small Queen Anne house to the east of Lichfield: a little man, gone bald, about her own age, who having once been refused by her had never married at all. On his staircase were a dozen large, fine pictures. I had not been taught by Gleadowe and Oakeshott for nothing, and recognised them as Canalettos – English scenes, never exhibited, never reproduced. I dared an inquiry. Yes, his great-grandfather had bought them direct from the artist. I have often wondered what happened to them, since he had no close relatives. In the worst case, the army requisitioned his house and soldiers burned them. I hope, instead, they are scattered round the farmhouses of Staffordshire and will one day come again to light.

My housemaster in College – called the Second Master – was Monty Wright, a contemporary of my father, a mathematician who had been in College himself, and had come back from the Western Front with a Guards MC. Unluckily, he and I did not get on. On the only occasion when I needed his help badly, I didn't get it; each of us thought the other a fool. I complained to him that I was being sexually bullied by one of his favourite pupils. He could not believe the charge, and I failed to convince him of it.

A great many years on, reading the Oxford Book of Sonnets, I came on one by John Davies of Hereford, who was a contemporary of Shakespeare's, which began with lines that fitted my case only too well :

When first I learned the ABC of love
I was unapt to learn.

I shall make no attempt in these pages to sketch out my private life, beyond remarking that being at a one-sex school did it no good. Some blame may rest with Leach, with whom I had had a formal talk about the Facts of Life (my parents hardly uttered a word to me about sex, nor did any servant I knew). Leach laid it on thick that this was God's way of propagating mankind; it was all rather ethereal, and he forgot to mention an essential fact – that the male must penetrate the female. This I did not discover until the summer of 1939, when I learned it from a Left Book Club manual.

Dickie had been away in Australia for six months in 1930, looking into the possibilities of founding a branch of Peek, Frean out there. His report was so strongly in favour that the firm told him to go out and get on with it himself, so back he went in 1931, and stayed there for four years. The only time I remember a serious quarrel between my parents, while they still lived together (I do not count bickerings after bridge parties), was shortly before he left on this journey. Nina wanted to go too, but he insisted that she stay in England to look after the children. When he came back, in the summer of 1935, he did not come back alone, Edith Carson his American mistress came with him. Nina refused to divorce him. As the law then stood, he could not divorce her. Paddy and I both stayed with Nina. Paddy hardly saw her father again, and I saw him seldom, except in wartime. We moved from the tiny flat opposite Olympia to a detached house in Esher, with a sizeable garden and a garage.

His desertion of my mother, which helped to unsettle my Christian belief, strengthened hers. She became a Christian Scientist, and now and again took me to Christian Science services. I dutifully read my Mary Baker Eddy, but remained unconvinced. I will say, though, that my mother's injunction to 'hold the right thought, dear' has often been a help since. I have been all but immune to the common cold, by dint of telling myself that I'm not going to have one.

Once, in the spring of 1937, I did go on a brief holiday abroad with Dickie. We went by boat to Esbjerg on the west coast of Denmark, and on to Copenhagen by train; he had business to do there, and left me to the city's fine museums. In one of them, from a sixteenth-century painting of the Expulsion from Eden, I discovered something then carefully kept out of sight in English art galleries – that women have pubic hair. From Copenhagen we flew to Schiphol near Amsterdam, in a Douglas DC-3 – my unforgettable first flight, made more memorable still by the sight of a chequerboard of tulip fields in flower as we came in to land.

That summer, I went for a few days to stay with Gordon Barker, Maurice's elder brother, who was a regular cavalry officer, to see whether the military life might appeal to me too. I lived in the camp mess of the 4th/7th Dragoon Guards, a very smart regiment, still horsed; but the military life did not take. Their manners were excellent, they were all charming and brave, brought up to feed their horses before their men and their men before themselves, but the whole ambience of the mess struck me as narrow, compared to the conversation to which I was used in College, and I privately decided that whatever I did with my life, I would not devote it to fighting unless I had to.

* * *

In the autumn of 1937 I sat the annual examination for closed scholarships from Winchester to New College, and was elected, placed to my own surprise third out of eight, senior to men senior to me in the school. One of the examiners was R.H.S. Crossman, with whom I had a protracted *viva*, arguing about current English poets. His younger brother Tom, two years my senior in College where he was known to be very bright, was killed in a banal RAF air crash during the war, out of which the man he was teaching to fly stepped unhurt.

I was looking forward to two more halves at Winchester, relaxing and enjoying myself, when my father came down to tell me that I was to leave the school in a few days' time, and the country soon afterwards. He handed me a wedge of traveller's cheques and a letter of credit (are letters of credit by now entirely obsolete?) and instructed me to go abroad – well away from England – for six months. Was there anywhere I particularly wanted to go? As a matter of fact there was. I had just been reading some articles in the *Sunday Times* about Constantinople (Istanbul), which sounded a most fascinating city, worth exploring. So I spent the Christmas holidays reading up Byzantine history and van Millingen's books on the walls and the churches of Stamboul.

The Christmas holidays were also enlivened by meeting a stunningly attractive girl, a blonde called Diana Robbins, whom I much enjoyed looking at. She seemed quite to like me, and one weekend I was invited over to stay with her family just outside Newbury. The family were taking no chances; several other very young men turned up, all put to sleep in the village pub a few yards from the house. Diana and I exchanged letters, intermittently, over the next few months, while I was abroad.

Dickie found me a passage from Liverpool to Athens, and I was off on a proper grand tour. I undertook to spend, on the average, not more than ten shillings (50p) a day for food and lodging; and to make sure that when on land I sent him, every single day, a postcard at least, to say where I was. The journey out to Athens, in a small Cunard cargo steamer, was uneventful, with brief stops at Gibraltar and Malta. The captain's previous command had been the *Berengaria*, which he had had the misfortune to run aground. Athens bowled me over, the Acropolis above all. By a stroke of luck, I called one evening on the William Millers – he was then the accepted English authority on Greek history – and someone remarked that the Acropolis was open every night of full moon. There was a full moon that February night. I went up; I was the only visitor. The porter let me in, for a few drachmae, and retired back into his sentry-box – it was bitterly cold. Having the whole place to myself, I climbed up the side of the Parthenon, to where the Elgin Marbles frieze used to hang, and revelled in the beauty of it. I have never since seen anything more beautiful, and recall the climb almost every day. Reading in 2001 Peter Hart's *The Heat of Battle*, an account of the 16th battalion of the Durham Light Infantry in Italy and Greece in 1943–4, I was taken by the tale of an infantry section sent up to spend a night on the Parthenon at the opening of the troubles in Athens. What had it been like? 'Nothing up there but bloody stones, and perishing cold'.

I also got out of Athens on to some of the great classical sites. The British Consul-General there, Sebastian, an Old Wykehamist, took me to see Cape Sounion and the battlefield of Marathon. I went by bus to Delphi – a scary ride, along the edges of precipices – and was duly impressed, both by Delphi itself, and by the olive groves beneath it down towards Itea, which had caused the Peloponnesian war. The water there seemed so dubious that I drank retsina instead, my first taste of wine; Dolly forgave me. In a bus on the way to Sparta, I got my first sight of snow-covered mountains, the Taygetos range. I saw a little of Mistra; enough to write a letter in German, when I got back to Athens, of protest to Authority about the state into which it had been allowed to decay. It was at a restaurant in Sparta that I puzzled out, from the local newspaper, the fact that Hitler had brought off the Anschluss between Germany and Austria, forbidden by the treaty of Versailles: a move that visibly threatened Czechoslovakia, now hemmed in by Nazis on three sides.

Greece in 1938 was an uncomfortable country, even for the passing tourist, because it was under the dictatorship of Metaxas, who put out the extraordinary slogan that 'Greek history began on 4 August 1936', the day he had seized power. Any English public schoolboy could tell him this was wrong, but he did not want his subjects to bother their heads with notions, that he regarded as essentially false, about freedom or democracy.

Before I left Athens, Reuters' man there, who had gone out of his way to be friendly to me, charged me with a message to take to an Armenian in Istanbul. I was to memorise both the message and the address. The Armenian, it turned out, was an acquaintance of Dickie's, and his address was already written down in my pocket book; all the same, I was not to write down the message, which I can still remember, and now write down for the first time – 'Michalokopoulos has been sent to an island'. I was not to bother myself with who Michalokopoulos was – when I had delivered the message I was to forget all about him, which of course I never managed to do. This I can now see to have been my earliest introduction to the actualities of secret service.

Istanbul was as staggering as Athens. I was captivated by Santa Sophia, then whitewashed all over inside, except for the pendentives of the great dome; the architectural feat remained astounding. One day, while I was revelling in it, I fell into talk with an American about twice my own age. After a few minutes, he invited me to step with him into the narthex, and showed me where he had been allowed to clear the whitewash away from

45

a space about three feet high by two wide, revealling a superb mosaic of the Virgin with the infant Jesus, inscribed with four letters in Greek, MPΘY – short for MHTHP ΘEOY, mother of God. Could I read the inscription? Of course I could. Had I Latin? How else had I got into Oxford? Would I care to be his secretary?

I said no, or rather not yet, on the ground that I would be a much better secretary after I had taken a degree. Had I said yes, I would still have been in Istanbul when the war broke out, would certainly have been swept up into one secret service or another, and was then so brash that I would most probably have ended up, quite soon, in a sack in the Bosphorus, tied securely at the neck. By the time I got a degree the war was over and I had entirely lost touch with Whittemore, my acquaintance who was allowed to take the whitewash off all the mosaics inside Santa Sophia, thus restoring it to most of its full Byzantine glory.

I paid a brief visit by train to Ankara, with a letter of introduction from Dickie to the second secretary in the legation there, written because all three of us were Wykehamists. His name was Chapman, and he seemed marked for advancement, till he was accidentally killed in an air crash late in the war. He was thoroughly charming to me, and informative, when I asked him what work as a diplomat was like. It all depended, he assured me, on one's head of chancery; at Ankara they were lucky, they only had to put in about four hours' office work a day. Surely this meant a very easy life? Not altogether, for one had to spend about eight hours more every day on duty tasks of entertaining and being entertained. I thus realised that the diplomatic career was not going to be for me, even if I could pass the Foreign Office exam.

In Ankara, I stood by a brand-new bronze equestrian statue of Mustafa Kamal, the liberator-dictator, looking down a brand new dual carriageway that led to the diplomatic quarter. Within a furlong lay a medieval gate of the old city. I walked through it, dust at once up to my ankles, and little light because the upper stories of the houses were so close to each other. A woman came round a corner, stepping straight out of an illustration to the Old Testament – flowing robes down to her ankles, coif round her head, a pitcher of water balanced above it. As she caught sight of a man, her hand flew at once to her coif, to cover her face. I had stepped back from the modern into the ancient world.

I wanted to go on from Istanbul to Roumania, where R.W. Seton-Watson (Hugh and Christopher's father) had given me a letter of introduction to friends of his; from whom, if I was lucky, I could borrow a pony, and ride all up the Danube valley to return the pony to cousins in Austria. I had also thought, out of mere curiosity, that it would be interesting to spend a few days in Odessa, having a glance at the Soviet system in action. I put this to Dickie; he cabled back 'CANNOT APPROVE ROMANY OR RUSSKY', and sent me back to Athens for my next lot of traveller's cheques. Who had tipped him off I never knew, but a day or two after I would have arrived in Bucharest there was a right-wing coup détat, with a lot of shooting, which I suppose I was better out of than involved in.

A short spell back in Athens gave me another visit to the Acropolis, and I could tell Reuters' man that his message had been delivered. Dickie approved a visit to Italy, provided I got clear of it in three weeks. I took a boat through the Corinth Canal, catching sight of what was then thought to be Homer's Ithaca as we passed, to Brindisi, bought, by gesture, a *Corriere della Sera* at Brindisi station, and learned enough Italian from it during a day's journey to get myself a bed in a small hotel in Naples that night.

I can specify when I became a convinced anti-fascist: it was during those two or three days in Naples. Mussolini had the Italians well buttoned up. Every fit male child had to belong to the *Balilla*, his *Hitlerjugend*, and wear a uniform. I saw and heard a boy of about seven being ticked off, with real nastiness, by a boy of about nine because the younger one, who was a private, had failed to salute the older, who was a sergeant, as they walked past each other. A system that could make children behave like that must, I thought, be irredeemably bad; nothing I discovered later made me change my mind. Indeed, a few weeks later, having seen a little of Rome and spent a day at Orvieto, I had another jolt. I was walking across Tuscany and came to the village, mentioned in Dante, of Monteriggioni. It was quite early in the morning, school was just starting. As I walked past the school, I heard the children chanting the eighth of Mussolini's Ten Commandments: *Mussolini ha sempre ragione*, is always right.

In Rome – nobody believes this any more – I lay down in the Sistine Chapel and spent an hour, almost alone, looking at the ceiling through a pair of borrowed opera glasses. I also saw what had so far been uncovered of ancient Rome, and recall the arena at the Colosseum, decorated by a plain wooden cross inscribed AVE CRVX SPES VNICA, a gesture of a sort by the church against the regime. In Florence I could enjoy Botticelli's Venus, before the restorers murdered her (why did that incident not create an international furore?), and be captivated by his Judith with the head of

Holofernes, which I resolved to loot if war and revolution and I happened all to coincide in Florence, as they never did. In San Gimignano I woke very early, in the Cisterna hotel, to see from my window a flat sea of mist with a dozen Tuscan villages poking their tops through it. I also had a day or two in Venice, sensationally beautiful, even if crawling with German tourists. I saw the wreck of Leonardo's last supper in Milan, and then took a train towards the Alps, pausing at Orta to walk by the lake, while the stationmaster stole from my rucksack the new sunglasses I had just bought. I took a train on to Domodossola, where I had my shoes re-soled. The soles wore out in the course of the next fortnight's walking.

I had not quite done with fascist Italy. I walked from Domodossola up the Simplon pass, where the road sometimes rang hollow under my feet, and the granite mountain sides seemed peppered with loopholes. At the frontier, several thousand feet up, the frontier police took my passport into their warm office, leaving me for twenty-five minutes to wait in the chill air till they had decided they would stamp it and let me leave. I walked on into Switzerland. No frontier police, no guards of any sort, indeed not a soul in sight; and no loopholes either. About a mile on, I came on a party of convicts mending the road. An army officer in uniform wished me good morning, in German; I replied. Had I a passport? Fine; he did not ask to look at it, wished me a good journey and turned away. At the top of the pass there was a small hotel, where I stayed the night. The views in every direction were terrific, the sense of freedom overwhelming.

I walked out of Switzerland, a few days later, over the Col des Montets into the Chamonix valley. At the frontier there was a little footbridge, with a sentry at each end. Each wished me good day, in French; nobody bothered about any formality. I walked through to Grenoble, where I met David Johnson – the first known face I had met since leaving England. Several weeks later, I was stopped on a country road near Toulouse by a pair of gendarmes. Where was my passport? I produced it. It showed that I had left Italy, into Switzerland, weeks before. But how had I got into France and what was I up to? I played the innocent schoolboy, which I was, and they let me go.

At Carcassonne, Viollet-le-Duc's restoration entranced me, but more modern politics bothered me. From the ramparts, I could see the Pyrenees in the distance. Was it not my duty to pick my way across them, and throw my lot in with the doomed republic of Spain? The civil war was now visibly drawing towards its end. I had no contacts of any kind, and a day's debate with myself convinced me that I would do more good to the causes I favoured by going back to Oxford, and learning to think, instead of throwing myself away in some futile final charge. I suppose I was right; I still rather feel I was cowardly, as well.

* * *

Soon after I got back to England, the international scene turned black, with the Munich crisis. I went round to Esher town hall to find out if I could make myself useful, and helped to fit gas masks together and to distribute them. Stronger men were digging slit trenches and sandbagging doorways. Day after day the newspapers and wireless bulletins seemed to grow more ominous; major war seemed imminent. Even in the depth of the crisis, John Hasted and I went together to see *Hamlet*, a ballet by Massine, danced by Helpmann, with music from Beethoven's seventh symphony. It was so powerful that we were completely transported away from the Berchtesgaden talks to Elsinore, although the moment we came out into the London street afterwards we bought another evening newspaper to find out what had happened while we had been out of this world. I do not much care for ballet, and have seldom been again, but that one performance I can still recall with delight. The Munich agreement was indeed a relief, but at the time felt to me a shameful one. We had failed to support the only democracy (bar Sweden) in Europe east of Switzerland, and had given in yet again to Hitler's bluster. Debate still goes on about whether it was a sensible move on Chamberlain's part. I now see why he did it, but still believe him to have been wrong.

I went up to Oxford a few days later, to be plunged straight into the by-election in which A.D. Lindsay, Master of Balliol, failed to win that then safely Conservative seat against a young barrister called Quintin Hogg. Andrew Ensor, a year senior to me at New College, and I canvassed a strip of the Banbury Road on Lindsay's behalf, and wasted an evening chatting to General Swinton, the inventor of the tank, a colleague of Hogg's (and of Andrew's father) at All Souls.

I got an allowance of £180 a year from Dickie, on which to keep myself at New College; and just managed to stay within it, except for a bill at Blackwell's bookshop, which he did not mind settling for me. I lived – because they were almost the cheapest rooms in College – in a late nineteenth-century block in the back quadrangle, on a staircase with five other undergraduates, none of whom survived the impending war. My scout brought me hot water every morning, to shave in. If I wanted a bath, I had a furlong to walk to the bathrooms behind the front quadrangle. In midwinter this was not much fun, but nobody thought of protesting.

My moral tutor was David Ogg, the historian of the 17th century, who explained to me that the school of Modern History stopped in 1878 for European history, and in 1914 for English. I therefore, to his disappointment, insisted on taking Modern Greats instead (now usually called PPE, politics, philosophy and economics), because that ran up to the present day, where my own current interests, sharpened by my recent journey, lay. Ogg told me to take Logic for Pass Mods. I went to a lecture by Pickard-Cambridge, on forms of the syllogism. Every word of it might have been delivered, in Latin, five or six centuries earlier. The hexameter 'Barbara, Celarent, Ferii, Dario, Baralipton' has stuck in my mind ever since – it plagues me sometimes while I am shaving – but I did not go to another of those lectures. I took German instead, which I had to teach myself (Schiller, *Geschichte des dreissig-jährigen Krieges*, perfectly straightforward). I also went to lectures by Ogg, on British constitutional history from 1660. On the first morning, he entered the lecture room as New College clock struck ten, and began to talk. A moment later, another undergraduate arrived. Ogg paused in mid-sentence till she had opened her notebook and got out her pen, and then went on. This happened twice. Neither latecomer reappeared; the rest of us were always thereafter punctual. Pass Mods, which I took at the end of my first term, presented no kind of difficulty.

A chance remark of Isaiah Berlin put me on to Freud, of whom I read a certain amount, particularly *The Interpretation of Dreams* and *The Psychopathology of Everyday Life*. From the second of those books I drew some comfort when Diana came to have tea with me (she was staying with an aunt on Headington), to break it to me that she was now engaged to be married to somebody else. Her father, who had been made a peer, had made a large fortune in Rhodesia, where she often stayed; she was to marry the Governor-General's aide-de-camp. She showed me their engagement ring, which she put away in her handbag, remarking that as the engagement had yet to be announced, she did not wear it. When she left, she left her bag behind her. I took it up next day to her aunt's, but was curiously flattered that she had left the ring behind. I don't think we ever met again.

The Spanish civil war was still grinding on, clearly drawing towards a victory for Franco. The British and French governments, anxious not to exasperate Hitler and Mussolini, continued to turn a blind eye to their and to Stalin's manifest interventions, and stuck to their own doctrine of non-interference. They would not even allow the Republicans to buy anti-aircraft guns to protect their cities against bombing raids; this specially exasperated left-wingers. Some time that winter, I was persuaded by Frank Thompson (my fellow scholar at New College) to take part with him in a demonstration march in London. We assembled in the roadway north of the British Museum, and marched down Shaftesbury Avenue and Piccadilly to the Spanish embassy in Belgrave Square. I was in the front rank, holding one end of a banner reading ARMS FOR SPAIN. Nobody seemed to take much notice of us, and I saw no press report of the event, but it did my conscience a little good to have taken part in it, and helped me to look revolting students in the eye thirty years later.

Always then one to swim against the tide, I decided in my second term to sleep by day and work through the night. I would get up after six in the evening, dine in hall at seven, talk to friends afterwards, and settle down to read at about eleven, having a quiet night to myself, till after College breakfast, when I sported my oak (locked my door) and went to sleep. On days when I had tutorials, I would stay up for them. It worked reasonably well; but come the summer term, I didn't go on with it.

That Trinity term, I was entangled in an odd emotional quartet. Iris Murdoch, later well known as a novelist, decided she liked me, though, so formal and distant were man-woman relations in the Oxford of the day, she said nothing directly about it to me. She was a scholar of Somerville. I meanwhile fell for a commoner at Somerville called Léonie Marsh, who in turn was much taken by Frank Thompson, who had fallen for Iris. Léonie toyed with me, sometimes hinting she would come and share a bed with me, usually putting me off at the last minute. I later found out that she had had transient affairs with four other undergraduates, and she threw us all over for a naval officer, whom she married.

I joined the Union, as a matter of course, and heard and even spoke in a few debates. Once I appeared on the order paper – I was a teller for a motion, easily carried in a thinnish house in the last debate of Trinity term 1939, that 'this house would go to war for Danzig'. Unlike the notorious motion of mid-February 1934 (for which Max Beloff had been a teller) that 'this house will not fight for king and country', this debate was unreported in any newspaper, national or local.

By that time I was already in the army, as a part-time soldier. About midwinter 1938/9, family history repeated itself. My father sent for me, and said that he did not like the look of the newspapers; he reckoned there was soon going to be another world war. Had I not better join his show? New College made no sort of objection. I believe about a third of the men who were up with me had already joined some sort of volunteer unit before war did break out in September 1939. I was commissioned a second lieutenant, Royal Engineers, Territorial Army, on 3 March 1939, and posted to the 35th Searchlight Battalion, which Dickie commanded. The unit had been the 1st Surrey Rifles, 21st London Regiment, and had fought as such through the Great War, taking part in September 1916 in the battle at High Wood on the Somme (along with David Jones in the Royal Welch Fusiliers, as he described in his matchless *In Parenthesis*) and in December 1917 in the capture of Jerusalem from the Turks by Allenby. Every year in peacetime there was a regimental dinner on the Jerusalem anniversary.

There were two drill halls, one brand new, in Lordship Lane, Dulwich, the other (to which I was posted) in Flodden Road, Camberwell: dull yellow brick buildings, cold and draughty. There were a few regular soldiers on permanent duty there, one of whom received 'two dozen buckets, fire, galvanised iron, eighteen-inch, 50% for water and 50% for sand'. He filled each one half with water and half with sand. A very few Sundays later, Dickie spotted this during one of his routine inspections; it has always symbolised to me the stupidest aspects of regular soldiering.

There was one obvious job I could take on, training soldiers in how to read an Ordnance Survey map – my first teaching task. I was also expected to mug up, by myself, out of army handbooks, the elements of electrical engineering and of searchlight operations, and I taught myself aircraft recognition. By the summer of 1940 I reckoned to identify any warplane in a western European sky, just as five years earlier I could have identified any motor car on any English road – the techniques were similar. Our technical equipment was not advanced. We had no radar sets yet; they came in later, few at a time and deadly secret. We located aircraft by sound. Even the large Mark IX sound locators were hard to come by, and my own section seldom had anything better than a Mark III, simply two pairs of wooden earphones about six feet apart, on a rotating stand. Even this presented its troubles; a sapper allocated to sound locator duties turned out when I tested him to be stone deaf in one ear, and thus unable to use a sound locator at all.

I went to one annual camp in peacetime. Instead of the usual fortnight, it lasted for a month. On the last day of Trinity term I went down into Sussex, and had the section deployed on half-a-dozen sites east of Petworth. Parts of AA Command were thus unobtrusively mobilised on to war stations, just in case the international scene, already very black, suddenly turned to war. In mid-July I went back to plain clothes, to a routine visit to White Hill, and to life at Esher punctuated by worries about Hitler.

CHAPTER 3

War

These worries turned out to be justified: the war broke out in the middle of my first long vacation. Had it not been for Hitler, Richard Pares would have been my tutor at New College, and I might have had a different career. I went into uniform for six years instead.

Anti-Aircraft Command mobilised, fully this time, on 24 August 1939. At Flodden Road there was an old-fashioned flurry, that I recognised from what I had read about the outbreak of the previous world war. Along the railings in the street stood stolid, silent women, waiting for their men to come and chat with them, exchanging endearments and advice. Inside, there was little effective to be done because there was little equipment. I spent a few days collecting stragglers, while the unit was packed off by train to a camp on the north Cornish coast for a few weeks. Once we got our ninety-centimetre searchlights, lorries and sound locators, we settled into sites in the mid-Thames valley. Battalion headquarters was, from the start, in a requisitioned house on the upstream side of Marlow, and I had a spell there – sleeping in a tent on the lawn – choosing sites before searchlights deployed on to them. (I discovered in 2005 that the ten-year-old son of the gardener, Mr Bond, who had stayed in the gatehouse to look after the garden, was my long-standing acquaintance Brian Bond the military historian, who succeeded Michael Howard as professor at King's College London. Mrs Bond, I'm glad to say, had always cherished a warm regard for Colonel Foot.)

On Sunday 3 September, in north Oxfordshire with a driver, knowing that the Prime Minister was going to address the nation, we simply went up to the front door of a large house in a village and asked if we might listen in as well. A dozen people assembled in a drawing-room, to hear a weary voice inform us that we were at war. A few minutes later, I walked up to a remote farmhouse at the end of a track, to make the usual inquiries about water supply and so on, that would cover the arrival of a searchlight detachment. I mentioned that we were now at war. 'Oh yes I know', the farmer's wife replied, 'we have just been listening to Mr Chamberlain on the wireless.' Many farms in those days still had no electricity, but hers was well found.

That night there was gloom in Mess; no wonder. We rose to drink the loyal toast, as usual (they in port, I in orangeade), and sat round silently. My father, still seated, raised his glass again, and gave us another toast: 'Damnation to him.' We all knew whom he meant, and drank up. It took nearer six years than five.

John Elcombe, the quartermaster, was an elderly lieutenant, Royal Engineers, promoted from the ranks, and let fall another evening that he had been a corporal in *River Clyde* at Gallipoli on 25 April 1915. Why on earth, I asked him, was he still alive? 'I 'ad no orders to go ashore.' He had spent the day leaning against a steel plate in *River Clyde*'s hold, listening to Turkish machine gun bullets drumming against the outside of it and wondering when they would start to come through. (He had been taught the formula, but had forgotten it.) At sundown the Turks did stop firing, for a few minutes, to pray; he got his orders and ran ashore then. As he did so, he saw the sea between V Beach and the ship for thirty yards out red with blood. Churchill must have heard of that blood, hence his doubts about whether the great seaborne landings of the next world war, particularly the one into Normandy, were going to work at all.

I had a few days at the army gas school at Fort Tregantle, just outside Plymouth, from which I can still remember the smells of phosgene and of chlorine, and the intense irritation caused by a tiny drop of mustard gas on the back of my hand. That course put me off red geraniums for good, for they smell like mustard gas. Most of the cold first winter of the war I spent under canvas in the Chilterns, near Lacey Green north of High Wycombe. At first Bob Burrows was the section commander. He then moved on, and I had about a hundred men to look after by myself, scattered round half a dozen sites. Nobody told us what we were there for. It is clear in retrospect that we were covering Bomber Command's headquarters near High Wycombe and the prime minister's residence at Chequers. There was no Luftwaffe activity; the only excitement arose when a townee night sentry, getting no answer to a challenge, opened fire on a cow.

In March 1940 I was briefly posted to work as a liaison officer in the RAF operations room at Northolt, where I extended my flying experience to include rides in Blenheims and Tiger Moths, and met one incident so extraordinary that I must record it as perhaps the stupidest thing government has done in my lifetime. Walking along the main road from London to Oxford, which ran past the southern side of Northolt airfield, I could see the Blenheims of 604 Squadron. Parties of airmen were busy on each, re-painting RAF roundels on top of what had been put there overnight: a thin light blue swastika on a white ground, the mark of the Finnish air force. I turned back, and went to see the station intelligence officer, with whom I had made friends. He explained that the squadron had just been 'ordered to volunteer' to serve in Finland; the aircraft had been repainted accordingly. But the station commander, having heard on the BBC that the Finns had just asked the USSR for an armistice, had cancelled the order. Had we gone to war with the USSR and with Germany at the same time, our chances of survival would have been slim indeed. Russian manpower organized by the German general staff, even with Hitler in overall command, would surely have been too much for us. I began to feel, with Francis Thompson in his 'Hound of Heaven', that,

> My days have crumbled and gone up in smoke,
> Have puffed and burst like sun-starts on a stream.

Gone up in smoke seemed all too likely to be an Englishman's fate under attack from the Luftwaffe in the summer and autumn of 1940.

In early May 1940 my company, detached from the rest of the battalion, went down – by road; it took all day – to the coast of Kent. I had five lights deployed on the sea fronts at Margate, Broadstairs and Ramsgate, with headquarters on what had been Broadstairs aerodrome. I treasure a letter from the Admiralty, which found its way all the way down the chain of command to subalterns, explaining that neither the army nor the air force nor local authorities were to try to obstruct Fleet Air Arm airfields: 'Any obstruction necessary will be provided by the Admiralty.' As Broadstairs aerodrome was not FAA, some telegraph poles went up on it. It was of course absurd to send so much paper round the army. In the German army we were then fighting, there were no written orders below corps headquarters – and look which side won the 1940 land battle. The Germans had advanced much faster than the British with radio-telephony, so did not need our masses of bumph. The War Office absorbed more paper annually, all through the war, than the entire London book publishing industry.

I assured the section (wrongly, since I did not know that 51st Highland Division were doing a spell in the Maginot Line) that they were the nearest

British troops to the enemy. To my soldiers' exasperation, I insisted on their wearing steel helmets whenever they were out of doors. They were less put out when a motor-cycle dispatch rider came back one day from a journey to company headquarters, at the Red Lion in Wingham, with a dent in his helmet, which had saved him from being killed by a bullet from a passing German fighter.

The morning of 10 May was particularly fine and clear, more an early summer than a spring day. Soon after dawn, a Heinkel 111 appeared over Manston, high up – too high for Manston's gunners to reach it – and then flew down over Caesar's landing-place to provoke equally ineffectual efforts from the guns round Dover. I suppose this to have been as much feint as reconnaissance, a way of making sure that home forces kept their minds on home, instead of paying any attention to the invasion that dawn of Belgium and Holland. The Ramsgate seafront site must have been eyewitness to the return of scores of thousands of soldiers from Dunkirk, at the end of May and in the earliest days of June. They were rapidly passed inland from the Kent coast, leaving little impression on us; it was not our part of the army, we could do nothing to help them, and were most use keeping out of their way. We had already fallen into the routine of stand-to at first light and last light. Most of us were up and busy most of the night, and learned to sleep by day.

Long afterwards I heard, from a man who had then been a sergeant in the Pay Corps, that his superiors had put out word to every unit that came back from Dunkirk that the Pay Corps would accept any foreign currency they had with them, at a better rate than one could get at a bank, and no questions asked. The state thus secured a large sum in francs (French, Swiss and Belgian), dollars, marks, lire and guilders, picked up by soldiers from the least disciplined units as they marched through towns in Flanders that had just received the attentions of the Luftwaffe, so that when they passed a bank they might be marching ankle deep in banknotes. My informant told me that he had himself driven the lorry that took the proceeds to the Bank of England: about £13,000,000 worth, most of it in notes of small denominations, exactly what the secret services were looking for. When, years later still, I tried to put this story into print, it scandalised the historical section of the Cabinet Office.

To believe Dolly, the great tragedy of Dunkirk was that someone stole the field glasses she had given Maurice Barker for a twenty-first birthday present while he (a subaltern in the 12th Lancers) was on his way to the beaches, which he crossed in safety. (Robin Negus had died young already). An acquaintance who came back from Dunkirk told me that he cast an eye over several hundred soldiers, lying like himself in the sand dunes waiting their turn for a boat; about half wore their steel helmets on their heads, the other half laid them over their genitals.

We were edging into the Battle of Britain, in which our own small part was inglorious; but it was something to have been there at the time. We had a lot of minor action, a little bombing, and not much sleep. One stick of light bombs fell slap across Broadstairs aerodrome. Luckily for me, the fourth bomb of the stick hung up, and never dropped. I paced it out next morning; it would have landed a yard or two from me. The others cratered the grass, hurting no one. On another occasion, quite a lot of bombs were dropped near by from Ju 87 Stuka dive bombers, making a ghastly row as they fell. One failed to explode, not far from me. I walked over to look at it. The noise came from cardboard streamers, attached to the bomb, still intact. I took all my sergeants to see, and told them to tell their men not to be frightened of a piece of cardboard; thereafter, the din was more bearable.

Next to my site was a water tower, which made a magnificent observation post, all the better once I had bought (they were the last pair to be had in Maidstone) a decent pair of French field glasses, with which I now watch birds or deer, but then used to distinguish a Spitfire from an Me 109 approaching head-on. On one Me 109 my site's Lewis gun and I both opened fire. The aircraft fired also. We all missed. It was the only time I ever fired in anger the .455" Webley revolver which had been my grandfather's constant companion in 1914–18, and was mine all through 1940. One accepted, as part of the job of being a junior officer, the certainty of being shot at and the likelihood of being killed. All my class contemporaries did the same. There was nothing heroic about this; it was commonplace, part of what James Joll (who was one of us) once called in a famous article about diplomacy the unspoken assumptions among which one lived. None of our fathers let us forget the expectation of life of an infantry subaltern on the western front in 1917: three weeks. Survivors were proud to discover, years afterwards, that the expectation of life of aircrew in Bomber Command in 1941 was even shorter. I was just extremely lucky.

I did volunteer for Fighter Command, because I was so impressed by its achievements in 1940, but was turned down, because I had already passed my twentieth birthday. Invited to volunteer for Bomber Command instead, I declined; perhaps just as well. Peter de Wesselow who had been in charge of me for my first fortnight in College went into Bomber Command, was twice shot down, and escaped each time, under his own steam. He had so clear and ringing a speaking voice (from having read the lessons so often in chapel, when he was Prefect of Hall) that he became a master bomber in the pathfinder force, helping conduct the raids both on Peenemünde and on Dresden – an unexpected consequence of a Christian education. As an elderly man he was often asked whether he regretted raiding Dresden. He did not: it was a vital part of German war industry as well as a major communications centre on the way to the eastern front. He had his orders, and did not hesitate to carry them out. As his epitaph said, 'He tried to do good.'

Our principal event on the North Foreland took place in the small hours of 19 June. Hathaway's light on the sea front by Margate illuminated a German bomber, a Heinkel 111, which was promptly shot down by a night fighter (I later met the pilot, the celebrated Sailor Malan, who was operating a Spitfire at night for the first time; this was his second kill of the night). The aircraft crashed in the sea, just off shore. By the time I got there, a few minutes later, all but one of the crew had come ashore and been arrested by Hathaway. I waded out to the wreck, which lay in about three feet of water, in case there was anything to be found in it. As I stepped up to it, a largish wave hit me, and I put a hand down to the aircraft's tail to steady myself – on to the face of a dead man. This was the missing member of the crew, who had pulled his ripcord too soon, and was lying on the port tail fin, still entangled in bits of parachute and cord. The clamber turned out to be worth it – I found some marked maps and a diary in the cockpit, as well as a small pistol, taken off me a short while afterwards at Manston airfield, where I was allowed to sit in on the first interrogation of the crew, whom the diary proved to have come from Merville, west of Lille. I kept the pistol belt for years, with its 'Gott mit uns' motto, and then gave it to the regimental museum. Paul Nash's painting of the tail of the wreck (without its corpse) is now in the cellars of the Ashmolean at Oxford.

Every morning, at first light, a Gladiator biplane would take off from Manston, climb laboriously to 10,000 feet, fly up and down for a bit, and return with a weather report. German radar (which we did not, at our level, know the Germans had got) must have noticed this. One fine morning an Me 109 appeared from the east, above the Gladiator, and dived gently down on it, out for an easy score. I was sentimental enough to take my helmet off, because I was about to see a man killed. I was, but not the one

I thought. The Gladiator pilot kept, as usual, a straight and level course, till, at precisely the right moment, he looped the loop, came down on the Messerschmitt's tail, and shot it down.

Over night, on 31 May/1 June, we changed regiments. The War Office (which might have been thought to have more important work to do at the time) reallocated all searchlight units from the Royal Engineers to the Royal Artillery.

At about this time, I was visited by Captain Chambers, the battery's second-in-command, who had fought on the western front in 1916–18. I asked him, 'Were things as bad as this in March '18?' – which I had been brought up to believe had been the darkest month in the army's history. 'Oh this is far worse than March '18', he replied, and indeed it was, as a map in any decent newspaper made clear. But I am sure that it no more crossed his mind than it crossed mine that we might have lost the war. We had clearly lost a big battle, and a great deal of equipment; but, invincibly ignorant, determined to go on fighting. On the continent, it was everywhere taken for granted that Germany had won the war – not a view much shared this side of the Channel. A current fashion among historians suggests that we would have been much more sensible to settle with Hitler, while we could, instead of standing out so obstinately against him, wasting untold lives and too much of the nation's capital, a fashion that overlooks a simple, fundamental point – how awful a Europe dominated by Hitler and his gang for many years would have been.

A substantial slice of the army's manpower was absorbed, all through the war, by Anti-Aircraft Command, over a quarter of a million men and women, under General Sir Frederick Pile, rumoured to have been put to this task because his expertise was in mobile armoured warfare, for which the army was not yet ready. But as life in AA Command was so dull – like so much of any war – little about this has come out on paper, and the nation's news media's memory no longer extends to cover it.

Much of 35 SL Regiment had been recruited from the staff of the Southern Railway. In my own troop, all the drivers belonged to the Association of Locomotive Engineers and Firemen, most of the soldiers to the National Union of Railwaymen, and the two troop clerks to the Railway Clerks' Association, the trade union arrangements being exactly mirrored by their military tasks. We were, I think, better off than the searchlight regiment recruited from Bentall's department store in Kingston, of which the CO was the shop's managing director, the battery commanders his four floor managers, and so on down.

At about this time, I inquired whether I would ever receive the actual document that formed my commission, and was assured that the King was very busy, and it would turn up one day. I long supposed it had been destroyed by bombing, during the impending turmoil. In the end it turned up, in the nineteen-nineties, in a cupboard in the old War Office full of commissions nobody had ever got round to forwarding to the officers concerned. It was found by a friend, John Sainsbury, while he wrote his fine history of Hertfordshire territorial units, and he sent it on to me. The king had indeed been busy, as he had signed it – with a rubber stamp; so, with less excuse, had the secretary of state for war when he countersigned it. It still contained phrases that had been used by Victoria when she commissioned Cunningham into her navy long before, exhortations such as 'herein fail not at your peril' that reached me rather late.

Dolly, as she ran a farm, did not have evacuees planted on her at White Hill. She and Miss Timson were at lunch one day when they heard the door-bell ring, and a few minutes later Camfield came in. A lady had called who only spoke French. His French was too rusty to understand her. Miss Timson went into the hall, to find out what was going on. Madame de Gaulle's housekeeper had called: Madame understood that Dolly sold the best milk in the neighbourhood, and wanted to open an account – she and her daughter lived close to Ashridge. Dolly thought this so secret that she never mentioned it to me at all. Miss Timson told me long afterwards.

August 1940 I spent at Hornchurch airfield, under Park's command in 11 Group RAF, working one shift in three in the operations room as an anti-aircraft liaison officer. Again, I made friends with the station IO, who allowed me, when not on duty, to attend the nightly showing of film taken in combat that day by the cameras that each fighter aircraft operating from Hornchurch had lodged, beside its eight .303" machine guns, in its wings. From Broadstairs I had been watching the Battle of Britain from the gallery. I now had a seat in the stalls. I have never forgotten, for instance, film taken by Malan as he closed in on a Heinkel 111, from which tracer could be seen arcing gently towards him. He took out in turn all the crew but the pilot, whom he left alone. 'Why did you do that, Sailor?' 'Well, he'd dropped his bombs already, and I thought it would do Luftwaffe morale no good if he found his way back to his base, if he could, and explained what the reception over here was like.' The pilots enjoyed commenting on each others' gunnery, and I picked up a faint impression that, as the month went on, the standard of the German pilots they were opposing was starting to fall.

I got to know, slightly, in the mess two other later famous aces besides Malan: Tuck and Deere. Tuck was having his Dostoevsky phase, and was pleased to find an intellectual to whom he could chat; unluckily, I had not yet reached mine, so was not of much use to him. Deere – like Park the group commander, a New Zealander – was less inclined to talk to soldiers, having been given a chill welcome by the retreating garrison at Dunkirk when shot down over the beach-head. On the spot, they had had no idea of the amount of effort Fighter Command had been putting into protecting them.

In the operations room it was clear how much depended on the reports from radar stations along the coast, where some six hundred young women (including Anne Miller) – who ought to be as famous as 'The Few', the six hundred fighter pilots with whom they were working – stood up to incessant minor and major attacks, and provided steady, certain warning of impending raids. This saved the RAF the need to mount standing patrols, and enabled controllers to have a squadron or two of Spitfires or Hurricanes waiting above a major raid, in time to split it up before it could drop its bombs. There were also most useful messages from the RAF Y service, which heard German pilots chatting to each other as they taxied out for take-off, and often gave the earliest warning of large raids. The results of these messages were plain to see, on the map table; their sources long remained secret.

I was glad I had had practice at New College in sleeping by day. I once slept through a whole squadron of twelve Spitfires taking off a few feet above the roof of my hut. Even my heavy sleep was now and again broken by the Tannoy loudspeaker, ordering all personnel not on duty to take shelter immediately. Once, during one of the worst raids on Hornchurch (on 24 August), I was thus dutifully sitting in a slit trench, wearing battledress over pyjamas, and not feeling comfortable – not because of the frequent bomb bursts outside, but because whenever the nearby heavy AA battery fired a salvo, we got a blast wave through the trench. Two pilots sitting near me looked at each other, nodded, and went out. I asked one of them that evening where they had gone. He told me that they disliked being bombed on the ground. They had walked round the perimeter till they found an aircraft with some petrol in it, and had flown round quietly, low, till the fuss was over. This raid put Hornchurch out of action for less than three hours, the time it took bulldozers to refill the craters on the grass runways. Taking off thereafter was bumpy, but feasible. Some damage had been done to the hangars, and to aircraft on the ground, but the operations room – half-underground and well protected – had not been disturbed at all, and when Park made his usual call by Hurricane that evening the station commander was able to tell him that the airfield was fully operational.

Coming off watch early one morning, I bumped into one of the controllers in flying kit. He said he was learning to fly a Spitfire; and a few days later, I noticed 74 Squadron taking off with thirteen aircraft instead of the usual twelve. That night, in mess, he said to me with a grin *'Got one!'*. He had felt he would be a better controller if he had taken part in an air battle himself.

After a month at Hornchurch, I was stood down, and sent back to 342 Battery, taking over a troop with its headquarters in a dugout close to the beach at Reculver, looking out over the flats where Barnes Wallis was later to test his dam-busting bomb. It was odd to live in a dugout, exactly as Dickie's generation had done for years in France. Unlike them, I had little mud and no shelling, so cannot really claim to have shared the experience.

Soon I was posted back to Marlow. My father arranged for him and for me to have brief leave over one weekend. He had found some petrol coupons, and took me with him by car down into Dorset. On the main roads all went well, but the quarter-inch map on which he was navigating did not show many side roads, all the signposts had been painted out – the invasion scare was on – and, after some twisting and turning, Dickie turned to me and said 'I'm sorry, old boy, we're bushed. I shall ask the next person we meet.' Round the next corner, an old man was trimming a hedge. 'Could you tell me please the way to Long Bredy Rectory?' 'Why do you want to know?', with a cold stare over us both. 'My great-grandfather was once Rector.' 'What's your name? Foot? Why, I remember Rector Foot: I sanged at his funeral.' It gave me an odd thrill to shake his hand; and he told us we were only half a mile from where we wanted to go.

My brother officers in 35 SL were agreeable, rather than brainy; most of them were south London business men. As an Oxford undergraduate, I was something of a lone wolf, and as a comparative newcomer, I was not too much attached to regimental tradition. I could therefore easily be spared for the staff, and was. Dickie went off to command a Z regiment (great clumps of three-inch AA rockets, hitherto all but untried) at Portsmouth.

I became assistant intelligence officer to 47 AA Brigade at Middle Wallop near Salisbury.

We lived in a requisitioned house in the middle of the village. Like many other houses near by, its garden had a thatched wall. I shared a room with the staff captain, Trofimov, a heavy smoker (not the Trofimov who was later in SOE). When our batman called him in the morning, a hand would appear from beneath his blankets, scrabbling on the floor for his cigarettes and matches. I would hear a match strike, and then see occasional puffs of smoke from under the blanket, before he got up. I worked with John Mullock, the brigade IO, and wrote a short piece to go in the brigade intelligence summary about the wickedness as well as the virtues of Metaxas, when that sturdy dictator – who had at least stood up to Mussolini – died early in 1941. Mullock answered a call for volunteers, and went off into Bomber Command, to report on enemy searchlight tactics, where he earned his Military Cross.

While I was at Middle Wallop, my twenty-first birthday arrived, and I was given a day or two's leave. My parents and my sister gave me a birthday lunch at the de Rougemont hotel in Exeter – my father claimed de Rougemont cousins – and I drank my first champagne, which I enjoyed, much more than the first glass of beer I drank, in a pub near Middle Wallop a few evenings later. I also disliked my first cigarette, but soon became a mild regular cigarette smoker, sticking to Cypriot or Turkish tobacco when I could get it, and sometimes smoking a pipe. This birthday was, I think, the last occasion when I saw my parents together.

Soon thereafter the brigade moved to Bognor, with a new brigadier, and a few weeks after that I was posted to headquarters, 5 AA Division at Reading. (One got used to being treated as if one were a parcel.) I was nominally ADC to General Cunningham, the divisional commander – the great Admiral A.B. Cunningham's brother – who soon left us for a partly successful career in North Africa, and then to his successor General Pargiter. I did no ADC work; I was simply used as an extra dogsbody by the G (operational and training) staff.

At about this time, I lost my step-cousin Maurice. The 12th Lancers took the long way round the Cape to Egypt, to reinforce the army in the western desert. He had a row with a fellow officer about a girl they both wanted, and shot himself dead in Durban: a great waste.

A fellow staff officer at Reading invited me to give up the Ship Inn, where I had billeted myself, and come and live in his house with some other colleagues. I heard later that the wife of one of them enjoyed variety in bed, and slept in turn with all the lodgers; it was perhaps as well that I took up another invitation instead. This was from Michael Pinney, one of the GSO3s, whose cousin John had been at Winchester with me. He was living just south of Reading in a sizeable country house, Hartley Court, which belonged to another cousin, Hester Marsden-Smedley. I went out there to dinner, liked it, and was delighted to be invited to come and live there. Hester had three quite small children, and a husband – Basil, later mayor of Chelsea – who said he was in the "ministry of economic warfare", working in some sort of censorship job. Years later, I discovered he had in fact been in SOE, of which I had never then heard.

Later still, I discovered the odd role played unconsciously by his wife, who had been the *Daily Mirror*'s correspondent in Brussels, and had escaped with difficulty in the turmoil of May and June 1940, giving up her passage in *Lancastria* to a man who swore he was wanted by the Gestapo, and drowned with that ship, with several thousand others, bombed off St Nazaire. Hester got out eventually through Cherbourg, and found herself in the train from Southampton to London with *The Times*'s man from the BEF, whom she hardly knew. They shared a bottle of champagne to celebrate their escape. She asked what he was going to do. He supposed, glumly, he would have to volunteer for the army. She rather took to him, said she thought she could find him something more interesting, put him in touch with her husband, and so secured him a job with SOE. Thus Kim Philby found his way back into the secret service world, where he did so much harm. (To start with, he did a lot of good: he trained agents in how to live under a regime they detested, without showing that they detested it.)

Hester had kept up her connections with the Belgian government in exile in London; once or twice she had Monsieur Spaak the foreign minister and Monsieur Gutt the minister of finance, as well as Monsieur Bech the acting Prime Minister of Luxembourg, to dinner. At least I shook hands with all of them, though I could claim no more than a trivial acquaintance. With all the wartime difficulties of rationing and staff shortage, Hartley Court was a far less comfortable country house than White Hill, and in any case I was away almost every day, and many nights, on duty. I did have occasional days off work. On one, I was helping Hester sort her books, and stumbled on a copy of Daudet's poems inscribed '*A ma chère petite Hester, en souvenir d'une soirée inoubliable*', signed off with a squiggle. Who on earth, I asked her, was that? 'Do you know, I can't remember at all.'

One of Basil's working colleagues lived in the stable block, Anthony Lousada, whom I much liked, with his wife Jocelyn, one of A.P. Herbert's daughters, whom I liked even more. Sometimes I went round there and talked, or read or recited poetry to her, after she had put the children to bed and before Anthony got back from London. At his request, these visits stopped. He heard some servants' gossip, perfectly baseless, which made him suspect Jocelyn and I might be having an affair.

It was a joy to know Michael Pinney. He had got a degree (though not at all a good one) from Cambridge, had dipped into Dante, had read Gibbon, had read Keats, wrote poetry – which he then kept to himself – and had most agreeable manners. A further delight that arose from knowing him was being taken down to stay at his exquisite small country house at Bettiscombe at the head of Marshwood Vale, in western Dorset. His wife Betty was one of the most wonderful women I ever met; though we were never lovers, I was and remain extremely fond of her, and remember her daily. She was the child of Canon Cooke of Christ Church, where he brought up his four daughters, all of whom ran away in turn on reaching the age of twenty-one, though before long they all ran back. Betty had been in Paris, teaching herself to paint, and retained a real talent.

The house had been built by a Pinney in the early 1690s, and included a large double bed to which Michael and Betty had treated themselves as a wedding present. They bought it for £50, rather more than they could afford, from an antique shop opposite the King's Arms in Oxford, where the new Bodleian now stands. During their honeymoon, they got a letter from the Duke of Marlborough: by an unaccountable error, his agent had let go to an antique dealer the day bed ordered by the first duke for his wife, to celebrate his victory at Blenheim. The duke enclosed his cheque for £400, and would be glad to have his bed back. The Pinneys returned the cheque and kept the bed.

Near by, Hester's father Sir Reginald Pinney (Uncle Reg to the family) lived at Racedown, where Wordsworth scholars discovered in the attic a revealing correspondence between the poet and his sister. During the catastrophe in France in the spring of 1918, Pinney had brought off a feat rather far out of the ordinary: his division, the 33rd, or rather his divisional machine gun company, managed in a single day's fighting to stop the advance of six German divisions, which had broken through at the junction between the British and French armies (weakly held by the Portugese) in mid-April 1918. The now almost forgotten action at Meteren, which at least

I have got the new DNB to chronicle (under Pinney, Sir R.J.), was a turning-point in the Great War.

Uncle Reg's son Bernard, a regular gunner, commanded an anti-tank battery in the western desert. In a forlorn action in November 1941, all his guns but one were knocked out. A subaltern called Gunn manned the remaining two-pounder by himself, and succeeded in knocking out several German tanks with it, at close range. Bernard put him in for a VC that evening, which Gunn eventually got. Who had brought him up his ammunition? Bernard and a sergeant, out in the open; Gunn at least had had such protection as the gun shield afforded. The sergeant got a Military Medal. Bernard got nothing, as nobody senior to himself had been present, and was killed by a shellburst next day.

I fondly remember Digby Coventry, a model of good manners and hospitality, to whom I still owe a dinner, though I have lost touch with him entirely (we had been up at New College together, but the college no longer has an address for him); and a charming white-haired administrator called Tottenham, quite content with his lot; as well as Michael Pinney's introduction to Pouilly Fumé in the Dolphin at Chichester, after a brief visit to Tangmere. At Tangmere there were a couple of Lysanders, painted black, sitting discreetly by themselves in a corner. I asked an RAF acquaintance what they were for, was told they were for searchlight training, and believed it. (At Hugh Verity's memorial service, I met one of the Lysander pilots, who had been flying Spitfires out of Tangmere in 1940, and next found himself rather looked down on by the WAAFs who served him in mess there, because he'd been taken off operations on to some transport job. He could not explain that the transport job, in and out of occupied France, was even more dangerous than flying a Spitfire; he could do nothing but look meek and keep silent.)

There was a GSO2 at Reading, a regular called Burnaby who remained a stickler for correct procedure. He would go slowly through a training instruction, pointing out errors in punctuation, while telegrams marked immediate piled up unattended at his elbow. I coined to myself the word burnabism to stand for any irrelevant attention to petty detail I encountered later. He got on his superiors' as well as his juniors' nerves; we all heaved a sigh of relief when he was posted to command a survey battery in west Africa.

Before this happened, he and I shared a disconcerting experience. We went to Imber on Salisbury Plain to watch a demonstration of attack against troops by fighter aircraft. There must have been several such – General Brooke in his diary reports having attended one which passed off calmly. Ours did not. We stood in a long line, perhaps a thousand of us, on a down. On the opposite down was an equally long line of lorries, large and small. Burnaby who was rather short moved backwards two or three yards up the hill, to get a better view, and I moved with him. A Hurricane appeared, low, to our right, heading straight for us. The front of its wings twinkled. I flung myself down instantly; so did most of us. It roared overhead and was gone, followed by cries of 'Stretcher-bearer!' Several of us were killed, including a large Scotsman beside whom Burnaby and I had been standing, who had shifted into our place. One of those badly wounded, I discovered over half a century later, was a Cecil in the Grenadiers, grandson of the Lord Salisbury who had signed RMF's Bateman salver, and eventual sixth marquess himself. The demonstration was cancelled, and we all trudged off to our cars. Before we were off the down, the rumour was circulating that, of course, it must have been a Polish or Czech pilot, no Englishman would have done anything so silly, a rumour that turned out to be untrue, but showed the bloody-minded patriotism of the old officer class. Burnaby took us, unannounced, to tea with some friends of his in the neighbourhood, to whom he did not breathe a word of the incident – so no more did I. They will have read of it in a brief paragraph in the following day's *Telegraph*.

The GSO 1 was far abler than Burnaby: B.P. (Bil) Hughes, a formidable military intellect (though he never rose above major-general – the army must be one of the chanciest of careers), and a splendid staff leader. From him I learned that it is always far better to go out and see, than to write memoranda; he insisted on all his staff, on which I became a GSO3, knowing how to ride a motor-cycle, as I had already learned to do at Broadstairs, and hounded us out of the office as often as he could. Once, when I had spent much of the night flying out of Tangmere, watching searchlights fail to catch the Blenheim I was in, I fell asleep on the way back to Reading by motor-cycle. Asleep, I turned a right-angled bend – for which I presumably changed gear, twice at least. The wind of moving fast woke me up. I was doing 82mph down the wrong side of the road, over Hartley Bridge flats. Fortunately, no other vehicle was in sight.

On another occasion, I got back to Hartley Court one morning to find the lane in which it lay closed off by a police ribbon, with a constable by it: there was an unexploded land-mine outside a cottage near by. I pulled rank on the constable, telling him I lived there, and went forward to have a look. I met a sailor, who told me his officer was at the bomb, and recommended me – if I must persevere – to leave my revolver with him, in case its metal set the bomb off. I did so. I got right up to and touched the bomb, a cold grey metal cylinder about six feet long and two wide, with a parachute attached to it that dangled over the cottage garden gate. A naval officer, younger even than me, was kneeling by it staring at its fuse. He recommended me to rejoin his sailor, which I did; he came back to us a few minutes later, paying out a piece of string, told us to lie down, and pulled the string. Nothing happened. He swore gently, told us to stay lying down, went back to the bomb, and returned soon thereafter, deathly white but carrying the fuse.

When on night duty at Reading, by convention the duty officer could dine in a small hotel on the other side of the Bath Road on which the headquarters lay. A large, gloomy, solitary staff officer from some other formation always dined there, by himself, speaking to no one. This was Churchill's cousin the then Duke of Marlborough, remote indeed from his great ancestor's or his great relative's ways of making war.

One of my staff friends, Geoffrey Rice, disappeared from AA Command into Whitehall. I knew him well enough to ask him out to a meal, when I had a day on leave in London, and inquired whether there might be any chance of joining him there. Reading was an agreeable place to live, decently remote from air attack, but the work there did not seem to have much to do with bringing the war to a useful end. Several of my friends were already dead, and I did not feel like remaining in AA Command for the duration. Geoffrey said he would see what he could do.

* * *

The upshot was a summons to London for interview by his boss, a Cuban marquis who had been a racing motorist before the war and had become Mountbatten's head of intelligence at Combined Operations Headquarters (COHQ). After twenty minutes' talk (devoted, I found out later, to discovering whether I was socially acceptable) I was sent away, and a few weeks later – no doubt after clearance by security – was posted to serve under him. His wife Freda, formerly Mrs Dudley Ward, was a constant companion of Churchill when the Prime Minister went down to Ditchley at nights with a full moon; this her husband never mentioned to us. A few months later he was sacked, dithered for a few days between a posting to SIS and his previous job, was rejected by SIS as well, and went back to running the Curzon cinema.

On the way to join COHQ on 20 August 1942 I read in the train newspaper accounts of the previous day's raid on Dieppe. The headquarters, when I reported to it, was about as orderly as an overturned beehive. Staff officers of all three services were marching up and down the corridors – this was in the New Scotland Yard building opposite Downing Street, a few floors of which COHQ had taken over – crying out the forenames of missing friends, and deploring that such a ghastly mess had been made by all of them. Frontal attacks on ports were thereafter to be avoided whenever conceivably possible. No doubt Churchill and Mountbatten had wanted to pull off some great stroke, like Keyes's raid on Zeebrugge in April 1918, to reassure the Russians that we were really trying to fight; but it miscarried. It is still vividly remembered in Canada. I had a Canadian pupil once at Trinity, Oxford, who told me over half his class turned up in black ties next morning, having heard their fathers were killed or missing at Dieppe. I was unable to confirm a rumour, that I never saw in print, that one of the Canadian battalions, bored with all these infernal night exercises, did not bother to take its ammunition with it when it went to Dieppe. Luckily, as it was in the reserve brigade, it was never ordered ashore.

My aunt Lindsey, who lived in Chelsea, had left the Women's Institutes and become number two to Lady Reading in the Women's Voluntary Services, working out of an office in Tothill Street, Westminster. She rather enjoyed working on through the air raids of the winter of 1940–41, writing once to Dickie to claim that she had been continuously under fire for fifty-seven nights on end. She enjoyed it less when her own house was badly bombed, but simply moved to a flat near Chelsea Town Hall, without missing a day in her office. Sometimes I called on her at her office, which was almost opposite 54 Broadway. Neither of us ever mentioned to the other what 54 Broadway was: as we both knew, it was then the headquarters of the secret service. It backed on to a house in Queen Anne's Gate which was C's private residence. He rather enjoyed varying the front doors by which he went to work, or left it.

Lindsey and my mother both busied themselves with fitting up a flat for me, when I found one in Rochester Row, above a printer's shop. (In recent times, the printer's shop has been replaced by a restaurant too expensive for me.) It had two floors, including one quite nice squarish room, facing south. I had it fitted with a bathroom, and found a splendid Cockney woman to come in and clean it for me once a week, giving her my meat coupons as well as a wage in coin.

COHQ was then under Mountbatten, who with all the faults of vanity that are so often nowadays attributed to him was a good man under whom to serve. We all felt that he looked after our interests, such as they were, and was giving us a set of serious jobs to do that were going to help to bring the war to an end. He also took the trouble to invite his cousin the king to come over one afternoon and inspect the building, shaking hands with all the officers.

The first Sunday I was there, I was made duty officer. Thinking how exciting this would be, I did not take a book in to work with me; it was not exciting at all, it was plain dull. Having nothing else to read, I fell back on the Admiralty telephone directory, which was on my desk, and found in the naval intelligence division an entry for McLachlan, Lieutenant Commander D. H. Next day I reached him by telephone; it was indeed the same one. We met for a drink off Piccadilly. He cross-questioned me carefully about the sorts of intelligence my branch handled, and where we got it from. Thinking we must not talk about me all the time, I asked him what he did? Oh, he had a dull job doing propaganda in the admiralty; and he changed the subject. By this time he was aware that I was not cleared to know what he was really doing: he was running *Kriegswellensender Atlantik*, a black broadcasting programme intended to make U-boat crews desert. How much effect it had no one was ever able to discover, though its scabrous tone upset Stafford Cripps, who once picked it up by accident on his home set, and was appalled to find it was run under government auspices.

I soon fell into a regular Whitehall warrior routine. Reaching the office at about nine as usual, I was once held up momentarily by a Wren rating, searching in her bag for her pass. She couldn't find it, but the sergeant on door duty, knowing her, let her through. Next day exactly the same thing happened, with the same girl. Third time round, she confessed – she had not mislaid her pass, she had exchanged it, for a half-pound coupon-free block of Cadbury's milk chocolate, long vanished from the open market. Who had given it her? A man she'd met in a pub? What pub? She was quite open about it all, and went back to the pub that evening, accompanied by a stout lady from Special Branch. As they came through the blackout, a man at the bar turned, saw her, and asked her what she'd like to drink. 'That's him', she told her escort, who rubbed the lobe of her ear, whereupon two heavies got up from the back of the bar and arrested the man. He turned out to collect passes, as a hobby, the way other people collect stamps. He displayed passes to all three service ministries, the Foreign Office, the Treasury, the Board of Trade, the Cabinet War Rooms, even – all secured by offering secretaries coupon-free half-pound blocks of chocolate, provided by his brother who worked at Bournville. Nobody was prosecuted, but the pass holders, all easily traceable, were moved to much less agreeable jobs.

The army's passion for short hair compelled me to visit a barber quite often. I used to go to Lock's, in the Royal Opera Arcade – rather like Endicott's in Dorothy Sayers. In the autumn of 1943 they put up a notice: to the great regret of the management, for the first time since the war of 1812 it was necessary to raise the price of a gentleman's haircut above a florin, to 2s 3d (now 11p). No modern barber believes this.

One evening in the bar at the office I was introduced to a captain, Royal Marines – Evelyn Waugh the novelist. We exchanged a few civil words. Next morning we happened to walk past each other in a corridor. He looked up at me and said 'Get out of my way, you horrible little man.' I cut him dead – there seemed nothing else to do. We never spoke again, and he was soon forbidden the headquarters as too insubordinate to be borne. He wrote matchless prose, but was not a nice man to meet.

I also met quite a lot of formidable characters in and near the Commandos, such as Richard Broad, who had got back from St Valery after the 51st Division surrendered, bringing seven Scottish soldiers with him, or Blondie Hasler who raided a blockade runner from Japan in Bordeaux harbour, getting in by canoe and walking out afterwards with the one other survivor – Bill Sparks, whom I met years afterwards – from his companions. (Those who were not drowned were murdered.) Such men had an aura of quiet bravery that I found daunting, but impressive; I am still impressed by it over half a century later. Broad's party had hidden for some weeks in a nunnery at Honfleur. After the war the mother superior secured a private audience with the pope, and absolution for having in this one case broken the rules of her order. Broad never breathed a word to us about his intermediate spell in Madagascar, impersonating a Texan oil tycoon for SOE.

There were occasional flashes of culture in the midst of war. The National Gallery brought one picture a month up from the Welsh mountainside that housed their collection. I particularly remember Holbein's Duchess of Milan, who had the good fortune not to be married to Henry VIII. It also provided occasional concerts. At one, Myra Hess was about to play

Beethoven when the air raid sirens went; we were advised to take shelter. We all looked up at the glass roof above us, and stayed where we were. Similarly, I was once among the dense crowds queuing at Waterloo station for a bank-holiday weekend train. Sirens went – same advice, same result. So preference for own convenience over fright about the Luftwaffe was not confined to the concert-going classes. Portal called up the Griller quartet into Bomber Command, and occasionally, when they were not playing to bomber crews, they too could perform at the National Gallery. They took us, motif by motif, through Beethoven's opus 131 before they played it; thenceforth, I have been captivated by the late Beethoven quartets.

One afternoon I was browsing in Zwemmer's bookshop in the Charing Cross Road, wishing I could afford some of the Phaidon books in it. An elderly lady came in, went up to the desk, and asked if she might have a Bible to give to her nephew, who had just been posted to Burma. 'O dear me no, madam, not here. Try Foyle's, madam, across the road; they sell all sorts of books'. Another day, during my lunch-hour, I was browsing in a little bookshop off Victoria Street, and so was the CIGS, then General Sir Alan Brooke. A major went up to him, saluted, and embarked on a rigmarole about a grievance. Brooke listened impassively for a minute or two, said, 'Go through channels, you fool', and went back to his book.

Sometimes on days off I would go and walk in the devastated City. By 1943 there was open space all round St Paul's, six or seven hundred yards' width of beaten brick, with nothing left standing in it at all except the church of St Stephen's, Walbrook – and that, badly damaged. It gave me an odd turn to step into its ruins and see that its dome, which I had told friends in Arch. Soc. was a model on which Wren had tried out his ideas for suspending the dome of St Paul's, had been made not of stone but of plaster. The rest was quite bare, save for occasional flurries of rosebay willowherb. It still gives me a frisson when I see patches of willowherb beside a railway line; as I still get a worse frisson whenever I hear an air raid siren's noise being made by a police car. Nowadays I suppose that might entitle me to treatment for battle stress, a complaint not much heard of in the early 1940s.

Geoffrey Rice with whom I shared a desk introduced me to London club life, telling me that the Reform would take on officers who worked in Whitehall at half-subscription, and without an entrance fee, if they could find a pre-war member to put them up. I wrote out of the blue to Charles Grey, descendant of the Lord Grey who had passed the great Reform Bill, who had been at Winchester with me; he was then serving in the Scots Guards, and was soon to be killed in action, but he put me up for the Reform first. This was an asset, in a lonely life.

The only oddity about Geoffrey was that he kept an iron box under the desk, which he never opened when I was in the room. Once when he was on leave a letter arrived for him, in a plain brown envelope, which I opened. Inside it was a second envelope, addressed to him, marked TOP SECRET. I opened that too. A third envelope was marked TOP SECRET AND PERSONAL, TO BE OPENED ONLY BY MAJOR G.G. RICE. I put it unopened in the office safe. When I handed it to him on his return, he heaved a sigh of relief, but did not open it in my presence. Many years later I discovered that he had been one of Combined Ops's men on the Double Cross committee, run by MI 5 and a still more secret service, the deceivers – of which, again, I had never then heard.

I had by this time heard of SOE; it was mentioned in a secret paper I was reading. What, I asked, was it? 'Oh, it's a secret organization of engineers, run out of the War Office by a sapper called Gubbins. You mustn't mention it on an unscrambled telephone.' Gradually I got a little better informed, and occasionally rang up SOE's F section, to fish for information about areas on which we were proposing raids. The same man's voice answered to several different surnames, but not much in the way of useful data ever emerged. I got even less out of SIS.

Most of my work at COHQ was routine, but it was interesting routine. I saw the weekly intelligence reports put out by each of the service ministries, took a minor part in commando training, and had some idea of which major combined operations might impend. One of these, HUSKY the proposed invasion of Sicily, precipitated one of many staff flaps: there was a major change of plan. The fresh plan was put on a map, and I was told to provide twenty copies of it for a meeting in ninety minutes' time. The map was in colour; our excellent draughtsman did not cope with colour printing. But I had a friend in the Admiralty basement who did. I rang him up; would he mind postponing his lunch that day? I walked across Whitehall, with the map rolled up under my arm, and handed it to him. He held it ostentatiously upside-down, ran off twenty copies, and handed them back, remarking 'Well if you does it as well as we prints it, we shall be all right, shan't we?'

At short notice, I had to provide a docket – a fat file of papers – containing all that was known about the Norwegian port of Haugesund, on which a small raid was proposed. I then spent a whole day briefing the raid's commander, Sub-Lieutenant John Godwin, RNVR, with whom I had an odd link: we had been born on the same day. He was a twin, thoroughly British, though born in Buenos Aires where his father worked. When the war broke out, both boys took the first ship for Great Britain, in which John announced that, as he was the elder, he was going into the navy. We went through the docket carefully, and I also spent an hour passing on to him MI 9's doctrines about how to behave if by misfortune he fell into enemy hands – something on which I had been trained by a one-armed MI 9 lecturer called Langley, who will reappear in this book. Godwin duly set off for Haugesund in a coble, with half-a-dozen companions, all in uniform. The motor torpedo boat (MTB) towing them cast them off near their goal; they found the island off the port he and I had spotted on an air photograph, and hid there. They started sinking ships, with limpet mines, sank several, but then attacked a small German warship, which was more alert than they had realised, and took them all prisoner.

They were not there on any of the occasions when MTBs went over to bring them back, nor were they reported as prisoners of war. Through the usual secret channels, we heard that a charwoman in a prison near Oslo had seen seven uniformed sailors under guard, who had been sent on to Sachsenhausen. There, it turned out later, the whole party – except for one called Meyer, who had been 'disappeared' early – spent fourteen months testing boots for the German army, marching round and round a cobbled track for fourteen hours a day; in good spirits, often singing, impressing their fellow prisoners with their high morale. They were then called for on the camp loudspeaker, in terms that made it clear it was their turn to be shot. As they were marched away, in a party some thirty strong, Godwin remembered the MI 9 doctrine I had preached to him: capture did not mean one was out of the war. At a hitch, at one of the camp's many steel gates, he reached across to the belt of the SS man in charge of the party, took the pistol out of it and shot him dead. He was at once mown down by the sub-machine guns of the escort; but it was a good way to go. As nobody senior to him had been present, the best the decorations system could do for him was a posthumous mention in dispatches. Both those lives are on my head: if, as I was told in my childhood, I have to confront St Peter at heaven's gate after I am dead, he will require me to explain – if I can.

Much of our work – most of it, indeed – was for projects that never in the end took place. Senior officers were much inclined to put down their juniors with talk of the reprisals likely to follow on the juniors' proposals. It fell to me to go down to the New Forest and break it to the general commanding the Royal Marine Division, which was contemplating a major raid on Alderney, that he proposed to approach that already well-gunned island in tank landing craft, which could make seven knots, in broad daylight against a six-and-a-half knot tide. The proposal was cancelled that afternoon. Reading tide tables, like reading charts or maps or air photographs, was a routine part of the work. Are Pacific tide tables wildly unreliable, or was there a major intelligence balls-up, never publicised, when the US Marines landed at Tarawa on the wrong state of the tide, and had to wade ashore for half a mile under fire? William Manchester was one of them, and has left an unforgettable account.

My sister Paddy was called up, on reaching the age of eighteen, in 1943. She pulled the family's naval string, a fairly stout one, to make sure that she was called up into the WRNS, not into the WAAF or the ATS or the land army. She sent a stream of letters and postcards about how strange it was to live on the front at Gosport, wearing odd clothes and learning odd drills. She moved on to a stone frigate near Winchester; the letters got sparser, she was working hard, learning Morse. She then moved to another stone frigate, and we heard no more, save that she never forgot birthdays, and sent parcels at Christmas. Now and again she went home on leave, but would not tell her mother either where she worked or what she was doing. My father, bloodier-minded than I, called at the Admiralty in his brigadier's uniform and asked 'Where is HMS So-and-so?' They told him – it was a block of flats on the top of Hampstead Hill, within a mile of his own current headquarters in Avenue Road, from which he then commanded London's anti-aircraft defences. He went and called on her captain, and asked what his daughter was doing. 'I am afraid', was the crisp reply, 'I cannot tell you.' A few days later, I asked him what Paddy was doing. 'Sorry, old boy, I can't tell you' was all the reply I got.

Almost forty years later, I was able to quote to Paddy Mr Callaghan's ruling, that if you had been doing something secret during the war, and were sure that mentioning it would do the nation's security no harm, you could now tell your nearest and dearest what it had been. She said she had had an inconceivably dull two years, listening to Japanese submarines' W/T traffic, which by a freak of skip could be heard loud and clear on top of Hampstead Hill. Though she spoke not a word of Japanese, she had mastered Japanese Morse – a lot more intricate than common or garden

Morse – and hardly ever missed a single dot or dash; the traffic was all enciphered, anyway. Nobody ever told her why she was doing it, or that her results were promptly deciphered, and helped the US Navy to win its war. Later still, when it came out in 2000, I was able to send her Michael Smith's *The Emperor's Codes*, which explained the strategic and technical backgrounds.

About the time the European war ended, my father rang her up, and told her to bring ten of her prettiest companions down to his HQ for a party for some returned prisoners of war, whom he was to entertain. The girls did not tell him that several of them were on watch again at midnight. One of the haggard airmen present, Jim Gowland, looked at Paddy across the room, and walked across to propose marriage. They had met once before, when both had been helping with haymaking at Hamberlins Farm. She asked for a little time to think; and on reflection, her heart being free at the time, accepted. They were happily married for many years, going out almost at once to Australia, where they had a son and a daughter, and settled in Queensland on the coast. They had a starting spell in a mining village in New South Wales. One of Jim's fellow prisoners had given him a half share in a gold mine; there genuinely was gold in it, but no one had yet solved the problem of getting it to the surface. While the men were away down the mine, the women of the village organized a rabbit shoot, and invited Paddy to take part. She had never had a gun in her hands in her life before, but turned out the best shot in the village – a short proof that some gifts are heritable.

Jim had been in the RAF before the war, and became a Wellington pilot. He read maps well; so did his navigator. They developed a private technique for map-reading their way, very low down, over north-west Europe, climbing to the set bombing height on reaching their target, and returning as they had gone out. On his thirteenth raid the station commander said, 'Well, Gowland, you usually seem to find your targets; I shall fly with you to-night.' So he supposed he had better obey orders; duly flew at 12,000 feet, and was duly shot down. He had a horrible five years in Stalag Luft I, helping Jimmie Deans whom he revered to organize escapes.

Dolly meanwhile had quietly gone on with farming. She got a letter from the Hertfordshire War Agricultural Executive Committee, telling her to plough up and sow part of Northchurch Common. But, she replied, that has been common land since before the Normans came; I couldn't bring myself to have it done. She got a riposte in a tone sharper than any she had ever heard before, outside the hunting field: if she did not follow the directions of the committee, she would be haled before the courts and sent to prison. So she complied, and got three excellent crops of wheat, before the war's end let bracken and gorse take over again.

Nina disliked the bombing of London's suburbs, and let the house at Esher to a knighted MP (Warrender who was a junior lord of the wartime Admiralty), moving down to the outskirts of Bournemouth. There she was badly shaken up by a chance stick of bombs that fell athwart her house, luckily without doing any serious damage.

Inner life I had little; private life I had, for a time, none. Léonie faded out of my existence, after I called on her once at Harpenden, and found her speaking sharply to her infant son. I fell in love with Iris Murdoch, who, on account of her first in Greats, had been taken on by the Treasury, and turned out to be living not far from me in Westminster. We had a brief, unsuccessful affair. Long, long afterwards, I discovered that she had felt sorry for the way she had treated me. In the shorter run, I felt ravaged.

Part of the trouble was that the burden of the Official Secrets Act lay so heavy on me that I couldn't tell her what I was doing at COHQ, or what I knew from secret and top secret papers about the course of the war (I read chiefs of staff's papers, but had never heard of the ULTRA secret, to which I think hardly anyone at COHQ was privy except for CCO himself, the winged Marine who was his chief of staff, Colonel Neville the planner, and Geoffrey). Nor did she feel she could tell me anything she did or knew in the Treasury. I was taken – as, I am sure, were thousands like me – by a stanza in Housman's *A Shropshire Lad* :

In the land to which I travel,
The far dwelling, let me say
Once, if here the couch is gravel,
In a kinder bed I lay,
And the breast the darnel smothers
Rested once upon another's
When it was not clay.

All the same, I do not think I had the nerve to quote it to her. Like Léonie, she seemed to alternate between beckoning me on and putting me off, and

I could not easily explain why sometimes I could, and sometimes I could not spend an evening with her.

In June and early July 1943 I was much involved in providing intelligence for a series of small commando raids, codenamed FORFAR, on the northern French coast. In retrospect, it looks as if these were intended by the deception staff to keep the Germans' interest pinned on the Channel coast while major operations impended in the Mediterranean. Nobody at the working level knew or dreamed of anything of the sort. On one of them I was allowed to go myself, on condition I did not go ashore.

Before the party left, I had gone carefully into what was known about the target, including calling at Norfolk House in St James's Square where the intelligence branch of SHAEF worked. (It was George III's birthplace, a point tactfully never mentioned to the Americans who thronged the building.) There I saw John Austin, head of the I(a) branch – a Magdalen don said to have understood Aristotle better than anybody else since Aristotle stopped lecturing – to seek his advice. He asked me to wait while he finished writing a paper, more than twenty pages long, which dealt – as I saw when he tossed it into his out tray – with the rate of reinforcement of the western from the eastern front by panzer divisions in the first two months after an invasion of the continent. He then turned, without a pause, from strategy to tactics, looked at the air photographs I had brought with me, and pinpointed which of the pillboxes at the target contained a mortar, and which contained a heavy machine gun. (Geoffrey could hardly believe this when I told him, but visited the site late next year, after the Germans had been driven off it, and found Austin had been right.)

An MTB took us from Dover to the mouth of the Somme. A few commandos went ashore in a rubber dinghy, and returned ninety minutes later, angry with me because they had found nobody in the strongpoint they had raided. (How did they know? Having thrown stones at a pillbox for twenty minutes without provoking a reaction, they had gone in, and found it empty.) They brought back some barbed wire and an anti-tank mine. Clarkson, commanding the MTB, said, 'Start engines' down his voicepipe; nothing happened. Nothing continued to happen for over an hour. It started to grow light. By the mercy of providence, there was a thick sea mist, which concealed us from over a dozen coastal battery guns – I was busy calculating how many – any of which could blow a stationary MTB out of the water. It was broad day before the engines did start, and we were out of range before the mist dispersed.

I was driven back to London, and went round to MI 10 at the war office with the wire and the mine. They were enchanted by the wire, which did not appear in the German engineers' handbook they had by them; would I congratulate the party on an important discovery? I didn't, because on my way in I had verified my own guess: it came from a roll of British Dannert wire left behind in 1940, and they had another roll of it round their own front door. Meanwhile the major in charge was inspecting the mine; and suddenly said 'Clear the room!' 'But sir, it's been made safe as you recommend, with a nail through the fuse.' *'Clear the room!'* We did. While one of his subalterns went back inside, he explained that the Germans had seen newsreel film of British sappers clearing mines at second El Alamein, turning them over as they did so, and had produced a new mine, which blew up if it was turned over. I had been carrying one of those round with me for some hours, usually vertical, luckily without turning it right over.

A very few days later, Iris let me know that she would at last come and spend the night with me. She could not know, what I could not forget, that she had chosen the night on which HUSKY the Sicilian invasion was to be mounted. So we got off to a bad start, as lovers; my mind couldn't be, as it should have been, wholly on her. Elias Canetti, whom she later adored, saw fit after she was dead to explain how unexciting she had been in bed. I took his point, though I had been brought up to believe no gentleman would discuss such a subject in print. Before long she ditched me, for Tommy Balogh, a Balliol don she knew, much older and sexually much more adept than I, who died a life peer. Much of this is set down in Peter Conradi's life of her (2001), including the long-term impact on her novels, which she had hardly then started to write. There was no sort of consolation at the time but to buckle down harder than ever to work.

That autumn, I was offered the posting of intelligence officer to a commando brigade about to be formed for service in the Adriatic, and jumped at it. (Michael Brodrick had just been killed, commanding a company of the Coldstream at Salerno, the day before Michael Howard joined it.) I was kitted out for the task with, among other things, a sleeping bag and an excellent wrist watch, for which nobody asked me to sign. Forty-eight hours before I was due to leave, Laycock, who had succeeded Mountbatten as chief of combined operations, intervened: I was too useful to him in Whitehall, he would not let me go. At the time I was angry, but am now grateful to Laycock for having saved my life, for the whole brigade staff took part next spring in a raid on the island of Brac, in which every one of them was killed or badly wounded.

Laycock had made an excellent escape march in the western desert, with a commando sergeant, saving their lives by imitating, as best he could remember, the habits of foxes on the run from hounds. As a gesture of gratitude, he never went out with hounds again.

A raid was projected on Gravelines, a spot so heavily defended that the intelligence staff all protested at the mere idea, and were told, curtly enough, to obey orders. Estimates of probable enemy strength varied unusually widely between the service ministries; we had to guess as best we could. (This set Geoffrey and me on to producing a paper on the need for an inter-service intelligence staff, which eventually developed.) In the end, the raid took place on Christmas Eve 1943. Having briefed the small commando landing force, which I was forbidden to accompany, I went down to Dover to see them off – again on Clarkson's MTB. It returned next morning with no troops on board at all – they had all vanished. The MTB had grounded, trying to get close enough inshore to pick up one or two swimmers, but without success. Months later, when I had been posted elsewhere, a teleprint reached me from SOE. One of their circuits, in the Ain, had been approached by two men, dressed as Royal Marine commando privates, who alleged they had been put ashore at Gravelines on 24 December after being briefed by me: could this possibly be true? They, knowing no French, had walked all the way there, sleeping rough and living on what they could steal on the way, a splendid feat for which I hope they got proper recognition; they stayed on in France to help train Heslop's maquis.

Combined Ops seemed pleased with my work. I was mentioned in dispatches and promoted major. A few days later, Ian Collins a GSO1 (Plans) sent for me, congratulated me, and asked me if I would mind giving my majority up. Had I heard of the Special Air Service? Yes I had. They were now forming a brigade, and needed a brigade IO; would I care to take it on? It would mean dropping a rank, then a rule in the army, to deter too many volunteers for SAS. Would it get me anywhere nearer the Germans? – for I was getting very tired of desk work. Yes it would. So I accepted on the spot.

* * *

It meant moving to Scotland – the brigade was assembling in Ayrshire, with its headquarters at Sorn Castle. There were two British and two French parachute regiments, each about 400 strong, a Belgian company which later expanded to a regiment, and a Phantom squadron under Jakie Astor, one of whose brothers had been up with me at New College, to handle our signals. The brigade commander, Roderick McLeod, had commanded a parachute artillery regiment in North Africa, but knew nothing of SAS's proposed semi-clandestine role; nor did his brigade major, the equally unflappable Esmond Baring, of the County of London Yeomanry, who had commanded the tank troop in the western desert that had been Montgomery's personal escort. The brigadier and the staff sergeant-major were almost the only regular soldiers in the brigade. McLeod's cousin, Bill Kennedy Shaw, attached himself as an extra staff officer; he was resting after having been intelligence officer to the Long Range Desert Group, so was able to inform McLeod of the essentials at least of semi-clandestine intelligence gathering, at which he had been a leading expert in North Africa.

David Stirling's brother Bill commanded one of the British regiments – David by this time was in Colditz – and had a memorable row with McLeod about what the brigade's strategy ought to be. McLeod gave him orders with which he disagreed so strongly that he appealed, over McLeod's head, to 'Boy' Browning who commanded all airborne troops. Browning sided with Stirling, so McLeod had to appeal over Browning's head to Montgomery, who sided with him. Stirling went to Eisenhower, who took the opposite view. McLeod had to go to Downing Street and get Churchill to resolve the problem in his favour. Stirling went back to Keir in plain clothes.

Of the two French regiments, one consisted of Gaullists who had escaped from occupied France to go into external resistance; the other was made up of men who had been in the Vichy-controlled army in North Africa, and had been ordered to change sides after operation 'Torch'. The war office, with its usual passion for economy, put the two units in a single hutted camp, with shared ablutions and kitchens, and could not understand why there were constant fights between the two sets of men, who were ideologically sharply opposed.

We grew used to watching, every weekday morning, an unexpected piece of United States Army Air Force drill. A B17 Flying Fortress would take off from Prestwick airport, near Ayr, and fly round low in a circle till it had collected a tail of a dozen or so P47 Thunderbolt single-seater fighters. The whole party then set off southwards, the navigator in the Fortress guiding them by looking at a map, which the Thunderbolt pilots, young men just arrived in Europe, had not yet learned to master over such unfamiliar landscapes. We did not foresee how grateful some of us were going to be, in the coming summer, that the Thunderbolt pilots soon learned to map-read fast and well.

McLeod decreed that, like the rest of his staff, I should learn to drop by parachute. There was no room for me at the airborne forces' parachute school, so I went instead to the SOE school, which treated an outsider with intriguing degrees of mystery. They started by meeting me at one of Manchester's railway stations, and then driving me round for half an hour in the closed back of a small truck, so that I had no idea where we were when allowed to get out. We were in fact at a requisitioned merchant's villa near Altrincham, where a couple of days' exercises got us used to the mild gymnastics needed to jump through a hole a yard across in an aircraft fuselage's floor. Luckily for me, it was too windy to jump on the evening when I should have made my first descent, from a balloon – the moment at which most refusals refused. The villa was much like a small boarding school, with one oddity. In the dining-room (so called, not the mess) all ranks mixed, officers, sergeants and privates at the same table. With a plate of fish and chips in front of me, I turned to my neighbour – in unmarked private's battledress – and asked for the salt. *'Bitte?'* he replied. I never knew whether he only spoke German, or was a member of the staff trying out his fellow diners' nerves.

We emplaned for my first jump in a Whitley, a cumbrous twin-engined bomber already retired from raiding the Reich. Brian Franks, then an SAS major, was sitting opposite me. It was an encouragement to me to see that his lips were turning so blue with fright that they matched the centre of his MC ribbon, because I had heard something of the gallantry that had brought him that award in the desert. If a man that brave could be frightened, so could I.

Once one's parachute has opened, parachuting is a tremendous, sensual thrill – nothing but love-making with the right companion can touch it. Till one's parachute has opened, anyone is entitled to feel scared. One of the many extra officers on the brigade staff, Pat Smith the banker, who was in charge of parachute training, got positively addicted to it, and after he had made about two score jumps was forbidden by the brigadier to jump again (he came back from Brittany, to which he went by sea, with a Military Cross).

McLeod set me to hunt for areas where SAS parties could conveniently interfere with German reinforcements moving towards the landing area. One of the sites I put up was the Forêt de Morvan, in north-western Burgundy, where SAS established a firm presence in June 1944. We were not allowed to go into France before the invasion had started, and in those days were forbidden to operate in plain clothes. As the invasion approached, SAS tactical headquarters moved to Moor Park, Rickmansworth (which had once belonged to an ancestor), where Browning had Headquarters Airborne Troops in the great house, and we had huts and tents in the garden. I divided my time between Ayrshire and Middlesex, and, from Middlesex could occasionally get to central London.

There, at the end of April, I met Iris's flatmate Philippa (Pip) Bosanquet, and my private life took an abrupt turn for the better. We took to each other instantly, each of us on the rebound – I from Iris, she from Balogh. Gradually, we became lovers. When we could, we spent nights together, in the gaunt flat she shared with Iris in Seaforth Place, off Victoria Street, when I could get away from Moor Park and Iris had gone to stay with Balogh in Chelsea. The flat was directly above the Circle line of the tube; one soon got used to the passage of trains a few feet away. Occasionally, Pip would come out after a day's work at Chatham House to Moor Park by tube, and we would walk up and down the suburb and talk. She knew that I was a parachutist, and would have one day to disappear abruptly on operations, without being able to say goodbye; we both took this as stoically as we could.

She was, I discovered, the granddaughter of an American president, Grover Cleveland. Her mother had been expected to make a suitable marriage to an American notable, but, visiting London during the great war, met and fell in love with a wounded Coldstream captain, Bill Bosanquet, DSO, whom she married instead. They lived in a big eighteenth-century house in north Yorkshire, where he managed a steel works. He was proud to be related both to the philosopher and to the inventor of the googly.

About the middle of May, my telephone rang: could we scramble? We did. My caller, who gave no name, said he worked in the same corridor as David Hicks, who was Austin's subordinate. I was to allot a codename, and call him back with it – he gave me his extension number – and to get one of the British units in the brigade to tell off two parties, of an officer, a sergeant and three men each, who were to report to RAF Tempsford by 1700 hours on D-2 for operation NEPTUNE, which was the assault phase of OVERLORD. I had just allotted most of my codenames; only TRESTLE and TITANIC were left. I chose TITANIC. David Hicks assured me that any request from the extension I queried with him was to be dealt with instanter, no questions asked. I went, having cleared the operation with the brigadier, to call on Paddy Mayne, the enormous Ulsterman who commanded 1 SAS, and put the point to him. He said, abruptly enough, No. But Colonel, I replied, *hakkum hai* – a Hindustani phrase to which the army was used, meaning 'it is an order.' 'I don't care whether it's an order or not, I'm not going to obey it' – and he told me why. The first operation in which he had ever taken part for the regiment, in the western desert, had been a parachute raid on an Italian airfield, which was cancelled. The troops for it were given forty-eight hours' leave in Cairo, and got back, nursing their headaches, to hear that it was on that night after all – 'and the bloody Eyeties were waiting for us. After that, I resolved to touch no more intelligence operations; and now will you get out?' (Long after, I discovered what had gone wrong. Shan Hackett had mentioned the intended raid, as a *fait divers*, to Colonel Fellers the American military attaché in Cairo, who had passed it on to Roosevelt in a cipher the Italians read easily.)

From the formidable Mayne I went to the slightly less alarming Brian Franks, who had succeeded Stirling in command of 2 SAS; he made no sort of trouble. TITANIC is remembered in the regiment as a disaster, for good regimental reasons, because only three of the ten men who went on it came back, but they made their impact on the war. Both parties were dropped a few minutes before midnight on 5/6 June, as the Normandy invasion was nearing the coast; each accompanied by five hundred dummy parachutists, supposed to explode on impact, and armed with Very light pistols and gramophones playing bursts of small arms fire interspersed with bursts of soldiers' conversation. One team went in not far from Le Havre, and at least gave the commandant there a fright. In the small hours, he telegraphed to Berlin – copy to every other headquarters he could think of – that he had been cut off, what was he to do? There was therefore a little flag in Le Havre, reading *abgeschnittet* (cut off), on the situation map of every German general in France next morning.

More importantly, the other party went in to a group of woods south-east of Isigny, which in turn is at the south-east corner of the Cherbourg peninsula. They made such a stir that the local unit sent a message to its divisional headquarters that it was under sustained airborne attack. The duty officer took it to the general, but he was away, at a senior officers' conference in Rennes on how to repel airborne attacks. So he woke the chief of staff instead, who, as a well trained Prussian staff officer, on being attacked counter-attacked. The reserve regiment of 352 Division was dispatched at three on the morning of Normandy D-day to repel the almost non-existent airborne forces south-east of Isigny, spent the morning beating the woods, and was thus unavailable to counter-attack promptly General Bradley's landing at Omaha Beach, which after much initial confusion got soundly ashore after all. (All this has been in print for over a decade, in Young and Stamp's book *Trojan Horses*.)

SAS's advance parties landed safely – I went as far as Fairford airfield, as far forward as I was allowed, to see them off, and sat in on the pilots' debriefings, so that I could tell the brigadier later in the morning at least that all the parachutes had opened. He, I noticed, took quite calmly the almost total lack of hard news, all day, about what was actually going on, having been trained not to show excitement.

Slowly, it dawned on everybody that the landings had been an almost unqualified success, dimmed only by the hitch at Omaha beach. We all settled down to establishing the bridgehead and getting ready for the break-out. It turned out that on the left flank of the landing the leading troops ashore (after the engineers who made safe the beach obstacles) were the tanks of the 4th/7th Dragoon Guards, by this time commanded by my cousin Gordon Barker who earned his DSO with them. They were supported by the guns of the 86th Field Regiment, RA, that had evolved out of my grandfather's original Fourth East Anglian Field Brigade, TF. These family touches I only discovered years later; there was more than enough to do meanwhile.

Brigade headquarters had an interesting staff rule: only the brigadier, or in his absence the brigade major, could send a message more than one army signals form page long. This meant that anything one said, one had to compress into thirty-two words – a refreshing exercise in terseness.

Among SAS units' tasks was that of reporting likely targets for air attack. The BULBASKET party near Poitiers sent word of petrol tankers in the goods yard at Châtellerault. I passed this on to the tactical air force working with the main landing forces; some of their Mosquitos attacked it, and started the biggest petrol fire they remembered. This gave SAS a useful credit balance with the airmen.

Late in June I took part, as an observer, in operation CADILLAC, a major daylight resupply drop by the USAAF, flying in a B-17 from an airfield in

Suffolk. Before dawn, everyone flying that day attended a briefing in a vast hangar. For ten minutes the Met men talked about the weather, while the navigators took notes and everyone else fidgeted. Station commander appeared, and tension heightened. 'First slide: to-day's bombing height.' Lights out. Slide appears, reading '800 feet'. Several hundred men take in their breath, at once, and hold it; a few cross themselves. 'Second slide: today's target.' New slide: 'Open field in France.' Several hundred men let their breath out again. Brief pep-talk by station commander about the virtues of French resistance, and we are off to emplane.

Sky over East Anglia, on a fine clear summer morning, crammed with four-engined aircraft looking for their friends. Our party of thirty-six sort themselves out, and set off southwards, joined by a B-24 Liberator who cannot find the rest of his squadron, and knows he has the legs of us. Wholly uneventful flight, save that we pass a shade close to Le Havre, and I smell a near miss from an HAA shell. No visible activity in the beach-head, and no trace, those bursts of AA fire apart, of the Luftwaffe.

As we get well into central France, we begin to lose height. Beyond Lyons, we make a sharp turn to port, and start to fly below the summits of nearby mountains. Liberator crew must begin to wonder what they have let themselves in for, but open their bomb doors with the rest. Luckily, they spot parachutes from leading aircraft, and close their bomb doors, discarding their bombs in the Channel on the way home. I have often wondered what they put in their operational record book.

By misfortune of war, all this party's 36 Fortress sorties turned out as useless as the single Liberator's. Everything dropped was hidden in the attics of a cheese factory near Dole, and discovered there a few days later by visiting German police. The organizer, F section's 'Scholar' de Saint-Geniès – of whom I had caught a glimpse as he strode across the dropping zone with his courier, Yvonne Baseden – was shot dead on the spot; she survived a spell in a bad concentration camp, and is still alive.

In the intelligence office at SAS I not only had the help of Kennedy Shaw, much older wiser and more experienced than I, but that of a Polish subaltern called Jasienski, younger even than myself, who had managed an escape from Poland and was longing to have another go at the Germans. He parachuted into Brittany quite soon after D-day, to help the French SAS unit there in its difficulties with the many local Wehrmacht units manned by renegades from the Red Army. I can now see how unsuitable it was to send a Pole to talk to Russians; he must have known, much better than anyone else at Moor Park, how unsuitable it would be, but he claimed fluent Russian, and off he went. He was soon captured, badly wounded, and was told by the Germans that as soon as he could stand, he would be shot. Luckily for him, the hospital where they kept him was overrun by the Allies before he was fit for execution, and he survived.

The Deuxième Régiment de Chasseurs Parachutistes, otherwise 4 SAS, under the one-armed Colonel Bourgoin, set up two main bases in Brittany, at one of which, near the village of St Marcel north of Vannes, they underwent on 18 June a set-piece attack by the Germans. At lunchtime that day Esmond Baring left me in charge of the office, while he went across to the great house for lunch. Jakie Astor looked in, also on his way to lunch, to remark that he thought a bomb line was coming through by W/T from DINGSON at St Marcel; a few minutes later it was in front of me, on an army message form. I reckoned that, even if a German agent overheard the message, he would have no time to get it across to his masters before the aircraft struck; so I rang up my acquaintance in the tactical air force, and read it out to him over an unscrambled telephone. Ninety minutes later, a party of P47 Thunderbolts attacked the Germans on the bomb line. Under cover from them, Bourgoin brought off a successful withdrawal, and word spread all over Brittany that SAS could get air support. We never in fact brought off this feat again, but to have managed it once was something.

The SAS unit in Brittany achieved, at a cost of about forty per cent casualties, a fine feat of arms. They organized armed squads in most villages, who each fell in, at five to midnight on a set night in early August, on the village square on hearing among the BBC's *messages personnels*, 'Le chapeau de Napoléon, est-il toujours à Perros-Guirec?' Most villages in Brittany were in Allied hands by midnight, saving a great deal of trouble to the United States army in its dash for Brest.

The army, like society at the time, was highly competitive; each regiment thought it was better than any other. Similarly, each special force tried to excel the rest. We all knew in SAS that the commandos had made a botch of trying to cut out Rommel in the desert – this was where Keyes's elder son had won his posthumous VC. When I discovered where Rommel's headquarters lay during the Normandy fighting, at the La Rochefoucauld château at La Roche Guyon, I put it to the brigadier that SAS could do better than the commandos, and might cut him out properly. There was what looked on air photographs like a passable Lysander landing ground not far from the château. A friend in the RAF made reassuring noises, the plan, rapidly formed, went ahead, and a small party dropped in.

Unluckily for SAS, airmen had got to Rommel first. Our party came up on W/T to report that he had been wounded by a passing aircraft and taken to hospital. The operation then degenerated into black farce; this is not one of the tales (already in print, if you know where to look) that redounds much to the regiment's credit. The team commander, on hearing that Paris had been liberated, went there by jeep, and called on his British girlfriend's sister, who had managed to live there through the occupation. She was delighted to see him, because her lover, a German business man living in her flat, no longer dared to go out. The SAS officer rose to the family crisis, let his driver loose in Paris in one of the business man's suits, took the business man back to England with him in the driver's battledress, and asked his girl friend – who worked in the aliens branch of the Home Office – to sort the imbroglio out. Love and duty had a brief conflict. Duty won. She turned the business man in, and reported her lover, who was cashiered.

* * *

Early in August, the brigadier went over to Brittany, to see what was going on. When he came back, I at last got his leave to go over to France myself. In a brief talk, he gave me a mission: to seize – or if necessary to shoot – a subaltern in the *Sicherheitsdienst* called Bonner, who had been doing dreadful things to SAS prisoners. He used to begin interrogations by stripping his victim, tying his wrists to his ankles behind his back with barbed wire, and leaving him to swelter for a few hours before coming in armed with a riding whip to make him talk.

I had a wholly uneventful journey over by daylight in an RAF Dakota, landing on the airfield at Meucon near Vannes which SAS had just taken over from the Luftwaffe (it had been a main pathfinder base in 1940–1). Where, I asked on landing, were the nearest Germans? 'Oh about a mile away, terrified of us; we shall have no trouble with them.' Nor did we. I got close to Bonner, in a couple of days' driving round south Brittany in a requisitioned motor car, with Adjutant (Sergeant-Major) Caplan of 4 SAS. It was Indian country – at any crossroads, there might be anybody, on either side. We were shot at once or twice – on the waterfront at Nantes I had several bullets close past my ear. Once we met an isolated United

States Army anti-tank gun and its crew, uncertain whether we and they were on the same side. Not far from Redon, we took a wrong turning, and came to a partly blown bridge. I got out of the car to see whether there was any hope of driving across it; and walked straight into half-a-dozen German parachutist machine gunners.

They promptly took me prisoner, and blazed away at Caplan (who was turning the car) without hitting him. He very sensibly drove off, retaining the car for the unit. Had the Germans not broken an ancient rule of war, by failing to post a sentry, they could easily have shot me as I walked up to them – had they known who I was (I was wearing British battledress with an airborne smock and beret). From snatches of their talk afterwards – none of them knew that I spoke fair German – I gathered that their uncertainty had been resolved when they caught sight of the Tricolor and Union Jack, which flew on the bonnet of our car to encourage any villagers we passed.

The corporal in charge of the machine gun (which they had stripped down for cleaning: I could smell the oil) was proud of having captured me, and remarked to his platoon commander – a sergeant – how young I was to be a captain. He was sent on with me to a higher headquarters, where I was delighted to hear him getting a rocket from a colonel for having failed to capture the car as well. That wiped the smirk off his face. This gave me early practice in keeping my face still, which I needed more at my formal interrogation soon thereafter, at corps HQ, through an interpreter.

I had Bonner's name down in my pocket-book. It turned out he had been messing with the unit that captured me up to the morning of the previous day, but had disappeared. No one ever found him; I suppose him to have run away with some of the ample SS office funds, and now to be in Egypt, or South America, or Hell – probably Hell. Who, I was asked, did I think Bonner was? Oh, he was the regimental transport officer (as indeed another Bonner, an English Jew, had been, four years earlier). So that passed over.

Otherwise, I did my best to stick to name, rank, and number. 'Ask him what calibre his guns are.' 'Captain Foot, what calibre are your guns?' 'If you were me, would you answer that?' It worked. I established a sort of rapport, as one officer talking to another. Just as well; for they worked down the signs on my arm, establishing my regiment (Royal Artillery, like about a fifth of the army), and mistaking Pegasus for 6th Airborne Division – it was not for me to correct them. 'And then', said the IO, 'his parachute wings'. 'No Sir', said the interpreter (the brighter of the two), 'Look, here are 6th Airborne's wings, a different shape'. They thumbed through the

Taschenbuch des britischen Heeres; luckily for me, they had not got an up-to-date copy, that showed SAS wings.

'Excuse me, Sir', said the sentry, speaking for the first time, and easing off the safety catch of his machine pistol, which he kept pointed at my navel, 'I can tell you what that gentleman's got on his arm: the same sign as was carried by all those terrorists we had trouble with at Pontivy last week.' *'Das ist ganz einfach, wenn er Terrorist ist, ist er sofort erschossen.* (If he is a terrorist then he will be shot straightaway) *Frage Ihnen, wann ware er letzt in Pontivy.'* 'Captain Foot, when were you last in Pontivy?' 'Pont-Ivy?' (brief pause); "where's that?" A white lie – I had spent part of the previous afternoon there; but enough to turn the trick.

They next went through my pockets, and I had another stroke of luck. I had been fool enough to take into the field – I had forgotten it was there, but a careful search revealed it – my cheque book, in the inner pocket of my battledress blouse. Two of the stubs, to pay mess bills, were made out to HQ SAS Troops, and would have been fatal. The interpreter glanced inside it, showed a blank cheque to the IO, said to me "You won't be wanting this, will you?" and dropped it in the fire. I had made another professional mistake. Bill Kennedy Shaw and I had countersigned each others' military identity cards. If the IO had been properly briefed, he would have risen to Shaw's name, and been much more suspicious of me. Luckily for me, he was an ignoramus in the intelligence world to which he had been posted, and missed that trick as well.

I then had a colossal stroke of luck, which preserved me from dire trouble. As I was hanging about – under close guard – waiting for transport, a passing sergeant cried, 'Oh, that's one I haven't got – excuse me, Sir', whipped out a pocket-knife, and cut off my SAS wings. He collected Allied insignia. If he survived the war, he may be showing them off to his grandson today. He left me dressed as a captain in airborne artillery, an easy identity to adopt.

I was put into a truck with over twenty Luftwaffe privates, all bristling with weapons, to guard me. I longed to join in when they broke into a sentimental song we used to sing at Winchester, *In der Heimat, in der Heimat, da gibt's ein Wiedersehen,* but stuck to my pretence of having no German. So began a disagreeable hundred days as a prisoner of war, in the wreck of a factory on the eastern outskirts of St Nazaire – now vanished under the abutment of a new westernmost bridge over the Loire.

To start with, I had four fellow prisoners. John Hill, an RAF warrant officer with a wounded leg, had recently been shot down in a Whitley minelaying off St Nazaire. Georges Guillard, butcher in the Breton village of Rochefort-en-Terre where he had been an active resister, in touch with SAS, who briefly had a headquarters there, told me he was the first civilian the Germans in Brittany had ever captured instead of shooting off-hand. There were also a Sapper captain and his batman, Goss and Tegg, captured in odd circumstances. When Patton broke the German left flank in Normandy, Goss secured forty-eight hours' local leave, and set off, with his batman, in an army truck, to call on the girlfriend he had made in south Brittany in 1940. They like myself had stumbled on Germans who took them prisoner.

He and I each at first thought the other a stool-pigeon. I asked him who had won the Boat Race in 1943; he did not know the Boat Race had not been rowed that year. In return, he asked me who had won the FA Cup. I was equally ignorant. We lived, cheek by jowl, in a little hut in the factory's forecourt, at too close quarters to remain at daggers drawn. I turned out to be the senior, and at once urged him to join me in escaping.

The hut had masses of ironwork over its window, which I inspected carefully, only to discover that the whole caboodle depended on four nails, two above and two below. I had with me an MI 9 hacksaw, with which I cut the two lower nails, while Sapper Tegg mounted guard for me. Deep in the night, I gave the ironwork a push; it opened, with a clang. I heard the sentry hurry over. He pushed the ironwork, inwards, found it firm, and went back to his sentry-box. An hour later, Goss and I got out of the hut and managed to crawl under the wire.

We shook hands and parted company outside the wire. He got clean away. I went in a different direction, up the right bank of the Loire, and stumbled into a quicksand. I was walking quite briskly, and went in first knee-deep, and with the next stride thigh-deep; for a moment I thought I was going to drown. One of the happiest moments of my life then arrived. I was wet through to the skin, unarmed, on the run behind enemy lines, but by throwing myself flat onto the quicksand surface had found rock, and was resting on that, not drowned after all. I staggered cautiously along the rock, got onto dry land, set off through the outskirts of the town, and blundered into a German sentry, who took me prisoner again. I had come upon the Wehrmacht defaulters' barracks. The Germans sentenced me to a few days in solitary confinement, on even less food than usual – quite bearable.

Goss's escape had a lucky result. He and I had each memorised the other's father's address. He wrote to Dickie (at Peek, Frean), and the family thus discovered that I was a prisoner of war after all. On Caplan's evidence, I had been posted 'Missing, believed killed'. I was allowed to write one postcard a week, and wrote alternately to Dickie and to Pip, who first met when he called at Chatham House to exchange news about me.

I cannot pretend I enjoyed being no longer in any way master of my own time. Moreover there was little to eat and no water to drink at all, nothing indeed to drink except about a pint per man per day of a dark brown liquid, called coffee, made from acorns, and turnip soup, which was our main nutrient. Sometimes it was made of parsnip or swede or mangel-wurzel instead. We got two or three small thin slices of black bread a day each, sometimes with a smear of margarine on them, occasionally a fragment of what passed for jam, and once a week, on Sundays, a slice of mule, our only protein except for what was in rotten potatoes. We were eating exactly the same rations as our captors, except that they sometimes treated themselves to rat, which they did not offer to us (nor would I have eaten it, had they done so, considering what it must have lived on). On that diet, it was not easy to keep fit. I got leave to run every day round an empty yard at the back of the prison camp, carefully watched over by a sentry as I did so. No other prisoner bothered to do anything of the sort; they all thought me a fitness fanatic, which I have never been. But it would be no good trying to escape when physically a weakling.

Gradually, our numbers increased. A French doctor called Leo Rollin turned up, with his girlfriend – she was promptly released. He was in Franc-Tireur et Partisan uniform, had been fighting in the Aveyron, was on his way to meet his Breton girlfriend's parents, and had had no idea there were any Germans left in the neighbourhood. James Silva, an American fighter pilot, was shot down between the lines and brought to join us; so were two more American air force officers, Keller and Norelius, who had fallen asleep in their Dakota on the third supply sortie to the Vosges of their day, setting an alarm clock to wake them when they got near their airfield at Angers, and forgetting to check wind speeds. At the height at which they were flying, there was a sixty-miles-an-hour easterly, which blew them well past Angers, so that they were woken up by a single flak shell which shot them down (a good shot). There were also a couple of score of French irregulars, captured (fast asleep, one of them told me) in a trench raid. We were moved out of our little hut into a larger hut, built inside the empty factory shell.

We got no Red Cross parcels. The British Red Cross, indeed, did not seem to know that we existed, and we had no incoming mail. The French Red Cross provided a few dog-eared novels in English and a little French poetry, and, once, a lemon for every man. Most of us, myself included, ate ours on the spot, as if they were oranges; mine tasted delicious. Till those novels arrived, I had nothing at all to read except a paperback copy of Shakespeare's *Antony and Cleopatra* which I had taken to France with me, and (rather to my surprise) been allowed to keep. I soon had swathes of it by heart.

Luckily, the German secret services took no interest in us. They may not have had much presence in a U-boat base, except as security guards. Once a couple of Waffen-SS privates strolled up to the camp, to have a look at us. I caught their eyes, while they were still outside the wire; we had a short staring-match, each of us conscious that we belonged to a *corps d'élite* within our countries' heavily organized armed services. I am still conceited enough to remember that I outstared them both in turn, and they went away.

A friendly Frenchman who heard in secret the BBC's news bulletins formed the habit of bicycling past the camp most mornings in September, crying out as he did so the name of the latest town the allies had captured; this gave us some idea of how fast the liberation of France was progressing. I recalled, too often, having seen a phase map of how the NEPTUNE landings were supposed to develop, which had had the mouth of the Loire in allied hands by D+100 – that is, by mid-September. A little distant artillery fire was all we ever heard of the fighting.

When out of earshot of the Germans I encouraged everybody to escape if they could, and am proud to remember that, while I was the senior officer in the camp, there were always more guards than prisoners, and there was never a fortnight during which somebody did not at least attempt an escape. Our main guards were the crew of a minesweeper sunk by the RAF, mixed in with some *Landwehr* soldiers in their forties. Their behaviour to us was 'correct' – no bullying or beatings, let alone use of prisoners for target practice. One German NCO, a cabinet-maker in peacetime, was not much of a Nazi, and extracted from me a chit that he had never behaved brutally towards any of us; but he lost heart after an extra fierce pep-talk to the prison staff by the commandant on the importance of loyalty to the Führer, tore it up in fright, and was still waiting for me to replace it when I finally left the camp.

One escape, which I witnessed, was a model of quick thinking. Every day a prisoner went, alongside a German, to fetch water from a well, which the kitchen turned into soup. One day I saw an elderly private (less than half my present age) go off to get water with a French lad who had told me he was just seventeen. The lad, quite abruptly, stopped, took off his yoke of two buckets, and ran away. The private unslung his rifle, rummaged in his pockets for a cartridge, loaded, and fired at him; by this time the lad was a hundred yards away, zig-zagging, and the shot missed. So did a second; the lad was then out of sight. The shots should have raised an alarm, but the Germans in the camp thought that the lucky private was shooting rat for supper. The lad ran for a couple of miles, took refuge with a local family, dyed his hair, put on a pair of spectacles, and was evacuated as a child under fourteen a fortnight later, under the nose of the German NCO who had interrogated him when he had been captured.

Another time, Leo and I were walking up and down the open space in front of the hut that served as the camp office, when a lorry groaned up. The sentry opened the knife-rest of barbed wire that closed the road, and followed the lorry over to the kitchen, hoping for something to eat. I nudged Leo. We did not vary our pace, but walked straight out through the open gateway. By bad luck, we had not gone a hundred yards before we met the German naval lieutenant-commander who ran the camp, who pulled a pistol on us and cried '*Zurück!*' In strict escape theory, we could have broken away instantly, one each side of him. He would hardly have brought both of us down before one was out of pistol range. But there would have been an instant hue and cry, chances of a complete escape nil. So we shrugged, smiled, and turned back.

On Armistice Day 1944 we decided we would hold the two minutes' silence to which we were used, at eleven o'clock. A minute or two before eleven, all the prisoner other ranks put down their wood-cutting tools, and fell in on the parade ground, where the officers joined them. The interpreter came bustling out of the office: what on earth was going on? I told him that we were remembering our war dead, and his war dead too. While he was explaining this inside, we held our two minutes' silence and dispersed. The commandant thereupon sent for me, remarked what a fool I had made him look ('No, no, don't translate that', but of course I understood), and packed me off to a few more days' solitary for impertinence.

A few days later still, Keller managed a trick with the keys of our hut, and he, Norelius, Leo and I all got out of the camp, this time by climbing a fourteen-foot-high barbed wire fence. We shook hands outside; the two Americans went off together, and got through eventually (with help from strangers) into the Allied lines. Leo and I settled to walk through the outskirts of St Nazaire northwards. It was a fine night for escape, drenching with rain. Suddenly, we bumped into an SS sentry, who asked who the hell we were. 'How dare you speak to an officer in that tone of voice?' cried Leo, in impeccable German with an upper-class accent. 'Stand to attention when you speak to me!' *'Zu Befehl!'* cried the sentry, clicking his heels smartly, and we passed on.

Almost as surprised as the sentry, I asked Leo who on earth he was? Was he an Austrian? (He was tall, long-headed and fair-haired.) I was not, he assured me, to worry; he was no more German or Austrian than he was French. He was the only child of a Russian surgeon, who had been sent to Berlin in 1930 with his wife and ten-year-old son in exchange for a German surgeon who went to Moscow. Leo had been at a good school in Berlin and picked up perfect German, as he had picked up perfect French when his father had been moved on to Paris in 1935. He had been conscripted into the French army, and captured in 1940, escaped, and had gone off to the Aveyron where he had joined up with an FTP unit who were glad of his medical knowledge – I knew the rest.

It continued to pour with rain. We got out on to the Grande Brière, the marsh north of St Nazaire, and moved roughly north, with the help of a tiny luminous MI 9 compass, swimming the odd canal or small river, which hardly made us wetter than the rain had done. About four in the morning we came on a lonely farmhouse, just as described in escape training – no sign of a motor vehicle, or enemy occupation, or a telephone – and tried a downstairs window. It opened, and we climbed in.

Someone lit a candle; we had got into the main bedroom, where the farmer and his wife stared at us from their double bed. Leo explained that we were escaped prisoners, looking for shelter. The farmer let out a bellow. Two strapping young men came in, in nightshirts, each bearing a pitchfork, and made for us. I was knocked out at once by a blow to my forehead, followed by another on the nape of my neck as I went down. Leo, badly cut about the face, got me back through the window, and carried me down the farm track till he found a haystack, into which he tucked me. He walked on till he found some Georgians in German uniform, to whom he could make himself understood in Russian, and packed them off to get me into hospital. One of them was cad enough to ask him for his papers, and so he got recaptured. I was taken, still unconscious, to a seaside hotel in La Baule which the Germans had turned into a hospital, and have hardly any memory of it.

I swam up from a profound coma, simply to be aware that I was alive – no more than that. Gradually it came to me that I was lying flat on my back. I could neither hear nor see nor smell. From schoolboy reading, there darted back a recollection from Edgar Allan Poe: perhaps I had been buried alive? If I had, then I must hammer on the lid of my coffin; but I *could not* move my hand to do so. Could I think of an easier muscle to work? Try an eyelid? By an immense effort, I got one eyelid open, for a momentary glimpse, of myself, flat on my back, covered in a sheet up to my neck, with all the hair shaved off my skull, and a white-masked stranger in a white gown beside me holding a pistol-shaped object to my temple. It seemed to be some sort of boring instrument – I could still feel nothing, but heard a faint hum. How was he going to know when to stop? I tried to speak, and must have moved a muscle or two, for I heard a quiet southern American voice remark 'Anesthetist, the patient seems to be coming round. Give him another shot, would you?' The thought had time to dart, 'What is he speaking American for? The Germans have got me' before I felt a jab in my arm, and passed out again.

I came round in a United States Army hospital at Rennes, having been exchanged while still unconscious. (Somebody, whether German, French or American I never discovered, had seized the occasion to relieve me of my issue wristwatch, though I still had the silver cigarette-case my mother had once given me.) All my fellow prisoners, Leo included, and a larger party from another camp near Lorient, had (I soon discovered) been exchanged too. For several days I was pretty thoroughly confused. Dickie came to see me. I recognised him, and grinned hallo with half my face – the other half was still paralysed. In retrospect, I give him a very good mark for not having shown how upset he must have been.

He had agitated for my release. Getting no change out of MI 9, whom he approached through friends in the War Office, he went over to Brittany, and called on General Molony whose 94th Division was helping the free French to besiege St Nazaire and Lorient. Molony's Red Cross officer, Andrew Gerow Hodges, drove in a jeep into the German lines and opened negotiations with their high command. By mid-November they got as far as producing him a list of their prisoners' names, which did not include mine. They said they had had to capture me four times, and if I was fit to be moved at all, they wanted four German majors in exchange. Hodges beat them down to a single German naval officer, a rank senior to me. Neither of the two U-boat captains for whom they asked was available. Instead they got *Kapitän-Leutnant* Karl Müller, a much-decorated E-boat ace whom a New Zealander called Hobday had recently rescued from a sunken E-boat off Dunkirk. (Sixty years afterwards, the exchange was put into a film, *For one English Officer*, shown on American television.)

Hodges told me later that he had been to see me in La Baule, and had asked me how much I had weighed before capture. I remembered that I had weighed about ten stone (140 pounds), but knew that stones meant nothing to Americans, who counted weight in pounds. Misremembering, I said 'Oh about 280 pounds'. No wonder his face fell. By then I weighed about six stone (84 pounds). As my brains started to settle at Rennes, a doctor came to see me, and told me I had a broken neck as well as a cracked skull. He offered me a choice: either I was to promise him, then and there, not to lift my head from the pillow till he told me I could, or he would put me in a plaster cast from my neck to my groin, to make sure my neck muscles stayed still. Pip had once been in such a plaster cast, and had described it to me as a lasting torture, so I promised not to lift my head.

As my paralysis wore off, I was moved into a large ward, most of it full of men who had been badly wounded in the Vosges. The senior patient, a staff major with an ingrown toenail, felt acutely our inferior. We had the Allied Expeditionary Forces programme on, rather loud, on the loudspeaker, all day and every day, with hourly news headlines, three-hourly news bulletins, and George Melachrino's or Glen Miller's bands in between. I got no fonder of either fare. Luckily, I was lent some books, including a fat anthology of poetry, in which I could immerse myself. There was plenty to eat, though the food was on the whole unappetising – American army rations, white bread included (the first I had seen for years), peanut butter with every meal. I benefited from General Eisenhower's promise that every soldier under his command was to eat turkey on Christmas day: I got for Christmas midday dinner a single slice of turkey breast, on the same plastic dish as peanut butter, mashed potatoes, and half a tinned pear.

About mid-December 1944, I noticed a lot of packing going on round me, and asked a nurse what was happening. 'Haven't you been listening to the news? The Germans have broken through; we're going back to the States.' What about the wounded who couldn't move? 'Oh the nuns next door will look after you, I'm sure.' I had heard too many tales about the SS shooting Allied wounded to feel at all comfortable. Luckily, this rear area flap caused by 'the battle of the Bulge', raging three hundred miles away, was soon over, and the hospital plant stayed in Europe.

A man dressed as an American air force sergeant limped up to me one day, and asked whether I spoke English? Yes it was my nursery language – why on earth did he ask? It turned out that we had been in the same ward at La Baule (he had been in Keller's aircraft), where I was usually unconscious, but when I talked at all, I only spoke German (except when talking to Hodges). Goodness only knows what I said.

A Frenchwoman of about twenty also came up to my bed. She was reading English at the local university, indeed was about to take her final exam, which included an oral test. Her professor had announced that he was going to fail anyone who betrayed the slightest trace of an American accent. She understood that I was English, not American; might she please listen to me now and again? This was Odile, Comtesse de la Varende, whose uncle had played a distinguished part in running escapers and evaders across Brittany, a story that I never unravelled properly, but gathered to have included some quiet work by his niece.

In February 1945, at last, the doctor told me I could lift my head, even get up. I did my best to leap out of bed. A medical orderly, knowing what was about to happen, caught me as I fell. I had to learn to stand and to walk again. It did not take long, and I saved everyone a lot of paperwork by begging a flight back to England from an RAF officer whom I met by chance, who flew me back in late February in an Anson to an airfield near Maidenhead.

On the way, I glanced at my medical file, which I was allowed to take with me; it opened on the words 'May pull through', and for the first time I realised how ill I had been. The operation turned out to have been the trephining of my skull – boring four little holes in it to inspect the state of the surface of my brain. Those are small scars I bear yet.

*   *   *

The army put me in its lowest medical category, and left me on sick leave. Pip had waited for me; she left Seaforth Place for Rochester Row, and we had practice in how to live together. Though I could hardly walk, I had mental energy to spare, and rang up Geoffrey. Yes indeed, COHQ would welcome it if I cared to look in, there was a job that needed doing.

This turned out to be working out, with the help of a naval colleague called Rich, the rate of casualty that would probably be incurred by a set-piece invasion of the Japanese mainland: another vast operation on the scale of NEPTUNE. I did not of course keep a copy of our report, and desultory searches for it at the record office have so far proved vain, but I have never been able to forget our conclusions. We had before us all the known casualties for major opposed landings, from Dieppe to Okinawa. We calculated about 600,000 allied and 900,000 Japanese dead – service casualties only, we took no account of civilians; and we reckoned that either figure might be out by as much as 100,000, either way. A butcher's bill of about a million and a half was in close prospect. With this report in front of it – shorn no doubt of our names, by the time it had reached so exalted a level – Churchill's cabinet gave its immediate agreement to the use of the atomic bomb, in an attempt to save lives. Those bumper-stickers that read 'No more Hiroshimas' have therefore always looked odd to me.

Dickie by this time was again abroad. AA Command had been swept through for everybody who had two eyes, two ears, two arms and two legs that worked. He was given command of one of the resulting infantry brigades, and marched with it into collapsing Germany. Accident made him one of the first general officers to see the concentration camp at Bergen-Belsen, by which he was so appalled that he could never bear to talk about it afterwards at all. Seeing and smelling it may have helped to prompt his reply when, many years afterwards, an Australian friend asked him whether he had ever done anything he was really proud of. He answered, 'Yes, I have twice marched into Germany with a conquering army.'

Pip and I were in London for VE day, which we spent in a daze, wandering round the densely crowded streets. It was wonderful to see, in the evening, the clubs along Pall Mall and St James's lit up with torches, some of which had been burning in 1814 and 1815 to celebrate the defeat of Boney, more of them in 1918 to mark the end of the Kaiser's war.

The garrisons of Lorient and St Nazaire were the very last German ground troops to surrender – they did not give in until the day after VE day. The local resistance then took his ceremonial dagger off the lieutenant-commander who had run the prisoner of war camp, and sent it to me, as a mark of respect for the stance I had often taken on the French prisoners' behalf against him. It was my most precious possession; again, stolen from me during a house move, by a thief who wanted to flog it for its plain curiosity value.

* * *

Soon after VE day, we decided to get married: a very quiet civil ceremony at the Caxton Hall, with no party after it and no relative of either of us present at all. Pip was supported by Anne Cobbe, a mathematical scholar of her year at Somerville who worked in the Home Office, whose brother Bill had been at school with me. He joined the RAF, and had long vanished on a routine patrol over the North Sea. Geoffrey Rice was my best man. Dolly only discovered I was getting married because Lindsey, whom I had told by telephone, rang her up. One of Pip's stiffer Yorkshire acquaintances asked her mother, 'Can they really be married? I never saw an engagement notice in *The Times*.' We had a few days' honeymoon at Bettiscombe.

We were still in London in early August, when we read in the newspapers that the first atomic bomb had gone off, and the second; and, almost at once thereafter, that Japan had surrendered. It was a shocking business, but I felt at the time – and have thought ever since – that the shock was necessary, to make even the most wildly militaristic Japanese realise that they were entirely overshadowed by their opponents, and must stop fighting.

Once the war was over, Pip was released by Chatham House, and we both went back to Oxford.

CHAPTER 4

Oxford

As I had an uncompleted university degree, like my father at the end of the previous war I was in the first batch to be demobilised from the army. I spent a single night at RA Depot, Woolwich – the last time in my life I had to wear uniform – and was let out next morning, after I had persuaded the bombardier in charge of my papers not to date my discharge 31 November 1945. I was already back at New College, which was by then used to married undergraduates, and had spent much of the long vacation reading quietly in Bodley. I got a thirty per cent disability pension, reduced to twenty per cent after a year. An army doctor then said, 'There's nothing really the matter with you, is there?', and it stopped.

The college put us into 8 New College Lane, just outside the west wall of the cloisters, to keep squatters from taking it over: a delicious tiny eighteenth-century house, supposed to be where Halley lived when he discovered his comet. It included a few pieces left behind by H.W.B. Joseph the logician, who had once lived there; I handle most days, lighting a candle for dinner, a now much worn matchbox cover of his. Christopher Hawkes who had been taught by him told me, "It was like drinking a pint of disinfectant – you felt awful at the time, and much better afterwards". We moved on in the spring of 1946 to a term in a house belonging to the historian E.L. Woodward in Keble Road, which he lent us while he and his wife were away in America, and then managed to buy a freehold in Park Town for something under £6,000. My bank lent me some of the purchase money. After I had signed a sheaf of documents, the bank manager gathered them up and said severely, "You should know that you have not only paid too much for this house; you have paid much too much too much." He did not then take in how far beyond his foresight house prices were to soar later in the century.

It was a five-storey stucco-fronted house in one of a gently curving pair of terraces built by a pupil of John Nash in 1853. Betty Pinney looked almost shocked when we told her we lived in Park Town, for it had been built on the understanding that an impending Universities Act would allow dons to marry. It did not, and the owner went bankrupt. Several dons bought freeholds for a song each, and kept their mistresses there. The neighbourhood still retained a slightly risqué flavour well into the 20th century. Our next-door neighbour on one side, an elderly maiden lady, was proud of having been born before the war – of 1870. Two doors away on the other side lived a grey-haired woman with an un-English accent and two russet-haired teenage daughters, whose only eccentricity was that she kept the curtains of her ground floor front room permanently drawn. Many years later I discovered why. She was Boris Pasternak's sister, and the room held dozens of paintings by their father.

We lived at number sixteen, and occasionally by postman's error got letters for R.W. Chambers the editor of Jane Austen, who lived at number six, a grander house. He kept a postcard pinned on his front door, reading NOT AT HOME. I could not help noticing his cold eye upon me, through his front window, when I delivered his misdirected mail. We had another neighbour, widow of the head of a house, who had preserved a grand manner, lived with her daughter, and had no tact. She was inclined to ring up in the early evening and say, 'We had *such* an interesting luncheon party today. You and Philippa are to come to supper at half-past seven tonight to help us finish the left-overs.'

A little of the furniture came from Lindsey, who died early in 1946. She had not felt well during the war, had been advised by her doctor to take six months' rest, had – being her – gone back on duty, and was carried off by a cancer. Dolly went round her cottage at Blewbury, ordaining which pieces were to go to me and which were to go to Paddy. The family solicitor then arrived and read her will, which she had made in 1915 and never bothered to alter. She left all of which she died possessed to Dickie, who was not at that moment on speaking terms with either of his children.

He had at last been divorced by Nina, who was so much struck by the trouble he had taken to get me back from a prisoner of war camp that she offered him the divorce as a way of saying thank you, and had at once married his mistress, from whom, again almost at once, he split. He met at a party at the Coopers' flat over Prunier's in St James's Street an Australian painter called Elaine Haxton. They fell for each other at sight. Dickie went through a second divorce, married Elaine, and went out to Australia with her. I did not see him again for over twenty years.

As I had passed the first public examination – by taking pass Mods at the end of my first term – and had been away for over five years on His Majesty's service, I turned out to be already entitled to take a BA and an MA, which I did, in late October 1945. My father had always promised that he would pay the bill for my first degree, so I sent it on to him. I had been brought up on a rule nowadays out of fashion: 'never read bills, my dear, that is rude – simply pay them. Tradesmen are honest.' As Dickie was paying this bill, I thought I had better read it first. There was an unattributed item at the end of it for £25.10.4. I queried it. 'Dear me,' said the bursary clerk, 'I have accidentally added in the date – I *am* sorry', and crossed it out. An ingenious racket, presumably dating back some centuries.

Though I had my nominal degrees, I thought I ought to buckle down to getting proper ones, so settled again to PPE. Another Wykehamist, Peter Wiles, senior scholar of my New College year, was doing as I did. (He had spent much of the war providing excellent tactical intelligence from decipher for the Eighth Army, till sacked for impertinence.) A tutor suggested to him that he might attempt All Souls; Peter did, and was elected. He went to ask his new warden what he should do about taking his final schools. The warden recommended him not to put temptation in the examiners' way, so Peter never took schools at all, though he lived to be an eminent professor of sovietology at LSE, one of the few intellectuals to see right through the Soviet Union, early, and denounce it as a sham.

Pip was teaching philosophy for Somerville, of which she soon became a fellow. With great good sense, she made no attempt to make a philosopher out of me; and Herbert Hart my philosophy tutor – later a most eminent jurist – exclaimed one day, 'Foot, you have not got the philosophic mind.' I accepted his verdict, and took a shortened version of the final schools. I did not discover till many years later that Hart had had an interesting war in MI 5, where he had been in charge *inter alia* of the case of the notorious double agent Déricourt, which I was never able to discuss with him.

Alan Bullock taught me history, and put me on to J.L. Hammond's *Gladstone and the Irish Nation.* A few books, in anyone's life, make the world not look quite the same shape ever after. This was such a book for me, and I became an ardent Gladstonian. He also put me on to Koestler's *Darkness at Noon* – 'Read it on a wet week-end. You'll want to throw yourself in the Cher afterwards' – and on to Lionel Robbins's *Economic Causes of War*, another good cure for infantile Leninism. I knew and liked, but was never taught by, Lightfoot, who had a wonderfully named chair – he was the

Dean Ireland Professor of the Exegesis of Holy Scripture. Not even he could persuade me to attend chapel.

Isaiah Berlin taught me as well – political theory. I had had a few tutorials with him in the summer of 1939, on moral philosophy, and had found him exceedingly hard to follow – I could understand about one word in ten. It was a sign to me that I had matured a bit during the war, that after it I could understand about one word in three. Difficult though it was to dream of keeping up with him, it was a delight to have encountered a mind of such terrifying swiftness. I have remained proud ever since to have known him, and when he died I planted an oak tree in his memory.

For a special subject on international relations between the century's two world wars I went to John Wheeler-Bennett, whom it was also a delight to know. He had been everywhere and met everybody; it was almost an embarrassment to be taught by him. For instance, he had been selling horses in Berlin in the early 1920s, and so knew most senior German generals of the 1940s. He had also been acquainted with Kaiser Bill, whom he strongly resembled, whose life he thought of writing, and whose illegitimate descendant the gossips made out he was, though he always maintained his mother had never met any Hohenzollern. (He once remarked that when he had been staying at a great house in Roumania, another guest asked if she might have the honour of kissing HRH's hand.) He did know the old Kaiser, and indeed was staying with him at Doorn the weekend Hitler's war began, when his host remarked, gesturing at the newspapers, 'You see, the machine is running away with him, just as it ran away with Me.' He lived in Garsington Manor, scene of Aldous Huxley's *Crome Yellow* when it had been inhabited by Lady Ottoline Morrell. Once or twice I was invited to visit him there. His study, a spacious square room, was crammed with books: all on a single subject, the history of Germany in and since Napoleonic times.

I had hoped for a first, but had no idea whether I was anywhere near getting one. Several of my contemporaries cherished similar hopes, in similar ignorance. The only man to take PPE finals from New College in summer 1947 and get a first was Wynne Godley, younger son of the Lord Kilbracken who had been Mr Gladstone's private secretary, whom none of the rest of us had ever seen with a book in his hand. He had brains.

Lightfoot saw the list early, and bicycled up to Park Town to tell me I had a second. I was out, in Bodley; Pip broke it to me when I came home. Ever since, I have collected notes of men, later much more eminent than me, who got seconds. A.J. Balfour, later prime minister and earl, I regard as the president of the club. Clement Attlee, also prime minister and earl, and J.L. Hammond and Michael Howard the historians are among the vice-presidents. Hammond told me once that when he went up to Oxford he had been reading Greek since he was eight; his future wife Barbara Bradley had to learn Greek on coming up the same term. He got a second, and she a first, both in honour mods and in Greats. The university made eventual amends, giving both of them honorary doctorates on the same day. Another vice-president of this notional body was Donald Mackinnon, who got a second in mods, a second in Greats, and a second in theology, was a fellow of Balliol before he was thirty, and a Regius Professor before he was thirty-five. But he, like Attlee and Hammond, was a man in a million.

It was Donald, who had taught Pip, who secured me a toe-hold in Oxford after schools. I had got a respectable second, with beta-alpha my highest mark and only one mark below beta plus. Donald arranged for me to teach politics at Keble, where he was then the philosophy fellow (he went to Balliol immediately afterwards). Maurice Hugh-Jones the economist and Basil Mitchell the new philosopher accepted this calmly enough. I did not have a teaching room in college, so taught at home, as did Pip.

Keble made me a member of their senior common room, reminding me not to lunch on Wednesdays, just before college meetings. The food was passable, the cellar good. Every Thursday during full term there was a black tie guest night, with good wine at table and better port in common room afterwards, as well as good conversation. During the war, the economics don in the board of trade and the bursar in the treasury had between them arranged for Keble to buy a pipe of 1940 and a pipe of 1942 port. No other college had then got either.

Following Peter Wiles's example, I was fool enough to put in for All Souls, in the teeth of the evidence that G.M. Young was the last fellow they had elected who had failed to get a first. My father cannot have improved my chances by writing to Warden Sumner to remind him that they had been at school together. Feiling was my host at dinner. As we sipped sherry before it, he introduced me to G.D.H. Cole, who said, 'Ah, Foot, I have just been reading your papers', in a voice of such perfect neutrality that I knew at once I must have failed. They offered up to three fellowships, but only elected one, a charming Thucydidean who never went into public life or wrote a book. At least I failed in distinguished company, that included Lawrence Stone and Peter Strawson, both later knighted.

And at least I could go to Sumner's classes on how to write history, a pale imitation of Marc Bloch's famous seminar at the Sorbonne, but a most useful piece of schooling for me. As well as doing some teaching for Keble, I was working on a further degree, in the history faculty, supervised by R.W. Seton-Watson whose sons had been my revered seniors in College at Winchester. He began by telling me to read Stern's *Geschichte Europas*, returning in a fortnight to discuss where I should concentrate. A few days later, we met by chance in Blackwell's bookshop, and he asked how I was getting on with Stern. I confessed I was still only halfway through the first of seven volumes in black letter. He replied, wisely, 'You will never be an historian till you have learned to skip.' I duly met him, next Friday week, having skipped to the end of Stern, and we settled on a subject for a B Litt thesis, on Gladstone, Granville, and the project to re-create an independent Lorraine with which they toyed in the late 1860s. I had a Gladstone memorial lectureship, sponsored by Christ Church, for a year (with little money and no dining rights), which helped to keep the wolf from the door.

Roy Harrod at Christ Church most kindly gave me an introduction to a friend of his, Sir George Leveson-Gower who was Gladstone's last surviving private secretary, and from Sir George I got one most useful sidelight on Mr Gladstone, which I eventually put into print in a pamphlet published at Hawarden on the hundredth anniversary of the great man's death. I had inquired what it had been like to live in the same house as Mr G, and got the reply that he was the most agreeable of men to know. But wasn't that, I replied, what everyone always said about Sir George's uncle Lord Granville? Sir George insisted that, of the two, Mr Gladstone had been the nicer; not the view of Mr G one acquires from most of his biographers.

Work for the B Litt gave me, as it was meant to do, experience in handling original documents. I got embrangled in the Luxembourg crisis of 1867, that almost led to a premature outbreak of the Franco-Prussian war, and needed to look at the papers of Lord Cowley, then at the close of his long spell as British ambassador at Paris – he had been there since 1852, the first one to survive a change of government at home. The proverb 'not what you know, but whom you know' here came to my aid. Wheeler-Bennett knew his descendant Sir Victor Wellesley, who had given Cowley's papers to the public record office, and put in a word on my behalf. I was first in to bat, since the papers were still in the packing-cases into which Sir Victor had had them bundled. Luckily I knew the handwritings I was looking for, and beyond them, came on papers by Cowley's private secretary, called Atlee (presumably no relation). I found out a good deal, enough to get a B Litt thesis together, of which Richard Pares persuaded me to summarise the core in an article for the *English Historical Review* on the Luxembourg crisis.

Teaching a few hours a week for Keble – mainly in one-to-one tutorials – provided a little income, but not much. Donald McLachlan provided a useful supplement, by introducing me to Stanley Morison who was then engaged in adding a couple of volumes to the in-house history of *The Times*, and needed a research assistant to prepare him the chapters on foreign policy. In 1948–9 I used to commute – at first by train, later by bus – between Oxford and Blackfriars on three days a week, working in *The Times* archives at Morison's knee. Morison once described me to a friend as the most donnish man he had ever met, and we parted company after a couple of years, when I had done as much work as he wanted, and when he sent me galley proofs of a chapter written on the understanding that Mr Asquith had still been prime minister in 1917.

He had a little office at the top of the Astors', originally the Walters', private house in Printing House Square, which you could approach through the Georgian front door and up a carpeted staircase, or – as I was to do – from the back yard, through a back door, into the servants' quarters, and up a mean back stair with crumpled linoleum. As he had so many friends on the printing side, who also used the back stair, we had lavish printers' back-up: one chapter, I remember, I saw seven times in successive galley proofs, before we went into page.

He played a lot of his cards close to his chest, but did let me see one file, about eighty pages long, of riveting interest. It contained the letters exchanged in 1936 between Geoffrey Dawson, the then editor, Alan ('Tommy') Lascelles, one of the new king's private secretaries, whose colleague Alex Hardinge had married Lady Milner's daughter and thus knew Dawson, and Canon Don of Westminster who spoke for Archbishop Lang. They all agreed that Edward VIII, as a king, was not doing his work, and that his infatuation with Mrs Simpson might lead to difficulties. Would Dawson sound out Dominion opinion about Mrs S's acceptability as queen? The point was so delicate that they did not want to take it up through the Dominions Office. All Dawson's friends in the four old Dominions agreed that she would be unthinkable. A meeting was arranged with Neville Chamberlain at Preshaw, a private house near Winchester, early in September. Partridge shooting provided the cover. (The host, Colonel Pelly, was Alan Brooke's brother-in-law.) The abdication followed.

The file was so interesting that I made a photocopy of it, which I took away with me. At the time it was of course unusable, all the participants but Chamberlain and Dawson were still alive, and each would have sued at the drop of a feather. I put it away in the bank. Changing banks, in 1959, I got a reminder that the Oxford bank held an envelope, contents unknown; were they to destroy it? I went to collect it, and reopened it to refresh my memory. Serve me right – due to the early photocopying process I had eighty sheets of nearly blank paper. No one can now find the original file, which someone has presumably confided to a kitchen boiler. Lascelles left the incident out of his recent autobiography, *King's Counsellor*, but I do not see why the secret of it should die with me.

It was a delight to see something of the head of *The Times*'s intelligence branch, J.S. Maywood. He had joined the paper at the turn of the century, as a boy clerk, working for Moberly Bell the manager. The paper was then in severe money trouble. One of its efforts to recoup lay in buying *Encyclopaedia Britannica* and preparing a new edition of it. Maywood was set to read every article as it came in; and if two articles contradicted each other, to put the authors of each in touch, so that they could resolve the hitch. That is why the encyclopaedia's eleventh edition (1911) is so good. Maywood got thanks, but no official recognition. It was obvious in the late summer of 1938 that a major international crisis was developing. Every evening the paper appeared in September he went down to the stone, and brought back with him into his office the manuscripts or typescripts from which the leading articles had been set (these were usually thrown away), thus providing me ten years later with a useful source for who had written which phrase.

I got one major historical lesson out of this spell at Printing-House Square: an introduction to the work of Alfred Milner, who had been Dawson's (then Robinson's) patron in South Africa at the turn of the century. He turned out to have left a diary, which his widow had deposited in New College, which in turn had loaned it to the Bodleian, where I read it. This led to an invitation to stay a night or two with her at Great Wigsell, her house in Kent. Pip was to come too, and I was to bring a dinner jacket. Lady Milner turned out to be formidably far to the right, denouncing for example Mr Justice Lynskey who had just been conducting an inquiry into supposed misbehaviour by junior ministers as an obvious left-wing appointment. She was upset when I pointed out that he had been put on the bench by the wartime coalition, with its large conservative majority; she had little use (any more than I had) for Simon the then Lord Chancellor, and she still had her knife deep into Churchill, for having ordered a battle cruiser squadron to Lamlash in an attempt to intimidate the more extreme Ulster unionists, shortly before the Great War.

Her father, Admiral Maxse, had been ADC to Lord Raglan during the Crimean war. To my disappointment, she did not confirm the anecdote that Raglan used to inquire at breakfast, 'Did the French do anything in the night?' – meaning not the French but the Russians – because he could not get the Napoleonic War out of his head. But I did get her leave to quote as much of Milner's diary as I wanted for Morison. And I treasured her remark that 'Kitchener was like another brother-in-law to me'. Whenever he was in England he stayed at Hatfield, where he was treated as a son of the house.

I also made a good friend at *The Times*, Peter Utley – whom Pip had met already in her Chatham House days – all but stone blind, but coruscatingly clever. He dined now and again in a Fleet Street pub with what called itself the Ex-Future Editors' Club, and let me join them. There I also met Donald Tyerman, who had not yet left *The Times* for *The Economist*. Peter told me that when *The Times* interviewed him, all they asked about his education was, 'You were three years at Cambridge, weren't you?'. He got no chance to show off his starred first in history. One of my Oxford pupils was also interviewed by the same paper, and only asked whether he had been three years at Oxford. He was thus able to conceal the fact that he had been ploughed in the final schools, and was also appointed.

In *The Times* history's third volume, most of it written by Disraeli's biographer G.E. Buckle, some passages on the Parnell Commission attracted the ire of Henry Harrison, who had graduated from being Parnell's bodyguard to being a Home Rule M.P, and was still alive. I went up to Hampstead to see him. He warned me, by letter, that he was stone deaf. When, following his instructions, I walked into his study off Haverstock Hill, he opened by remarking that I was lucky to find him alive. He had just gone out to buy some tobacco, and had paused as he walked, to try to remember in detail something he was going to want to say to me. He forgot that he had paused in the middle of the main road, and was roused from his reverie by a bump on his thigh. 'I looked round. There was a motor bus leaning against me; the fellow seemed to be sounding his horn.' We were able to put in an appendix to rectify Buckle's errors.

Harrison had been present in committee room 14 of the House of Commons when the Irish party met to elect its leader for the session, in

1890, just after the fact of Parnell's adultery with a fellow MP's wife became public. He told me that when Parnell said 'It is simply a question of who is to be master of the Irish nation', T.P.O'Connor broke in, 'No, Mr Parnell, the question is who is to be mistress of the Irish nation', and Parnell rose to strike him, but was held back.

When Morison's history of *The Times* from 1912 to 1941 – the series dated its volumes by changes of editor, not by world events – appeared in April 1952, I got a copy, and was pleased to find myself in respectable, if anonymous, published print. I grangerized my own copy heavily, inserting from spare galleys everything Morison had cut out of my drafts.

In the Bodleian's upper reading room, where I spent a good deal of time, there was one fixture, an eminent Arabist staff member, who once got engaged in a long, loud conversation with a visiting scholar, in a mixture of German, Arabic and English. A.L. Rowse, sitting not far from me, picked up one of Bodley's signs that read PLEASE TREAD LIGHTLY AND TALK LITTLE, and plonked it on the Arabist's desk. It worked.

Philippa thought she ought to do some sort of good works, and early became a strong supporter of Oxfam, which was then starting up. Among the people she met there was Robert Castle, who was one of those invaluable men who is always there, has always got a box of matches handy, and can see his way promptly though any small practical trouble. In his teens, he had been printer's boy to T.E. Lawrence's printer while *Seven Pillars of Wisdom* had first been set up in type (apart from the celebrated version run off on a New York newspaper press, of which a few copies were put on sale, none bought, for a vast sum in US dollars). I could not resist asking the inevitable booklovers' question, how many copies had they printed? He replied that no one had ever known but Lawrence. Several times, first in in the mornings, he had been aware that during the night at least one more copy had been run off (Lawrence had a key to the shed). How many, only the author knew, and he would never say. This seems to me a sound example of a properly kept secret.

Philippa persuaded me to pass on to Oxfam something that had reached us from White Hill: a large set of cone-shaped copper vessels, running in size from half a pint up to four gallons. The maids had dutifully polished them, but they had been too big even for White Hill's big kitchen, and were quite unfit for ours, and besides, we had no maids. She kept one, to put flowers in. It did not break my heart to part from the rest, which had been familiar from early childhood, and it did Oxfam a little starting good.

Not long after the war, we went to stay with Leo Spanin – Rollin's real name – at Cahors, where he was a schoolmaster, preparing for the *concours de l'agrégation*, the exam every French schoolteacher had to pass before he or she could teach at a university. We met and liked his Gascon wife Janette, *née* Laboubée (the Bretonne had not waited for him). I am proud to say they named their only child, a son, Michel after me. We also greatly took to a colleague of Leo, who taught medieval history. Why on earth, I asked, had he not become a don? *'Il ne sera jamais reçu: il est royaliste.'* As a routine precaution, the Republic inserted in every history paper a question no royalist could bear to leave unanswered, thus ensuring none became dons, to upset the political balance. Another time, we visited his in-laws, in the small town of La Romieu, down towards the Pyrenees on one of the pilgrim roads to Compostella. His father-in-law boasted an elderly Citroen, a double petrol ration as a cultivator both of vines and of peaches, and almost the only house in La Romieu more than two storeys high, which he kept plastered with communist party posters. When I dared inquire why the principal local kulak supported the PCF, he said *'Jeune homme, vous ne savez rien de la politique. Mon père a appuyé Gambetta jusqu'au jour de sa mort; ma famille se trouve à l'extrême gauche.'* For that conservative reason, he always voted communist.

In the summer vacation of 1948 I was sent to Germany by the Foreign Office, to take part in a holiday course for undergraduates at Bonn about liberal ideas; I was to talk about Mr Gladstone. The devastation, still hardly touched, was appalling. In Cologne, I walked for a mile along the main boulevard, upstream from the cathedral, and saw only six or seven buildings with a habitable ground floor, nothing taller. Bonn had been chosen to be capital of West Germany because only half of its houses had been destroyed. I was put up in a requisitioned hotel, and at dinner on the first night noticed an irregular line of blobs along the window. What were they? 'Oh they're children's noses – they like to look at the food.' I discovered that my audience existed on a daily ration of about 900 calories, while the control commission staff got ample army food, quite three times as nutritious. I managed to leave the hotel, taking a ration card with me, to get put up with my audience in a bunk in a vast concrete air raid shelter, and to eat the same food as they did. Some days later, I had to revisit the hotel, for a word with a colleague. Waiting for him in the bar, I was proud to overhear someone else murmur, 'Bad business … foreign office lecturer … gone native'.

At a *vin d'honneur* shortly after I reached Bonn I was introduced to Professor Curtius, one of the university's eminences, to whom I mentioned how shocked everyone in England still was at the recollection of the Nazis' concentration camps. He assured me that he was as shocked as I was; they had come as a total surprise to the general community. A few minutes later, when he had been buttonholed by someone else, and I happened to be standing back-to-back with him, I heard him remark to the German to whom he was talking that if one had taken such-and-such a step during the war, one would have been packed straight off to a camp, and everyone knew what that meant. I spun round, and confronted him with the contradiction. 'Forgive me', he said, 'the Rector has just arrived, I have business to do with him', and eased away. But I did not forget.

At Oxford I used (in spite of Monsieur Laboubée's remark) to teach political institutions, for the routine PPE paper, as well as British history since 1830; and, if anybody wanted to take it, the international relations special subject I had taken myself. Gradually I extended the scope of my teaching, to cover British history since 1660, and European history since 1815, and taught occasionally for other colleges than Keble. Eventually Trinity took me on also, to teach politics, and I got a university lectureship. I enjoyed teaching in one-to-one tutorials, preferring them to seminars, and understand why so many dons say you can't write unless you have taught. Certainly I later found it useful, when composing a paragraph, to ask myself whether some of my stupider pupils could understand it.

The cleverest person I ever taught was, I think, Joan Stolper Campbell of St Hugh's. She was so bright that quite often, when I put her a question, she answered not the one I had asked, but the next one I was going to ask after that. She had been brought up partly in Berlin, where her father Gustav Stolper had edited the *Berliner Tageblatt*, and partly in New York to which he had had the good sense to move his family in 1933. The intelligentsia of both cities had clearly struck sparks off her. She missed a first, not having done an inordinate amount of work. One of her examiners is said to have proposed giving her a long *viva*, because she answered routine questions so brightly, but to have been turned down by the chairman. Another bright spark I taught was Anthony Nicholls, who went on to a distinguished career at St Antony's and married C.S. Nicholls who did so much for the *Dictionary of National Biography*.

When a new special subject was impending in the history school, which I also intended to teach, on British policy and the making of the Ententes,

1898–1907, I happened to turn in to Thornton's bookshop in the Broad. Mr Thornton himself greeted me; he had put on one side for me, knowing I would want them, the four volumes of Gooch and Temperley that were among the set books, and could let me have them for twenty guineas. I had the pleasure of telling him that I had just bought them, at cost price, from HMSO, for they were still in print, at half a guinea a volume.

I met a worse shopkeeper's racket in the High. Among the scraps of furniture that came to me from the family was a shapely oval wine-box, mahogany, probably Irish eighteenth-century. Central heating in Park Town cracked its lid. Yes, certainly the antique dealer to whom I took it could repair it; would I leave it with him for a few weeks? Three weeks later I looked in to inquire progress, entering the shop as other customers left and the telephone rang. The dealer, with his back to me, was talking on the telephone; yes, he happened to have one in the shop at the moment – he had his hand on it at that instant – and he put his hand out to caress my wine-box. 'Oh about two hundred and fifty.' He then turned, saw me, and offered me £25 for the box – which I got mended elsewhere.

Most of the papers I needed to see for my B Litt were in the old public record office in Chancery Lane, or in the vast Gladstone collection in the British Museum library. Knowing no better, I had begun by going up to Hawarden, expecting to find the Gladstone papers there, and was advised by Warden Vidler at St Deiniol's Library to work on Disraeli instead, for his toils at *The Orb and the Cross* had so distressed him that he could hardly any longer bear the sight of Mr G's handwriting. That advice I am glad I ignored.

I also ranged as far as Chatsworth, where there were some points I needed to hunt up among the papers of the future eighth duke. Francis Thompson the librarian, who lived across the park at Edensor, was kindness itself to me. The great house was empty except for him and the butler, who would not be parted from the gold plate and slept on a camp bed pitched across the door of the safe. The then duke preferred Eastbourne, and the family had not got round to re-opening the house since the war, when a girls' school from Eastbourne had lived in it. Thompson received me in his study; he had the Chatsworth Head beside him, a bronze head of Apollo attributed to Praxiteles. When I admired it, he said, 'Pick it up.' 'I wouldn't touch it !' *'Pick it up !'* So I did; it was made of papier maché. He had the original and two dozen papier maché replicas scattered round the house, an ingenious security precaution. (It is now in the British Museum, in lieu of a quarter of a million pounds of death duties.)

I was staying in the Peacock at Baslow, right at the gates of the park, only twenty-five minutes' walk from the house. I persuaded Thompson to come and dine with me there one evening. As we moved through from the dining-room to the coffee-room, I mentioned that there was a men's room just round the corner. He said, 'I'm quite comfortable, thank you; but how I envy you being able to say that. When I was your age –', but at that moment we entered the coffee-room, where ladies were present, so of course he changed the subject. This shift in manners has I think gone unmarked among social historians.

I wandered round the empty house, admiring the superb furniture, and noticed on the main bedroom floor a brass handle in a splendid Chinese wallpaper. Fitted cupboard? No, it opened a small door onto a spiral staircase, that led upwards. I went up to the servants' floor. Abrupt change of key: linoleum or bare boards, plain iron bedsteads, rickety wash-stands, and no windows – it was thought unsuitable for the servants to look out over their betters, so their floor was lit by skylights.

Work among the Gladstone papers was not perfectly straightforward: to see his notes of what passed in cabinet, one had to get leave from the current cabinet secretary (they are all now in published print). I had had a run in with the manuscript officials already, while working for Morison, when I wanted to see a paper of Balfour's on the defence of England against seaborne attack. For about a year, I was put off with various excuses – gone to the binders, not yet back from the binders, reserved for another reader, and so on. As I persisted, I was taken behind the scenes to meet the Keeper of Manuscripts, who gestured to his blazing fire, and told me that was where he was going to put the Balfour papers if I continued to make a nuisance of myself. There was a paper among them, on how to defend this island against seaborne attack, written in 1915, which the general staff had had copied out (not being allowed to borrow it) in the summer of 1940; the keeper was not going to have strangers peeking at it.

I made one precious friendship in the old British Museum manuscripts room. One morning when I went up to the desk to ask for a Gladstone volume I had pre-ordered, I found myself standing next to a reader much older than myself, who had, it turned out, asked for the same volume. He insisted I was to have it first; I did my best to make him take it. It ended up by my reading it first, and then lunching with him at the Reform. This was Lawrence Hammond himself, whose book had so much influenced me.

All things considered, and not even excepting my grandfather, he was the nicest man I have ever met.

Hammond had served briefly as an artillery officer during the Great War, but was invalided out on account of a weak heart, and later taken on by the *Manchester Guardian* as its correspondent at the Paris peace conference, and then in southern Ireland during the Troubles. His dispatches from there, which C.P. Scott made sure that Lloyd George read, did a lot towards persuading that prime minister that he would have to come to a settlement with the Irish, instead of trying to browbeat them. I am not sure that Hammond has ever been given the full credit that was his due. He lived at Piccott's End, beyond Hemel Hempstead, in a small house he and Barbara had bought for themselves before the Kaiser's war, not knowing that an army rifle range was about to be set up opposite them. This gave their friends, for decades, the odd experience of going to call on a marvellously pacific couple and having their conversation punctuated by intermittent rifle fire.

He continued to review for the *Guardian* long after he had ceased to be a working journalist, and had a fatal heart attack brought on by reviewing the volume in Woodward and Butler's official series of foreign office documents that included the tale of how the Foreign Office had sidled out of the arrangement Chamberlain thought he had made with Hitler at Munich that Czechoslovakia's frontiers were to be guaranteed. On his death-bed, he asked Barbara to ask me to finish the short life of Gladstone that he was writing for Rowse's 'Teach yourself history' series; and I did.

He had put about half the book into typescript already. One chapter, on the social and economic conditions in which Gladstone grew up – the core of his past work with his wife – he had written three times over, in variant versions which I had to conflate. Beyond that I had nothing, beyond a few words scribbled on a single quarto sheet, to indicate where he meant to go next, but it was not too hard to guess. This was my first book. I did my best to follow the lines he had laid down in his big book on Gladstone, and to make my prose as indistinguishable from his as I could. Nevertheless, when I sent a copy to my mother, the least intellectual of women, and she wrote to thank me for it, she picked out correctly the page at which I had taken over from Hammond.

Once I had asked Hammond whether he had read Mr Gladstone's diary. He only replied, 'You can't see it'. The family had asked him not to mention that they had shown him the sawn-off version of it which Herbert Gladstone

My grandfather with both his children, my father and my aunt, on the Western Front ca. 1917.

Brigadier-General R M Foot, late 27th Inniskilling Fusiliers, my grandfather.

My grandfather, myself and my father, outside my grandfather's study door at White Hill, ca. 1926.

White Hill, my grandparents'
house, where I spent much of
my childhood.

My Mother as a member
of the Gaiety Chorus.

Self on Dinah, held by Brown, the groom, in the stable yard at White Hill.

Winchester College Archaeological Society on tour in Normandy, 1935. (L to R), Monsieur Liétard, Hall, Barron, Aris, Foot, Birbeck, Joll, the Reverend S S G Lesson, de Wesselow, Andrew, Major Hamilton, Baines, Brodrick, Barnes.

Stewart Menzies, the wartime C.

Colin Gubbins, the
mainspring of SOE.

James Langley,
Coldstream Guards,
my co-author.

Marie Madeleine Méric (later Fourcade): from a false identity card, made in London, depicting her as a French housewife.

Victor Gerson in uniform about 1942: in plain clothes. He ran the 'Vic' escape line, that never lost a passenger.

Norman Crockett, who ran MI9, in his office at Wilton Park, Beaconsfield.

Harry Peulevé, TV cameraman turned saboteur, who crossed the Pyrenees as a cripple, ran SOE's 'Author' circuit in the Corrèze, and later escaped from Buchenwald.

Kapitän-Leutnant Karl Müller, 1943, the year before he was exchanged for me. For many years he supposed me to be my namesake the erstwhile Labour Party leader. *(IWM photograph HU48338 courtesy of the Imperial War Museum, London.)*

My sister Paddy; studio portrait, perhaps for her engagement to Jim Gowland in 1945.

In my study at East Finchley, ca 1980.

In New Orleans, May 1990 with (L to R) Colonel Hans von Luck, Mrs Mary Mohs and Professor Stephen E Ambrose.

Martins Cottage, Nuthampstead: deep in the country, within forty miles of Charing Cross.

Self doing a crossword with grandson Matthew; I then eighty, he then eight.

had dictated during the Great War to a lady typist, leaving out anything he thought unfit for a lady's ears. After I had read the diary myself, the publisher let me amend Hammond & Foot slightly, There were not many changes to be made, for Hammond had got to the core of him already.

After his death, I once asked his widow why neither he nor she had ever mentioned the Webbs, whom surely they must have known? Yes they had known them well – very well; had even been on first-name terms with them. 'But when the South African war began, Sidney said to Lawrence 'Society must move from the less sophisticated towards the more sophisticated; therefore in this struggle I take the side of the crown.' So of course we never spoke to them again.'

I took little interest in politics during Attlee's governments, but when the Labour Party was beaten in 1951 thought I ought to rally round, and joined the city Labour Party, of which (to my surprise) I rapidly became a vice-president. Pressed by my Labour friends, I stood for the city council (aware, as they were not, that I was following, a goodish way behind, in the footsteps of T.H. Green, Dick Crossman and Frank Pakenham). In 1954 I was elected councillor from the south ward – mainly the slum of St Ebbe's – as junior colleague to Arthur Kinchin, a robust retired railway worker. He had got his first job, as a child of nine, scaring crows in north Oxfordshire at sixpence a week; this brought the family's weekly income up to half a crown (12½p). He had gone on to a career as a railway porter. He was so likeable a man that I invited him one evening to a Tuesday dinner in Keble (Tuesdays, also guest nights, did not involve black tie). Accident put him at dessert next to Robert Hall, then a senior personage at the Treasury, to whom Arthur delivered a lengthy disquisition on how to make up a train. Robert said to me afterwards that though he had had to teach practical economics at Trinity, he had learned a good deal from Arthur. Robert by this time was a Treasury knight, one of the half-a-dozen people who could ruin the country by a few minutes' indiscreet telephone talk with a Zurich banker. The responsibility weighed on him, he was troubled by a recurrent dream. He was back at being dean of Trinity. The college had gone head of the river, was having a bump supper, and the victorious crew were trying to burn the college down.

My spell in local politics soon disillusioned me with politics altogether. Extreme, personal pettiness seemed to play much too large a part, and the actual party machines seemed to be run at the agents' personal whims. Once we needed a new parliamentary candidate. One of the contestants for it sailed over every formal hedge, till it came to interview, because his trade union offered to pay the whole of his expenses. The moment we saw him, we dropped him – he was unelectable in voice, manner and appearance, but the union's money had carried him that far without effort. As soon as I had a decent excuse – Mr Gladstone provided it – I bowed out. I recall one or two fragments with interest, such as a tense debate on the subject of the proposed inner ring road, on which the council divided exactly equally. The town clerk reported accordingly to the mayor. "Wait a moment," said the mayor, "I haven't voted yet myself. I vote for the motion, and therefore declare it carried." The proposal then went to a public inquiry, parts of which were exceedingly dull. I walked out of one session, because it was so dull; so did the mayor. He remarked that the inquiry still left him in doubt about the ring road, but had made up his mind definitely on another point, the death penalty: he was now against it, for he was not going to put any man's life at the mercy of people who argued with the slipperiness of the barristers we had just been hearing.

I remember also having every single door in a street slammed in my face, when I went canvassing down it on the Labour Party's behalf – not in the part of the ward that voted labour. The party suspected that the wards had been rigged in the Conservative Party's interest, and once on the parliamentary committee the Labour members persuaded the town clerk to suggest alternative ward boundaries. He brought to the next meeting, and presented with a straight face, a revised set of ward boundaries that would undoubtedly have given the Conservatives not the slight majority they then held, but an overwhelming one. We did not pursue the point.

It was fun to take part in a formal inspection by the council of the city's defences. William of Wykeham had made an arrangement with the mayor of Oxford, when he bought the site of New College in the fourteenth century, that the mayor could from time to time come and inspect the part of the city wall that ran along the college garden's northern and eastern edges. It had settled down to a once-in-four-years ceremony, and had duly taken place both in 1940 and in 1944. I was able to be there in 1956.

Davidge, the bursar of Keble, was so upset at my sitting for a town instead of a university seat, and in the Labour interest at that, that he did not speak to me for a year. He was a devout Anglican, and long held out against his colleagues when they sought to delete from the college statutes a clause – originally inserted I suppose at Mr Gladstone's suggestion – that every fellow had to be a communicant member of the Church of England. In the end he gave way, on the insertion of a new sub-clause: fellows were to retire at 68, but the bursar at 75. Years afterwards, going through the papers for an impending college meeting with his clerk, he came on an agendum: 'Fellowship vacancy.' 'But what fellowship is vacant?' he inquired. 'Yours, sir: you retire in seven years' time as bursar, but your fellowship runs out at the end of September.' He took the hint, and retired, so that he could hunt five days a week instead of three. He died aged seventy-nine, from a fall in the hunting field.

One met extraordinary people in Oxford, as a matter of course. I once had an hour's talk with George F. Kennan, over dessert at Keble, which concentrated on his time in Czechoslovakia. Dining out, chance threw me next to an American psychologist of about my own age, who during the war had been in charge of a radar station on a Trobriand island. He was the only officer there, and was bored, so he learned the local language. When he was fluent in it, he asked some of the old men he knew whether they remembered Malinowski. They all burst out laughing; Malinowski was warmly remembered as the man who would believe anything. As for what the women told him – they laughed louder than ever. As much of modern social anthropology is founded on Malinowski, this talk did my professional scepticism good. Another evening, dining in Worcester, was memorable: my neighbour this time had only got one arm. As a conversational pawn, I asked why. He had been a subaltern in a German armoured car regiment, and had been counting the turrets on the Kremlin – had counted up to thirty-seven – when a soviet anti-tank gun got him, because he had stayed still so long.

We also got to know Gilbert Murray, who lived on Boar's Hill and was still in his early nineties a fount of sharp and interesting anecdotes about Mr Gladstone and others. He in turn introduced us to his grandson Lawrence the artist, who invited us (and scores of other acquaintances) to a party to celebrate his purchase of a vast piece of canvas, quite twenty feet by twelve, on which he was going to paint a major work. It bore a coat of whitewash. Had he bought it like that? 'No, it had a daub on it by a fellow you'll never have heard of, called Alma Tadema.' Gleadowe and Oakeshott, again, had not been in charge of me for nothing: I recognised the name. But the picture has never surfaced.

Pip and I were among the earliest of the million tourists whose breath began to rot the cave paintings at Lascaux. It was a magical experience to see them; like the Parthenon, they have stayed with me for good. Afterwards we went to a farm just above the site, where we ate a five-course meal, fish, meat and wine included, all of which except the salt had come from the farm. On another holiday, in Italy, the white of one of my eyes suddenly turned scarlet. We went to see an eye doctor, who declared, '*E molto serioso*' – we were to go into his clinic for a month for tests. We cut short our holiday and flew back to England instead. At the Radcliffe, it was determined that I had iridocyclitis, instantly curable, by a brutal method, a cortisone injection straight into the eyeball. I have never been able to forget the sight of that needle nearing my eye. Further research – a dozen injections into each forearm in turn – revealed that I had an extra strong allergy to goat's milk cheese, which I have done my best not to touch since.

F.M. Powicke, the medieval historian, was dining one Thursday in Keble, and happened to be sitting next to me at dessert. He invited me to write a book in his series for Hutchinson on aspects of history. I chose British foreign policy since 1898, and finished it quite soon – closing in summer 1956 with a reference to the Suez crisis, about to break out. Powicke also taught me how to review a book. Say whether it advances knowledge, and if it does, indicate how, in a sentence or two. Say whether it is scholarly in method and well written, then stop. I have done my best, over the years, to copy this laconic advice.

Occasionally, accidents of friendship brought me work of interest. Bert Goodwin, the modern historian at Jesus, secured me a few pages in a revised *Encyclopaedia Britannica* on nineteenth-century worthies, including Gladstone, Granville and Aberdeen; and Peter Utley introduced me to Patrick Bury who had been his tutor at Corpus, Cambridge, and was looking for someone to write up the outbreak of the Franco-Prussian war for the volume he was editing in the *New Cambridge Modern History*. This task took me into several odd corners. I looked up in Bodley the relevant volumes of the French official history, their pages till then uncut. Of course I read R.H. Lord's standard text on the subject. With professional scepticism, I got hold of a continental Bradshaw, to check Lord's train timings, which stood up well. Pottering round in it, I found something else – Bradshaw's account of the climate of Ems, almost intolerably stuffy in July and August. This explains an oddity of the crisis – the sharpish tone of the original Ems telegram, before Bismarck had doctored it. It was written by a courtier in full court dress and consequent discomfort.

I also paddled briefly in Acton's papers, which John Morley had given to Cambridge, and found him marvellously well informed on this as on everything else. From him I discovered the role of Versen, a cavalry officer who had distinguished himself at Königgrätz, and was sent by Bismarck to corrupt the Spanish general staff, with money Bismarck stole from the deposed king of Hanover. Versen did his work thoroughly, but when he returned to Prussia he found that the Hohenzollern family had turned the whole plan down, as too much trouble; and leant on Bismarck to revive it, with the results we all know. I enjoyed this, as an instance of the impact of small events on great, something that those who believe in iron laws of history cannot stomach. (Spanish generals have got more expensive. Versen only spent £50,000, in sterling. SIS ran to $20,000,000 to keep Franco's generals neutral in the war against Hitler, using as intermediary Juan March, who took five per cent.)

Keble's modern historian John Bromley re-introduced me to his friend Richard Pares, who had spent the war in the Board of Trade, and had had to give up his chair at Edinburgh because he suffered from an obscure form of muscular dystrophy. Like Lindsey, he had been advised by a doctor to take six months off work during the war, and like her had refused to do so (he was an assistant secretary); he emerged ill, and got steadily iller. All the same, he continued to edit the *English Historical Review*, and to write books. All Souls took him back, and he lived in Holywell Street, where his wife Janet – one of Powicke's daughters – looked after him.

He gave the best set of lectures I have ever heard, which turned eventually into a book – *King George III and the Politicians*. By the time he gave them, he could no longer turn a page; one of his daughters stood beside his wheelchair to do it for him. Against normal academic nature, there were more people at his last lecture than at his first. Soon afterwards, he woke Janet in the night; he was having trouble breathing. She restored him briefly with a portable breathing machine, and rang up the Churchill hospital, which took him up to Headington by ambulance, calling out as they left that she should look in in the morning to see how he was. She went up, but no one seemed to be about. A doctor met her – 'Ah, Mrs Pares. Richard would like his fountain pen please, he wants to finish a footnote.' He died later that day. I think of him as having been killed in action.

Another set of Ford lectures I remember was given by A.J.P. Taylor, one of the quickest-witted and one of the least likeable men I have ever met. Max Beloff buttonholed me in Blackwell's and asked me to lead the recent history group's discussion. (Afterwards I discovered that eight dons had already refused.) I prepared, with some help from Pip, a brief, hostile paper, pointing out where I thought Taylor had misled his audience. He and I dined with Beloff in Corpus beforehand, and walked in silence up to Balliol, where the meeting was to be. As I read my piece, Taylor slumped lower and lower in his armchair, till he was almost horizontal, shaking his head from time to time. Complete silence followed, for several minutes, broken at last by an American voice from the back of the room: could somebody open a window? A few weeks later, my book in Powicke's series came out, and was greeted by a twenty-line review in the *Manchester Guardian*, initialled AJPT. My publisher rang me up to condole; she had never known so much vitriol compressed into so short a space. Twenty years later, Taylor had forgotten all about it, and we were more or less reconciled.

Another odd chance brought me an invitation from the *Dictionary of National Biography* to write a short piece for one of their supplements on Hamar Greenwood, the last chief secretary for Ireland, infamous as the instigator of the Black and Tans, which I duly did. I began it by giving the date and place of birth he had given for himself in *Who's Who*, confirmed from GEC 's *Complete Peerage*. DNB wrote back to ask whether I had seen his birth certificate? I had not; would they pay my fare to Toronto? They would not, but their man in Canada looked into it. It turned out, they told me, that he was born Thomas Hubbard Greenwood, and changed his forename to Hamar when he ran away with a circus in his early teens.

While preparing this article I met his brother-in-law L.S. Amery, who had kept up his own connection with All Souls. I mentioned to Amery that I had seen some of his letters to Dawson, written in 1917 when Amery had been a junior secretary to the war cabinet. He told me that when he was appointed, Hankey said to him, 'Your duty is to record the decisions of ministers; and if ministers natter for an hour and a quarter, and decide nothing, your duty remains to record their decisions. Do you understand?' This seems to me the kernel of the cabinet system of government, at times when the civil service is strong and ministers are less so.

I continued not, as a rule, to go to church or chapel – I am not sure that I ever entered my parish church in north Oxford, SS Philip and James. But I do recall a few occasions that saw me on consecrated ground. Harry Pitt of Worcester, who was a friend, organized a set of talks on great religious figures of the nineteenth century, and persuaded me to give the one on Mr Gladstone. This I did from the pulpit (I had hardly ever stepped into a pulpit) of a small church near the Cherwell. It was disconcerting to find out afterwards that one of the very old ladies present was the widow of one of

Mr G's ministers; fortunately for me, she had enjoyed being transported momentarily back into his era. And once at least I went to a university sermon in St Mary's, because the preacher was Spencer Leeson. I remember nothing of what he said, except that he referred quite often to Plato, and every time he named Plato, Berlin who happened to be sitting in front of me waggled his ears. Once I attended an armistice day service in the City church, arrayed in a councillor's gown, and was shocked to hear from a Christian pulpit a sermon in praise of war. On reflection, this was in the mid 1950s, when the cold war was in one of its crisper passages, and the fighting in Korea was in recent memory; I am no longer as shocked as I was, but I remain surprised.

Historians of England are familiar with tales of how Society used to split down the middle, at times of intense crisis, so that Whig and Tory families no longer met socially till the crisis was resolved. This happened, for instance, during the reform crisis of the early 1830s, the home rule disputes of the late 1880s, and the Lords v. Commons crux of 1909–11. A miniature version of it appeared in Oxford during the Suez crisis of 1956. Colleges split, in odd ways. In Keble, the senior common room (myself apart) were stoutly interventionist, the undergraduates on the whole opposed; in Trinity (where I also taught, and had a room) the reverse was the case. One Trinity man, founder's kin, went down sooner than suffer the indignity of being taught by me.

Colin Leys of Balliol and I wrote a letter to the *New York Times*, published prominently on the first Sunday in November, drawing its editor's attention to the strength of anti-Suez currents in a Britain that the foreign press seemed to be treating as unanimously in favour of the war. I made the mistake, which I have never made since, of signing for publication with my first and last names only. This raised a small hornet's nest in England. The *Daily Mail* reminded its readers that I was not the Michael Foot who was prominent in the Labour party (who is I think my twelfth cousin), but a dim don of whom they would never hear again. A question was even asked in the Commons, by a double-barrelled Tory backbencher, and the minister who answered it described the letter and its authors as deplorable.

The next Thursday, I was – by long pre-arrangement – to have dined in Keble with a friend from another college. He rang me up, late in the afternoon, to say that he was damned if he was going to dine with such an infernally interventionist common room as Keble's. I had of course booked in a guest; it happened I had already put on a dinner jacket, before teaching at five and six, so went in by myself. Nobody spoke to me.

Sir George Clerk, then the head of the historical profession, happened to be dining that night in Keble also, with John Bromley (with whom my close friendship took time and trouble to mend). Clerk saw me, came across the room, and held out his hand – one *never* then shook hands in an Oxford common room – and said, 'Foot, I want to shake your hand: you have been called deplorable by a member of the present government.' It was one of the proudest moments of my life.

Though in principle I had left politics, I took part in a non-party demonstration when I was among a bus-load of Oxford citizens who went up to Westminster to lobby our MP. It was rum to be in the cellarage of the House of Commons on Guy Fawkes' night, rummer still to find myself having to act, a shade hectically, as spokesman for our group when we eventually cornered our MP. He dithered; there was a brief pause. A quiet man in the corner, wearing a Guards tie, whom none of us knew (he turned out to be a lecturer in French at Magdalen, called Pring-Mill) spoke up: 'Mr Turner, I voted for you at the last election. I came here to tell you I can never vote Conservative again.'

Pip meanwhile was wrestling with a fund, of which she was treasurer, to support in Oxford colleges students who had managed to get out of Hungary. The initiative for this came from Balliol, where an undergraduate remarked out loud, one lunch-time in the junior common room, that he thought something ought to be done to look after Hungarian students who were being oppressed in Budapest, and raised £300 in cash on the spot. Pip's appeal to senior common rooms brought in about £40,000, quite fast. We had several Hungarians staying with us in Park Town, two of whom settled in in the top flat, which happened to be empty.

One of these refugees had brought his girlfriend with him, who was charming, but no intellectual. A job was found for her at a shoe shop near Oxford Circus. She too played a part in Hungarian resistance. The Soviet ambassador's wife came in, with an interpreter, to buy some shoes, and left, a long time later, in tears, having bought nothing. The Hungarian girl had served her consistently with shoes two sizes too small.

There were two very able brothers called Zador, who had both been prominent on the student revolutionary committee in Budapest. One read mathematics at Balliol, the other read PPE at Trinity, and was a pupil of mine. His landlady found him stone dead one morning, at his desk, with a half-written essay in front of him, and a gas fire turned on, but not alight, beside him. I was reminded of the KGB proverb – 'any fool can commit a murder; it takes an artist to commit a natural death'.

Meanwhile again, I had got involved with an inter-university body of students who were anxious to intervene on the anti-Soviet side in the troubles in Hungary. We collected about £400, to be taken to Belgium and spent on small arms. One of us tried to steal it for himself, and was only with difficulty persuaded to disgorge. I found, by map-reading, a conceivable target for sabotage, a big railway bridge crossing a main road not far from the Austrian border; but we had no explosive and no local knowledge. I wrote to General Gubbins (whom I had never met – his address was in *Who's Who*), who had, I knew, been the wartime head of SOE, and got a sensible reply advising me to drop the whole idea. I was able to persuade most of my colleagues that it would do far more harm than good to persevere, and the affair lapsed. The best of us, a Kebleman called Austin, got the warden's leave to go down early, and spent some weeks running refugees across the Austro-Hungarian border, till he became the subject of a minor international incident, which he survived. Two other Keblemen, ignorant both of his and of my involvement in the project, insisted on going off to Hungary to fight, and were quietly picked up and sent back home by the Austrian police as they reached the Austrian frontier from West Germany. The ex-sergeant in the international brigade who, I strongly suspected, represented the Soviet interest on the guiding committee, and the unobtrusive man whose name I also do not remember who, I supposed also, came from MI 5, both went back to whatever their cover jobs had been, and I went back to teaching. I never heard a word from any of them again.

In those days Keble and Trinity were both, frankly, in the intellectual slums. Not many first-class brains seemed to apply to get in to either. Trinity men had a manner towards me that puzzled me for a moment, till I recalled what it was. They used exactly the same tone that my grandfather used to use to Duncan Lindsay his gamekeeper: full respect for his professional knowledge, tempered by the assurance that he belonged to a different social class. It took time and temper to break this barrier down.

Trinity at least provided me with a room to teach in, the ante-room to the fellows' library, which had a delightful view from its eastern window into a garden where the president, A.L.P. Norrington, grew an astonishing mixture of irises.

One Trinity pupil I cannot forget: a French Canadian called Bourassa, descendant of an earlier contestant for Québecois independence. He was absolutely charming, but not bright, and insisted on taking political theory for his special subject. Normally I sent Trinity men who wanted to read political theory to John Plamenatz at All Souls, whom I couldn't bother with Bourassa. So I taught him myself. We spent a whole term going through Hobbes's *Leviathan*, on which, for the first time ever, there was no question in the finals paper. Bourassa took in Hobbes's doctrine thoroughly, all the same, and rose to be Prime Minister of Quebec and a sharp thorn in the side of the federal government of Canada.

Another Trinity pupil, Hamilton Richardson, a Rhodes scholar from Louisiana, had a name that rang briefly round the world: he was seeded at Wimbledon. Unhappily, because he played so much tennis he did not do quite enough work to get a first, and because he was hoping for a first, his tennis was not quite up to the mark – he was knocked out in the first round. He and his charming wife went back to America, and I believe were among those who were going to lunch with Mr Kennedy at Dallas in November 1963, when the President was shot.

Agatha Ramm, who became the leading historian of late-nineteenth-century England, and I ran a small class together in Keble on British foreign policy in the days of Clarendon and Granville as foreign secretaries. For me at least it was an interesting experience, and I hope some of those who attended it learned something. I certainly learned a great deal from Agatha, who set new standards of accuracy for the editing of Victorian statesmen's papers in her edition of the Gladstone-Granville correspondence.

For several years running, Pip and I used to spend the long vacation at a cottage in Connemara which we found through an advertisement in the *New Statesman*. It was wonderfully beautiful, and equally primitive. From the seat of its Elsan closet you got one of the finest views in Europe, over the Twelve Pins; on the other side lay the Atlantic. It had a turf fire which, once we had learned to tend it, never went out. Our next-door neighbours one side – half a mile away – were a pair of brothers called Coyne who had had to skip at the end of the civil war in 1922, one to Glasgow where he made steel and the other to Detroit where he made motor-cars. After the amnesty, they came back. Neither could marry, as there would be no room for a wife and their mother in the one cottage, and after she died they felt they were too old. They seemed perfectly happy. They amused themselves in the evenings by reading Walter Scott's novels to each other – they had a complete set. I saw them once reaping their three acres of oats (which fed their pony) with a sickle, and called a few days later to ask whether I might handle their flail – I had seen flails in museums, but wanted to know how they felt in the hand. 'It would not be with anything as new-fangled as a flail that we'd be threshing', one replied; they threshed by hand, crouching down to bang the oaten stalks against a flat stone and winnowing with the side of the other hand. It took about three weeks.

Margaret Crum, on Bodley's staff and a friend of Pip's, came over one year to stay for a few days, bringing a pair of field glasses with her, and paused while out for a walk to look through them at a chough. She passed the glasses to me. I was at once captivated, and have been an enthusiastic (though not madly well-informed) watcher of wild birds ever since.

Our Irish peasant landlord looked in one day, put a dripping pile of cloth on the table, remarked, 'They're fresh off the strand', and left. They turned out to be a dozen oysters. We had several cookery books with us. 'After opening' or 'When you have opened' your oysters, all the recipes began; no one told us how to do it, and it took twenty minutes and a lot of chipped fingers before we found out the simple trick. Over half a century later, I read in Missy Vassiltchikoff's memoirs that the cream of central European aristocracy were in exactly the same predicament, when a hundred oysters fell to them as they were recovering from the air raids on Berlin in late November 1943.

Once I went into Clifden, the nearest town, to buy some oranges. A shop had a pyramid of them in the window, so I went in and asked for some. 'Not for you', the shopkeeper told me. He would serve nothing to anyone who spoke with an English officer-class accent. A greengrocer a few doors away sold me all I wanted. They had fought on opposite sides in the civil war; one at least of them could not forget it.

That cottage provided the site for a test I had thought was going to be awkward: giving up smoking. I had taken to smoking more and more, while I taught, and had got up to about sixty cigarettes a day, plus an occasional pipe. Pip, who also used to smoke the occasional pipe, had given up. A scare about cancer of the lung got through to me: odds on my survival, at the rate I smoked, were down to about 4–1. I therefore stopped, abruptly, at the end of Trinity term 1956, managed the two-day drive to Connemara without tobacco, and thereafter was faced with a forty-minute walk, even if I took the short cut over the hill, before I could buy any more. When next term started, I managed to teach for a week without smoking, and then for half a term, and then for a whole term; and have not touched the stuff since – not daring to, in case I again get addicted.

Out of the blue, a letter turned up in Connemara from Tilney Bassett the Gladstone family archivist: I was not to be surprised if the next day's post brought a letter from the Archbishop of Canterbury – as it duly did. He found himself the custodian of Mr Gladstone's diaries, and would be grateful if I would give him an opinion on their publishability. This started me off on what I thought was going to be my magnum opus. When I got back to London, I went to see Dodwell the librarian at Lambeth, who soon moved on to be professor of art history at Manchester. He recommended me to talk to Canon Claude Jenkins at Christ Church, which I did. Jenkins, that notable eccentric, told me that while London was being heavily bombed in 1940, he had taken the Gladstone diaries down to Christ Church with him, as likely to be safer for them, remembering to tell his archbishop afterwards.

The diaries, which I was allowed to keep in my room at Trinity, gave me an entirely new insight into Mr Gladstone. I was able to take in a great deal that Morley had thought it prudent – or proper – to leave out of his great biography, and to get much closer to the character of that astounding personality; as well as discovering something of his intricate relationship with Laura Thistlethwayte, formerly Laura Bell the courtesan, who had set her cap at him – without success – when he was first Prime Minister. I broke the seals – four successive seals, in black wax – on an envelope he had left behind, containing a document signed in the presence of his son who was Rector of Hawarden, in which he declared, knowing he was in God's sight as he did so, that he had never been unfaithful to his wife. Colin Matthew who succeeded me as the diaries' editor was not quite convinced by this. I was, knowing who Mr Gladstone had been and what he thought of writing in the presence of God.

I was able to persuade Oxford University Press to embark on the project, that turned out to be vast, of putting the whole of the diaries into print. This in turn involved raising some money, not a task at which I have ever been much good. I had an acquaintance, from a graduate class at St Antony's, who had gone over to America to work for the Ford foundation. With the help of a friendly letter from Mr Justice Frankfurter, a sound Gladstonian, I got the Ford foundation interested; they cabled offering me $5,000. This cable I took to the Pilgrim Trust, who offered to match it. The Calouste Gulbenkian foundation was still more generous; and the archbishop put in £1,000 he had been given by Henry Gladstone with the diaries in 1927, that had tripled since. As the project now seemed to be nearing take-off point, I wrote to my friend at Ford to ask for a cheque. How much, he replied, have you got? I was fool enough to tell him; Ford did not subscribe at all.

In 1959 the great Henri Michel, already the doyen of resistance historians, organized a conference on European resistance at Liège. He circulated every don teaching history or politics in every British university, inviting them to come. I was the only one to respond. It was a passably good conference, spoiled by the insistence of various interested parties that only their own fragment of resistance had been of national importance, and by the refusal of the eastern delegations – all under strict communist party control – to admit anything to the discredit of the USSR. There was a small official British delegation, consisting of Dick Barry who had been chief of staff in SOE in 1943–5 and Monty Woodhouse who had been much my senior in College at Winchester, and had gone on to be chief of the British subversive delegation in Greece; there were also two tall minders from the Foreign Office, both reluctant to give their names, one of them clearly a gentleman although his face had duelling scars, the other with a noticeably un-English accent. Robert Maxwell, who claimed a connection with SOE, eventually published the proceedings.

CHAPTER 5

Ructions

At the end of the 1950s my marriage to Pip broke up. I remained passionately interested in having children; she turned out not to be able to have any. Feeling a fearsome cad, I walked out on her, necessarily in those days walking out also on my Oxford appointments and career. I supposed I could move easily from Oxford to a teaching job at LSE, but was wrong. An acquaintance, with an Oxford first, put in for it, so there was no point in my even applying.

My second wife, Elizabeth King, much younger than I, also came from a broken home – her father went away to the war in 1939, rose to be a captain Royal Engineers, survived, but never returned to his wife. Elizabeth's mother Aileen divorced him and made a career for herself in the world of home economics, running two domestic science colleges in turn, serving as an inspector of schools and retiring (like Lindsey) with a CBE. We were married in 1960, and had a daughter next year and a son eighteen months later, but the marriage did not turn out the success we had hoped it would be.

We found a flat off Russell Square, within five minutes' walk of the British Museum reading room where I was hard at work on Mr Gladstone. Much of the early work on his diary was, like so much scholarship, merely clerical, and I soon got the hang of identifying most of his schoolboy and university friends (as Namier once remarked, a great many profound secrets are already in print if you know where to look for them). As he moved forward into parliament, and began his long official career, the work grew more complicated. By this time I had been allotted a shelf in the BM's North Library, thus joining an informal group of scholars who were getting on with the real work of imparting knowledge in printed sources, out of which the academic world could later teach.

A total stranger once came up to me there – an elderly lady. She understood I could read Mr Gladstone's handwriting? I could. Would I please come with her? We went through, silent, to the manuscript room. She confronted me with a passage Mr G had written in the autumn of 1894, with his eyes shut, because his cataract was so bad. Luckily I could spot that he was writing in Latin, and was quoting Horace. I gave her a word or two, referred her to the *Lexicon totius Latinitatis* which was on the open shelves in the great round reading room, and went back to my own work.

Various Oxford scholars, much my senior, took an interest in the diaries project. Alan Bullock allowed St Catherine's College's name to be used as a formal academic base, and sat on an informal committee, chaired by Kenneth Wheare, and including Robert Blake, Pat Thompson and the librarian at Lambeth, who interviewed me from time to time about how I was getting along. I got used to the facilities for scholars in central London, one of which was so odd that it deserves mention. In the men's room in the basement of the Institute of Historical Research there was a rather grubby roller towel near the washbasin for the use of hoi polloi. Beside it hung three linen towels, one for The Secretary, one for THE DIRECTOR, and one for **PROFESSOR NAMIER**. And I enjoyed the marked courtesy and efficiency of the staff in the old public record office, that dark neo-Gothic building in Chancery Lane, as well as in the British Museum.

Now and again I would stop work, and wander through the museum's many marvellous galleries, resting my brain while my eyes and my soul enjoyed the sights. Before the ethnographic collections were taken away to the north side of Burlington House, the passage connecting the King Edward VII gallery's east end with the older main building held, for a time, a case showing primitive methods of starting fires. When the cold war was at its worst, there would be a few earnest housewives poring over these ancient methods, in case they survived a nuclear catastrophe and ran out of matches.

Alastair Buchan whom I knew slightly – I was an early member of his Institute for Strategic Studies – invited me to write a short book for him. As this solved the immediate problem of income, I did. It was called *Men in Uniform*, and gave a politics don's view of the ways in which industrial societies organized their armed forces. It was fun to write, and involved a little foreign travel (for which Alastair's institute paid), which included a visit to Max Waibel, the Swiss intelligence officer at Lausanne. 'Just ask any taxi driver for my house', he told me by telephone. I was swept out to a large country chateau, full of portraits of ancestors in uniform going back several centuries. We make a mistake when we think of the Swiss, once the finest infantry in Europe, as an essentially civilian nation.

Work on the book also introduced me to the closing stage of a form of inter-city transport that was about to be suppressed – I suppose by early environmentalists, who could not abide the noise – but was a marvellous convenience at the time. In central Brussels, I had a few yards' walk from my hotel to a helicopter pad, and was flown at about 500 feet, on a clear day, to central Cologne where again I had a very short walk to my hotel. I was the only passenger in an eight-seater, and had a series of spectacular views of the cockpit of Europe.

I had already been taken round the battlefield of Waterloo, by a Belgian staff captain detailed for the purpose by Henri Bernard, a notable ex-resister who then commanded the staff college. Was there any part of the battlefield I would particularly like to see? Yes there was: the spot where the 27th Regiment, in which RMF later served, were found on the morning after 'lying dead in square'. We saw it; I thought suitable thoughts. The farm of La Haye Sainte was just below. Would I care to look at that too? I would. We pressed on the great gate, and went in. A Belgian boy in his late teens was walking across the farmyard, carrying a load of dung. Who the devil were we? My companion explained. Oh yes, there had been a battle there once; they often found bones when they dug in the orchard. And here was this boy, living on the site on which Napoleon's fate had been decided, yet he had never heard of him. This I have often later remembered, as a military historian, a sign of what little impact we make on mankind in general.

Writing the book also involved meeting a strong supervising committee, including Liddell Hart, Michael Howard, Mark Abrams, Ivelaw-Chapman, John Pringle and Donald Tyerman; all but Michael Howard older than me, and all powerful figures in their own fields.

Alastair knew Henry Kissinger, who had not yet gone into politics. Kissinger ran an international seminar every summer vacation, at Harvard, for foreigners likely, it was supposed, to become eminent later, either in politics or in academe. For the 1960 seminar, Alastair put up my name. I was accepted, one of three English members (Timothy Raison, later a leading left-wing Tory MP, and a Cambridge college chaplain called Walker were the other Englishmen). Most of us travelled westward across the Atlantic on the same liner, so that we could get to know each other informally before the course began. We reached New York, suitably impressed by its skyline, and were met by two Harvard dons, who saw the whole party through customs and immigration in an hour. Each then remarked to the other, at once, "You did order a bus, didn't you?" An extra two hours' hanging about gave us time to reflect on the limits of America's proverbial efficiency.

A favourite remark of Berlin's was that society needs a reliable barometer, yet to be invented. I could have used one at Harvard: one of the dreariest people I have ever met was on the same course, but – the libel laws being what they are – I had better be no more specific. I shared a set of rooms with a Pole, who was not the bore, but was as dour as one might expect from a young don who had been let out from behind the iron curtain.

One delight of life at Harvard was to go to a small café off Massachusetts Avenue to hear a new voice singing folk songs; her name was Joan Baez, and she later became famous, but at the time her following was only a score strong. She had a marvellous gift for wrapping herself round the heartstrings of her audience, and plucking at them gently; she was also as sound as the politically correct would have it about atomic bombs.

On a lamp-post in Harvard Square I noticed a sticker advertising a meeting, at noon the next Sunday on Boston Common, to discuss the bomb, and went, arriving early. Already there were several groups, mixed student-age and middle-age, arguing on a corner of the Common. It turned out that two bodies had each agreed to meet there, one the enemies of the bomb, the other Polish-Americans who supported it and wanted it used on the Soviet Union. I wandered round from group to group, listening, without hearing a voice or seeing a fist raised in anger, though clearly the two parties had remarkably little in common. Two cops, leaning against a nearby wall, made no move except to shift gum from cheek to cheek. At about half-past twelve, a young man got up on a bench, clapped his hands, and called out that he was going to walk to a naval base at New London, Connecticut, to protest against the launch of a Polaris submarine. He hoped anyone who agreed with him would come too. Most of the student types fell in behind him. At the tail of the procession were two attractive blondes, locked in argument with a Pole in his forties who was still carrying a banner that read SUPPORT POLARIS. It was a fine illustration of how a free society can work.

Of the Harvard faculty I saw few people beyond those who were teaching for Kissinger, but did bump into Sam Beer, whom I had met in Oxford. We were walking across campus together when Arthur Schlesinger passed, to whom Beer introduced me. They had both been at the recent Democrat Party conference, both on inside tracks. Neither could agree about how Lyndon

Johnson had secured Kennedy's vice-presidential nomination. This was a neat example of the weakness of the best-informed inside authorities.

Anne Henry, one of the Harvard rare books librarians, whom I had also met in Oxford at a party in John Roberts's rooms, it was a real joy to meet again. She took me along on a weekend trip with some friends of hers to Bar Harbor in Maine, where we ate lobster fresh out of the Atlantic. On the way back, we stopped at a field that had a bus shelter in it. Two of our party got out of the car, paused at a little desk beside the bus shelter, and stepped into a light aircraft which carried them off to California: a small eye-opener for me on the flexibility of transport. Earlier, she had taken me to hear a Hungarian string quartet in the Isabella Gardner museum, on a stiflingly hot day. Four chubby, squat men in dinner jackets, all wearing thick glasses, attempted a Bartok movement scored *prestissimo*. After twenty bars, all their spectacles steamed up, so that they could not see their scores. They had to stop, wipe their glasses down, and start again.

I had still not quite finished the book for Alastair. There was a muddle about my passage back to England, again by sea. I travelled in a French liner, with a shared berth in its bowels, close over the screw. I got little sleep, but was able to write the concluding chapter in quiet corners of the ship, while all the other passengers were out of the way.

When I got back, my wife remarked that someone with an odd accent had rung me up from the Foreign Office; would I ring back? I did. Did I speak French? I did. Had I heard of SOE? I had. Might I be interested in writing a part of its history, from the secret papers? I might indeed. I was called to an interview at the Foreign Office, which turned out to be with the two minders of the SOE party at the Liège conference. They had forgotten me, but I remembered them; it gave me a slight edge. Harold Macmillan, it turned out, had ordered the Foreign Office to get SOE's history in one country written up. They had decided on France or Yugoslavia, and dropped Yugoslavia because so few people spoke Serbo-Croat. They asked, in turn, three friends of mine at Oxford to do it: James Joll (who had himself been in SOE), John Roberts and Philip Williams. Each of the three refused, but suggested me. Fourth time round, they asked me.

I am still not at liberty to say where I worked on the book that turned into *SOE in France*. It amused me to see a PRIVATE EYE IS WATCHING YOU poster just outside its front door, but I don't think even *Private Eye*, then in its early heyday, knew what the building was for. My supervisor, Eddie Boxshall, had for part of his cover that he was not very bright; he lived that part of it conscientiously. I had been working on the book for over a year before I discovered, not from him, that he had been in SOE. When I taxed him with it, he admitted it, but added at once, "I was on the Roumanian desk; it had nothing to do with France, and therefore has nothing to do with you." Nor of course did he mention to me that he had been MI 6's head of station in Roumania, where another of his covers was that he was manager of the royal estates.

In a more relaxed moment, he mentioned that he had spent December 1917 in Moscow. "That must have been fascinating." "What do you mean, fascinating? It was damned dull. And do you know, one morning in the best hotel in Moscow *there was a cigarette-end in my bread* at breakfast?" When I had to teach the theory of history, this was a useful example of the witness on the spot who does not know what to look out for. He had been waiting for a train – run out of Roumania, where he had been assistant military attaché, by von Mackensen's army, he wanted to get to Vladivostok and so to England, but the Trans-Siberian railway was closed for weeks on end.

To write the book, I had access to most of the SOE files I cared to call for – once I had discovered how to call for any. They were in a fearsome muddle, and were only reachable through the prism of Boxshall, a sort of Cerberus barring the gate (I believe he thought that any published history of SOE must be a grave professional mistake). Eventually I got on terms with him and with the system, and read avidly, making some, but not always much, sense out of the papers. These included a typescript handbook of SOE's independent French (F) section circuits in France, just compiled by Boxshall and his PA (who had also been in SOE). I would have been sunk without it, but my own copy of it soon got black with annotations, as I found it so unreliable in minor detail. This has not stopped its quite widespread distribution; contradictions between it and my eventual book must continue to puzzle young researchers today.

I pressed hard to be allowed to talk to survivors. I had had on my desk for years an invitation to join the Special Forces Club, but Boxshall told me that if I tried to take it up, the office would use its veto to block me. Gossip at the club bar was not the sort of source they wanted to open to me. After about a year, I got leave at least to see Sir Colin Gubbins, who had inspired the whole show, and was then allowed to meet some surviving agents.

The book caught fire when I had dinner with one of them, Pearl Witherington, in Paris. Her father had been the last male survivor of an old Northumbrian fighting family. She had had an ancestor at Otterburn, who lost both feet in that battle and went on fighting on his knees. Lubricated by a bottle of Burgundy and a decent meal (for which the taxpayer paid), we talked till late, and I grasped what it had been like to live in clandestine conditions. Thereafter – I wrote that night till dawn – I got on with writing, and was allowed to meet several other valuable sources, including Vera Atkins and Tony Brooks. I once confronted Boxshall with the London telephone directory, which included an entry for an Atkins, V.M., whom I threatened to ring up on the spot; he eventually allowed me to see her, without mentioning that she had been one of his best sources when he had been running secret intelligence in Roumania in the 1930s (as I only discovered from Sarah Helm's life of her in 2005). Though the press expressed astonishment at the restrictions placed in my way, I saw in fact a larger proportion of the members of SOE than Dr Gallup's organization sees fit to see of the adult electorate when it prepares a national opinion poll.

Not till the book was in proof was I allowed to meet Maurice Buckmaster, long the head of F section that worked into France, and by the time we did meet, each of us had a solicitor at his elbow. Buckmaster, in his Old Etonian tie, engaged me in a staring match. How was he to know that my son Richard had just turned one year old, and was having staring matches with me quite often? It gave me a little quiet pleasure to win that first round against Maurice. We were able to agree on a few changes of phrase, and correspondence with Lord Selborne later persuaded me to make the anti-Buckmaster tone of my book still less sharp.

Towards the end, I had to go through what had happened to the captured agents, most of whom were massacred in concentration camps. Trying to find out where the order had come from that a dozen women agents were to be killed, I put in for files on Himmler and on Hitler. I was given a short file on Gebhardt Himmler, a brother of Heinrich's, who had been a major in the SS and was of no clandestine importance; Boxshall clearly thought I was not old enough to see any file on the Himmler who mattered. Nor was he going to let me know that MI 5 and MI 6 between them had turned Horst Kopkow, the SD authority for the killing of most of SOE's captured agents, to use him back against the Russians – a ploy successfully undermined by Kim Philby, then head of the anti-Soviet section of MI 6. This disagreeable fact only went public in 2005, from Sarah Helm's use of indiscretions in Vera Atkins's private *Nachlass* of papers that Vera ought not to have kept.

I put in also – there was by this time a cyclostyled chit for the purpose – for a file on Hitler, Adolf, son of Hitler, Alois, otherwise Schicklgrüber, born Braunau 1889, died Berlin 1945. The chit came back promptly, marked 'N/T'. I marked it 'pl try again' and put it back in my out tray. Forty-eight hours later it was back, now annotated 'N/T = No Trace'. At this point I rang up the archives officer; who told me 'There was a file once, old boy, but it's been weeded'. The file on operation FOXLEY, SOE's plan to kill Hitler – dropped because by late 1944 he was more use to the allies alive than dead – was perhaps then buried too deep for that archives officer to know of it; it went public at the end of the century, and is now in published print. James Joll, I believe on stylistic grounds, had written most of it; having had the good luck to get on to the staff of X section, which covered Germany, after being trained to drop into Hungary – the Germans got there first, so his Hungarian mission was cancelled.

My book was put into galley proof by Her Majesty's Stationery Office, and I waited many months while those proofs were circulated round a group of which I was never told the membership, some of them most eminent and some of them fully informed. With the galleys I got a message from the compositor to the author: it had been more interesting setting this than doing his previous job, which had been setting the London telephone directory. There was also a row about capital letters. The controller of HMSO, passing through Paris on holiday, paid a courtesy call on the ambassador, and noticed a pile of his galleys on HE's table. The book had been compiled strictly in accordance with Hart's Rules, then current at the Oxford University Press; the ambassador complained that his predecessor had not been given a capital A (no more would he have been, had he been an archduke or even an archangel). The controller put in a strong minute when he got back to London, and I had yet another dispute with Boxshall. We agreed in the end that Ministers and Government Departments should get capital letters; and that all the donkey-work of inserting them in proof should be done by an unlucky secretary, not by me. So the ambassador kept his small a, and the king his small k.

Doubts were evidently expressed about whether the book should be published at all. J.R.M. Butler, knighted Cambridge professor and senior official historian, was allowed to see it, and minuted that on historical grounds it ought to appear. Burke Trend, secretary to the cabinet, arranged to meet me privately at the dinner-table of his Blackheath neighbour Hugh Hanning, whom I had met at Buchan's institute (and whose elder brother John had been at The Wick and Winchester with me); and Trend, once satisfied that I was an honest man, put in a long minute to Wilson the prime minister recommending that the book come out. Wilson scrawled that he agreed. I read the minute nearly forty years later.

I had been outspoken, in the text of the book, about how bad I thought many popular accounts of SOE were, and how inflated I thought some newspaper reputations of former agents. I had also gone in detail into the catastrophe of the PHYSICIAN circuit, based on Paris, usually called by its leader's codename 'Prosper'; and had, I thought, proved that the catastrophe had not been caused by 'Prosper' himself but by 'Archambaud', his wireless operator and friend, whose real name was Gilbert Norman.

The day before the book came out, I had a raging toothache, which I took to a dentist in Knightsbridge; he was sorry, he had run out of anaesthetic, and pulled the tooth out for me without it. That evening, Vera Atkins took me to see Odette Hallowes, GC, formerly Churchill, whom I had never met, whom the newspapers had presented (and often still present) as a great heroine of the secret war, and who had, I indicated, done very little to bear this reputation out. She had been given an advance copy, and was much upset.

The day the book came out, my telephone at home rang twice. An elderly man with a cultured voice told me there were one or two things in it he needed to discuss with me; I should present myself at the Savile Club at noon next Friday. I did, and was greeted by Selwyn Jepson the novelist, a successful recruiting officer in SOE, who spent half an hour at hammer and tongs with me about why I had said what I did about Odette. Evidently I satisfied him that I had written honestly. He kept me there for lunch, and said at the end of lunch it was time I joined that club – he would arrange it, and duly did.

The second call, also from an elderly man with a cultured voice, was odder. He made an appointment to come and see me in a few days' time, and rang off without giving his name. He turned out to be Gilbert Norman's father, aged eighty-two: why had I not had the decency to wait until he and his wife were dead, before I published my indictment of their son? It was a moment when I wished my father had never met my mother. I could do nothing but explain, as gently as I could, how overwhelming I had found the evidence about his son's treachery. The father was long dead before further research convinced me of it even more thoroughly, and never knew that his son was thrown in with forty-odd captured Dutch agents, all massacred together at Mauthausen in September 1944. Research, later than my own, by 'Prosper' (Francis Suttill)'s younger son and namesake has now convinced me that Norman had had bad luck; the Germans rumbled his address, perhaps through a mistake of London's, and called on him just at the moment when he had spread out over a table most of his circuit's false identity cards, which he was about to amend to suit a new bureaucratic rule. That still does not excuse all that he did while in their hands.

The book was an unexpected success. Three months, to the day, after it appeared, the head of publications at HMSO rang me up; he had just sold the last copy, out of ten thousand, that morning, and had never known a book sell so fast at the price (forty-five shillings, now £2.25). Certainly he would call it a best seller; but when reminded of the promise I had had from the Foreign Office, that if it were a best seller the author's interests would be looked after, could only say, "But my dear sir, we cannot fritter the taxpayer's money away on royalties." There the matter rests, though, as I write, I have lately revised the book, which is now translated into French, and this time I have some prospect of a return.

Almost all the papers on which the book was based have now, sixty years and more on, gone public among the national archives at Kew. I am currently quite often rung up by newspapers which read me back once familiar fragments, and ask for comments. Young graduate students can see whether they can trip me up by finding points that I had missed.

At the time, there were several threats of libel actions, all settled out of court. Boxshall told me that the office was not going to have me appear in court, in case I got asked a question to which they did not want the answer made public. What that question was, I have yet to discover. Luckily for me, an exchange of letters with the Foreign Office covered me against libel damages, which the taxpayer paid for me. In both the serious cases, I was sure I could have stood up for myself well in court, but never had the chance to do so.

Once the book was out, I was allowed to join the special forces club after all, and met there a fair number of ex-resisters, whom I incline to regard as a social class quite by themselves, the salt of the earth. By no means all of them were perfectly clubbable, but they were – the survivors are – never dull. Later on in this book, I will give an opinion about what my work on SOE did for my understanding both of it, and of war, and of history.

We left Bloomsbury when Elizabeth was pregnant, lived in two successive flats in Hampstead, and then managed to buy a freehold house in southern Kentish Town. I had to pay about £12,000 for it. The seller, a railway worker who had just retired, cut out of the deeds what he had bought it for in 1942 – something under £100.

It was from that house that all four of us set off, by car into the city, to watch Churchill's funeral procession; forty years on, Sarah tells me that was the first public occasion she remembers (and she remembers nothing public about it, only sitting on a wall eating sandwiches). Several men round me were weeping. When we were passed by three extremely senior officers, not impeccably dressed, whom I recognised as the three chiefs of the armed services, Mountbatten strode alone behind them, his ravaged face clearly indicating, 'Gentlemen don't cry in public, but if they did, I should be in floods.' That broke me down, and I wept too. I don't know whether Richard, who sat on my shoulder, noticed.

After both babies, Elizabeth was attacked by post-natal depression. Our Kentish Town GP, Grant, put her in touch with a fellow sufferer, Catherine, wife of John Freeman, MP and television presenter, believing that two intelligent women might benefit from talking over their similar symptoms. There was an odd historical sequel, after John Freeman had suddenly moved on to be British high commissioner in India. He discovered that Lord Curzon, when viceroy, had subvented the training of archivists in medieval scripts, so that they could puzzle out the histories of their states in Mogul and pre-Mogul times. By the 1960s those of Curzon's protégés who were still alive were old men; not much had been done to train on successors, and several centuries of the past were about to vanish, for lack of interpreters of scripts. Freeman could find no official to take an interest, and asked Catherine to find an English historian to take it up; she turned to me. I passed the hot potato on at once to Dame Lucy Sutherland, principal of Lady Margaret Hall, whom I hardly knew, but knew to be an expert on the East India Company at least. It would be interesting to know whether anything useful got done.

Now and again we went on agreeable holidays. I remember one in Brittany, in a small hotel near Dinard. I can still see Richard's face, as he declined to eat any more of a plate of sea food that included a cockle which was walking towards the edge of the plate. I can't say I blame him. On the whole both children were reasonable sleepers, and passably behaved. I remained much preoccupied with literary work, getting on as best I could with Mr Gladstone – whose diaries had had to be left largely on one side, while I concentrated on SOE in France. By the time the French book was out (it appeared in April 1966) the diaries' finances were in a better state, and I could start offering the OUP some text.

John Bromley meanwhile had enabled me to keep my hand in at teaching. He had moved on from his Keble fellowship to a chair at Southampton, where he secured me a part-time lectureship – I went there one night a week during term – for classes on nineteenth and twentieth century diplomatic history, staying overnight in a hall of residence. I have never forgotten one musical moment – he and Jean his wife invited me to go with them to a concert, at which I heard Schubert songs sung by a young baritone near the start of his career, Dietrich Fischer-Dieskau.

There was an odd professional sequel to this job. John told me that the department had advertised for a full-time lecturer in east European history, but had had disappointing replies. If I could find him some references, he would rename the job one in central European history, and appoint me to it. I duly went ahead. On the day nominations closed, a man put in for the eastern European post who had a first-class degree, a doctorate, and bilingual English and Polish – Stepan Pawlovitch – whom of course they had to appoint. He was so good an historian and so nice a man that I could not feel disappointed.

Elizabeth had a fine soprano voice, and sang in an excellent small group of Bach enthusiasts, the London Bach Society, whose concerts I could sometimes enjoy, if we could find a baby-sitter. As a schoolboy I had been devoted to Beethoven, but by now was inclined to revere J.S. Bach even more. While living with Elizabeth, I heard a great many of his cantatas.

I also from time to time went over to France, to check points arising out of my book. A few days after it had come out, Maurice Hutt whom I knew slightly from Oxford accosted me in the British Museum reading room: some agents I had written about had been using 'his beach' in Brittany. What did he mean, his beach? He was working on British clandestine work into France in the 1790s; and yes, it was true. I got him and Peter Deman the agent concerned together, in the BM map library, round a chart of the north Breton coast. Hutt's characters and Deman had indeed been using precisely the same beach for the same purpose, in 1793 and 1943. When eventually I visited the beach, I was shown round it by the local director of education, who as a schoolboy had been an active resister, marshalling agents on the spot. He took me up the path from the beach to the safe house close above it. By a nice example of nature imitating art, it was thick with scarlet pimpernels.

CHAPTER 6

Manchester: more ructions

Accident led me to a seminar in the Connaught Rooms on the diplomatic history of the 1920s and '30s. I happened to sit next to Bert Goodwin, who had left Oxford for Manchester where he was professor of modern history. He was looking for a colleague, but they had had a disappointing set of applications. Whom was he to ask? Would he, I enquired off hand, think of me? He certainly would, if I could get references to his registrar by the following Tuesday.

With a scramble, I managed it, and was summoned for interview. The train paused at Stockport station for several minutes before reaching Manchester Piccadilly. Rain poured down. I could see nothing in any direction but filthy red brick, interlarded with smoking chimneys. The loud-speaker called on passengers for London Euston to go at once to platform 5. A voice inside me said, 'Go!' I stayed, and went on to an amiable interview, at the end of which I was offered, and accepted, the chair. I rang Elizabeth up to tell her; she groaned.

We moved to Didsbury, on the southern edge of Manchester, where I bought a house from Norman Hampson who was moving off to a chair at Newcastle. We paid for the house by selling the Kentish Town one, for what we had paid for it, to a friend of Elizabeth and her mother, who wanted it. There was a decent day school for both children near by, odd though it turned out to be walking them to the school in pitch morning darkness during some of Harold Wilson's experiments with the clock.

It was odd too to begin work in the room in which, it was said, Namier himself had taught; odder still to find, tucked away in a basement, a lady whom Namier had once employed as a typist, who was still retained by the university though she seldom had any typing to do. There still hung round the Victoria University a faint tang of nineteenth-century schooling, emphasised by a dreadful bell that tolled from time to time to summon us from one lecture to another. We soon shed the bell, and after a year the whole department moved to a new building with more modern facilities (such as telephones at one's own desk). One perk I cherished: for the only time in my life, I had a secretary, who would type letters and reviews for me.

I had tossed into my lap as I arrived, by John Erikson who left for a distinguished career at Edinburgh, a plan for a degree course in politics and modern history. The arrangements for this were concluded by what my great ancestor once described as the ideal committee – three members, two of them unavoidably absent. Neither Goodwin nor Chapman, the professor of politics, was able to turn up at the time I had fixed for settling the syllabus, so I settled it by myself, and understand that forty years later it is still up and running.

We next revised the modern history syllabus, to make it different from history as taught in schools, and yet still historically valid, by concentrating on major themes and on episodes. Remembering the rule absorbed in my childhood, that you must never set other people tasks you shrink from undertaking yourself, I picked on a theme – revolution – and did what I could to lecture on it. I could find no colleague willing to take up a set of episodes I proposed, on assassinations, and had left Manchester before I had to embark on that one as well.

Goodwin had remarked, when I was appointed, that he supposed I would offer a special subject, and I agreed, without having taken in quite how dour a teaching task I had set myself: undergraduates (called students at Manchester) who took it had to pursue original sources and write them up, and needed some finely tuned supervision. However, Anglo-Irish relations 1879–1893 turned out perfectly workable, over several years, and I hope I made a few friends among those who took it on. I had envisaged, when I got bored with it, moving on to Anglo-Irish relations 1893–1922, but never got that far.

The department included several professors: Goodwin and I for the modernists, John Roskill for the medievalists, Willan for the economic historians and Smith for the ancient ones, and we soon promoted Barry Jones to profess archaeology as well. Willan, a neighbour in Didsbury, had a nice anecdote about his predecessor, who had a special subject on rivers. One week, one of his pupils missed a class. A few days later he passed her in the corridor; would she care to look at his notes? 'It's quite all right, Professor, I've got my mother's.'

Late in the 1960s many universities had uprisings. Manchester's was odd. A rising at the new university at Warwick had settled some rioters in the registrar's office. One of them had just read in an Ian Fleming novel how to open a locked filing cabinet, so they opened the registrar's. In it they found an exchange of letters between Dear Jack (Butterworth, former New College law don, the vice-chancellor of Warwick) and Dear Bill (Mansfield Cooper, vice-chancellor of Manchester). Both agreed that a candidate from Manchester would not do as a political theory don, because he was a red. The local socialist society published the letters, and sent a copy to their opposite numbers at Manchester, who did the same. Mansfield Cooper and his registrar agreed that this document was libellous; the registrar was to have libel writs issued against the socialist society's officers. He issued the writs all right, but against the wrong people – against the previous term's officers, one of whom had at all material times been away in Ireland collecting material for his next degree. This provided motive enough for a sit-in.

They began in the registrar's offices. He pointed out that his floors were marble. Would they not be much more comfortable if they sat in in the great hall, where degrees were conferred and there was a carpet? They did, several hundred at a time – to start with. In faculties where people were taking out professional qualifications – such as dentistry, engineering, or medicine – no one was interested; the mathematicians did not bother either. About two-thirds of the history and three-quarters of the politics faculty were actively engaged, dons as well as students. In one department everybody took part, from Hugh Hunt the professor down to the freshmen – drama. The whole affair petered out, into a protracted dispute between the bursar and the socialist society about who would pay for damage to the carpet. Once I went over, lateish at night, to see what was going on. A couple of resolute men could have cleared the great hall of its sparse inhabitants in minutes, but I was by myself, had some residuary sympathy with the rioters, and did nothing. So ended the Manchester Rising.

It left a legacy: the presence of a student at most faculty boards, and so on, to give the student body some sense of participation in the way the university was run. So far as I could, I tried to run the modern historians democratically. We spent a great deal of time in sub-faculty meetings, but at least no one was left feeling he had been bossed about by a dictatorial professor.

When I arrived, one colleague was away on a year's secondment to Kenya, while an admirable stand-in did his teaching for him. The colleague liked Kenya, where he was offered a chair, and wrote to say that he was going to stay there. So we advertised a lectureship in modern history; everyone took for granted it would go to the stand-in. He was interviewed for it, but was outshone by an even abler candidate, who had to be appointed – Judith Brown, eminent in the Cambridge historical faculty.

My modernist colleagues sent me a round robin: before my time there had only ever been one woman lecturer in the department, who was still too vividly remembered as a Mistake; how dare I appoint another? I replied that (a) half our students were women, and (b) they should meet the newcomer before asserting that another mistake had been made. Judith's capacity, good sense, and good manners soon made mincemeat of their doubts; she left Manchester later for a chair at Oxford, which she still adorns. I had to do something for the stand-in, Andrew Porter who was left with no job. I wrote him a white-hot reference for a lectureship at King's College London, where he too eventually became a professor, also of imperial history, so that story had two happy endings.

After a year, Goodwin left to write a book (that, alas, he never finished). A strong internal candidate, John Western, succeeded him. Toward the end of the next summer term, he rang up the office: he was not feeling well, would somebody please collect the papers for his special subject that were being written that morning? We did not hear from him again. If one rang up, his Danish wife simply said he was not at home. I had to mark his special subject papers. In September, Ian Kershaw's wife who was a nurse at the hospital across the road came to see me: Western was in her ward, which dealt with incurable brain tumours, and was not expected to live out the month. Indeed, he died soon thereafter. I organized a *Denkschrift* for him, a collection of essays entitled *War and Society* that we managed to get published on the second anniversary of his death. In it I put a chapter of my own on 'the IRA and the origins of SOE', of which more in a moment. The book only came out so promptly because I warned contributors that if their pieces did not arrive on time, however eminent they were, they would be left out. This harsh stroke worked. I still mourn John Western, a good historian and a good friend.

Military studies were not quite inactive at Manchester. Fred Ratcliffe the librarian got me involved in a correspondence with Field Marshal Auchinleck, who lived in Morocco, of which the end result was that he gave the university his papers, a valuable collection. As an appendix to them, I was put in touch with Eric Dorman-Smith, by this time Dorman O'Gowan – Hemingway's 'Chink' – who had been Auchinleck's acting chief of staff at the time of First Alamein, and had been sacked with him. I went over to see him at his place in Co Cavan, a lovely house put up in the mid-eighteenth century by an Earl of Bellamont (his ancestor) round a Guercino of the death of Dido which he had picked up on his grand tour. There was still a clear glacis for a musket-shot round the house, and all the ground floor windows had indoor sills at the right height for a musketeer's elbows – just in case.

He gave me a suitcase full of his papers to take back to Manchester to place beside Auchinleck's; and with them, a map which I carried rolled up under my arm, which he told me he had unpinned from the wall of their battle caravan the day they were dismissed, 10 August 1942. It showed the layout of their army, and the presumed layout of Rommel's army, and from it the subsequent battle of Alam Halfa, always presented to the world as the fruit of Montgomery's unaided genius, could be inferred. I looked at it closely on the plane on the way back to Manchester. In the bottom left-hand corner a note read: 'G[eographical] S[ection] G[eneral] S[taff]. Cairo, September 1942.' The note made me suspect that Dorman-Smith had forged it, but he was dead before I could confront him on the point.

Shortly before he died, he had put me in touch with the Irish military historical society in Dublin, to which I read a paper to work out an idea I had discussed with him: that part of the origin of SOE could be traced back to the streets of Dublin during the Troubles, when two young English majors called Holland and Gubbins had been struck by the comparative efficiency of gunmen working singly in plain clothes over soldiers working in massed battalions in uniform. I was taken out to an early dinner before my talk, which I supposed would be given to a couple of dozen people. Four hundred turned up to hear it, three black rows of priests and nuns at the back, several personages looking distinguished in front. As we walked in, my host murmured, 'The British ambassador's coming; he was parachuted into Siam for SOE.' So I began, 'Your Excellency, ladies and gentlemen', getting an awk look from the chairman. His own exordium was 'Riv'rend Fathers, Riv'rend Sisters, M'Lord Bishop, m'lords, y'r excellency, ladies and gentlemen', which was the formula I ought to have used. Those present included, I was told afterwards, three large silent men in the front row who were survivors of the Twelve Apostles, Michael Collins's personal bodyguard, and one of the two detective sergeants in Dublin Castle who had doubled that task with being an agent for the IRA.

I also secured a lectureship in military studies for Mike Calvert, the 'Mad Mike' of SOE in south-east Asia, column commander under Wingate and McLeod's successor at the SAS brigade. He had been disgraced (on evidence that in the end turned out bogus) from a brigadier's command in post-war Germany and had gone almost utterly to the dogs. He told me that he cast up among the meths drinkers in Glasgow, who turned him out, because he was an educated man, unfit for their society. He abjured alcohol, and gave some interesting talks, then retired to the Charterhouse, went back to the bottle, and died.

Several times I went over to France, to interview former members of resistance movements. One of them, the great Colonel Basset, asked me whether I was proud of my Croix de Guerre. I said yes, very. He remarked that he had four of them; the first was given him for a feat of arms performed by him and three companions, for which twenty-seven people were given the Croix de Guerre. I felt suitably humbled.

He told me how he had first gone into resistance, automatically, with the help of a childhood friend, Jarrot, who lived on the opposite side of the demarcation line near Chalon-sur-Saône. They ran messages and people to and fro across the line ('Nobody is going to search every milk-churn in a van carrying thirty-two'). A sub-agent betrayed him, and he was arrested. The Germans strapped him down and pulled out one of his teeth with a pair of pliers, rather enjoyed it, and pulled out the rest. After the first one, he would have told them anything they asked. By the time they pulled out the last, he was furiously angry. He escaped that night, and did not rest till he had shot dead one German for every tooth he had lost. Similarly, the great George Millar told me once that he happened to be a very good shot, had shot a great many Germans, and regretted he had not shot many more.

Among others I saw was Maurice Southgate, who had run a vast F circuit in central France – Pearl Witherington had been one of his couriers – till he got arrested, by a stroke of bad luck, on May Day 1944. He was held for weeks, unidentified, because he had called at an address the Germans suspected. A much more junior SOE agent was caught near by, through one of the Gestapo's wireless games, was much upset by leaving his dropping zone in handcuffs, and was shown a pile of photographs of prisoners, in case he knew any of them. Southgate's face was among them, as a mere makeweight; but the boy said, 'Oh, that's 'Hector'. I met him when I was training', thus giving the prize away to the enemy. Southgate made fine furniture for a living, and so survived his concentration camp, for he was neat-handed enough to be useful in the tailor's shop at Buchenwald. He was outspoken, when he came back, about the wireless games. Buckmaster, his section head, tried to write this off as the report of an extremely tired man, but history can do better.

I was persuaded by Robert Lyon ('Acolyte') that I ought to have named him when printing a picture of him in my first edition – I did, thereafter. He threw in a telling anecdote. He and his courier got very fond of each other, as often happened, and she found she was pregnant. As good Catholics, they could not dream of an abortion, nor did they want the child to be illegitimate. So he gave her a month's leave, she settled in a village in a quite different part of France for the three weeks needed by French law to register to be married, and they were married there in their own real names before they went back to work under their pseudonyms. (She lost the baby, but they had others later.)

Mr Gladstone still took up a lot of my working time. The first two volumes came out in 1968, at a price that then appalled me of fourteen guineas, and were respectfully received. Much later, they brought me a compliment I cherish. Roy Jenkins, by then a peer and chancellor of Oxford University, wrote to me out of the blue in 1991: he had only just picked up these two volumes, and found my introduction 'the most fascinating thing I had ever read about Gladstone', as well as the best essay of its length he knew.

None of my Manchester colleagues were Gladstonians, but two of them did work in nineteenth-century history, each from as proletarian an angle as he could manage: Iori Prothero and the still more marxist John Breuilly, who later moved on to a chair at Birmingham. Peter Lowe was a twentieth-century historian, specialising in problems of the far east; Judith Brown worked on the Indian Raj and its enemies; Frank O'Gorman worked on the late and Riley on the early eighteenth century, Brian Manning on the English civil war, and Michael Bush mainly on the Tudors. We all got on passably together, united in the belief that the sub-department was doing some good.

Shortly before I left Manchester, one of the medievalist dons, Kershaw, came to ask me whether he could become a modernist instead. He offered fluent German as well as fluent Latin; I encouraged him to change, not foreseeing that he would become the nation's leading expert on the Third Reich and a knighted biographer of Hitler.

A Japanese graduate student turned up, who wanted to work under Riley. His grasp of English customs and spoken English was a lot weaker than his grasp of the language in print. The Rileys of course asked him round to dinner, and he presented to Mrs Riley a small silk object, roughly H-shaped, she could not conceive for what. Writing to thank him, she called it a scarf. 'Do you think', the Japanese asked the student with whom he shared digs (who was an Afghan) 'Riley will call me out, for offering an item of dress to his wife?'

It was Something to be a professor at Manchester, to have one's name in *The World of Learning*, to be asked to nominate for Nobel prizes, to be consulted as an Authority by the local newspaper. Now and again I was asked to examine for other universities, and here I claim one distinction. I have failed a candidate (not the same one) for a doctorate both at the university of Oxford and at the university of Cambridge. In both cases, my fellow examiner was senior to me; in both cases we agreed that the candidate, though worthy, had not produced a thesis of doctoral quality, and would have to re-submit or go down. Both went down, one back to the United States – spurning the B Litt we offered him, the other into the television world, where he rose to prominence.

I have never cared for sitting on committees – it was one of the reasons why I had been glad to give up being a local councillor; but having a Manchester chair necessarily involved me in several. I was invited for instance to join the council of the Royal Historical Society, on which I sat under the most incisive chairman I have ever met, Dick Southern the medievalist who was president of St John's, Oxford. He had matchless gifts for getting quickly to the heart of any problem, however tangled, and for not letting bores catch his eye. I was also taken on to the board of trustees of Mr Gladstone's library, named after St Deiniol, at Hawarden, unique as a residential library in which residents could pursue divine (or any other serious sort of) learning.

By telephone, I made friends with the reviews editor of *The Economist*, Gordon Lee, for whom and his successors I did a lot of work. This kept me up to date with some of the subjects I taught, and some of the things I knew about, clandestine history especially, in which Gordon and I were both interested. I think it was he who introduced me to Ronald Lewin, much my superior as a scholar and a military historian, and am sure it was he who re-introduced me, at an *Economist* party, to Jimmy Langley, the one-armed expert on escapes, of whom more in the next chapter. Many years later, I was at a conference in Washington, DC, to celebrate the release of three thousand cubic feet of OSS documents into the American national archive. I there met Constantinides, who had just written a short guide to books on intelligence and related subjects, which frequently quoted *Economist* reviews, every one of which I had written. George C. Chalou of the national archives, who ran the conference, published its proceedings promptly in a book called *The Secrets War*, to which I contributed a chapter on how SOE had got on with OSS.

Dickie came over from Australia, with Elaine, because he wanted to look over his grandchildren (who found him rather forbidding). After all the trouble he had taken about my accent when I was small, I could not bear to tell him that his own officer-class accent – which used to be indistinguishable from mine on the telephone – had developed a slight but perceptible overtone of Strine. He told me then that, having reached his seventies, he tended to wake between three and four in the morning, without being able to go back to sleep. In order not to disturb Elaine, he had developed a technique of lying quite still, without fidgeting, and keeping his mind occupied by extracting square roots.

While in Manchester, he took me to call on the mathematics department, where we found a large oil painting of Sir Horace Lamb, once professor there, who turned out to have been RMF's first cousin, as well as the father of Henry Lamb the painter, whom I can thus also claim as a relative. I do not think Dickie had ever known Henry Lamb; he rather disapproved of the Bloomsbury set, in any case. Philippa had bought (and kept) a splendid drawing of a horse by Henry Lamb, one of the delights of the Park Town house.

Early in my time at Manchester, I was sent a review in Swedish, which I do not read at all easily, of something I had written, and wanted it translated. I asked an acquaintance in the North Library; he indicated a stunning blonde at a neighbouring desk. She turned out to translate from Dutch, French or Latin, but not from Swedish, but an acquaintance thus began, which – thank goodness – I cultivated. In Henry Miller's immortal phrase, one thing led to another; in 1972 I married her.

She was Mirjam Romme, the youngest child of Professor Carl Romme who was a sort of Dutch Gladstone. He came from a Brabantine patrician family, Roman Catholics by long tradition, and observed that in Holland the Catholics were treated as a lesser minority by the dominant Protestant ruling class. He went, through law, into politics, and had been a minister in Colijn's cabinet even before the war. He played a major part in establishing the rights of the Catholics, and in persuading the Dutch they could not hang on to Indonesia in the late 1940s. He was long leader of the Catholic People's Party, a friend of Jean Monnet and a co-founder of the European Economic Community, and died in 1980 a minister of state.

His wife, *née* Antonia Wiegman, was a banker's daughter, brought up in a French-speaking convent school, always impeccably mannered and impeccably tidy, who had shown great talent at drawing as a girl. Indeed in 1917 she won the Prix de Rome, an annual drawing prize for the talented young; Modigliani, who put in for it the same year, was unplaced. Like my mother, but for quite different reasons, she gave up her profession on marriage, and devoted her life to bearing Carl children and looking after him and them. Luckily for Mirjam and me, there had been one divorce in the family already: her eldest sister Carla, seventeen years her senior, had had to divorce her Franco-Russian husband, with whom she had lived in Paris (and, incidentally, taught Mirjam to cook). So, eventually, the parents consented to meet me and approved our marriage. It became clear to me that I was marrying above me when it slipped out, in chance conversation, that in their country house at Bloemendaal they had had a man who came in once a week to wind the clocks.

For much of the war against Hitler, Mirjam's father had been held as a hostage in prison or internment camp, and she herself played a tiny, unconscious part in Dutch resistance. She was born with defective hips, for which part of the treatment included putting much of her torso into a plaster cast. She was in her cot, with a blanket over her, crying, when a routine house-to-house search by the Germans came to call. They were hunting for boys (such as her two brothers) on the run from forced labour. Several such refugees, including some Jews, were hiding in the cellar at that moment. The Germans asked what was wrong with Mirjam. Meningitis, her mother replied, whereupon they bolted, leaving the house unsearched. Mirjam never forgot that, during the last winter of the war, there was *nothing* to eat for some weeks but sugar beet and tulip bulbs.

I was able to introduce her to Dickie and Elaine in Paris, on their way over to England.

Philippa had made no difficulties about a more or less amiable divorce, once it was clear to her that I had moved out; whatever she felt, she made no kind of awkwardness, for which I have always been grateful.

She remained at Somerville, later became a professor of philosophy in California, and long philosophised from a house Anne Cobbe left her in Oxford. She and I sold the Park Town house, for about twice what we had paid for it, and halved the takings. Elizabeth – or rather her solicitor, a young Manchester woman of feminist leanings – was much more awkward. I was only anxious to get clear, and again made no appearance in court. The court found that Elizabeth was to have the freehold of our house, and to keep the car, and to keep custody of both children, whom I could see on alternate Sunday afternoons, and to have all my academic pension rights as well as alimony. I have spent the rest of my life living on my wits, on my old age pension (once, at seventy, I became entitled to it), and on Mirjam. This life sentence to comparative poverty has not been agreeable – no tropical holidays, no shooting or hunting or winter sports, no grand cars, no fine wines, no serious collections, never travelling first class, seldom taking a taxi. Living with Mirjam has more than made up for it. And the tsunami catastrophe in the Indian Ocean at the end of 2004 has cast a blight on tropical holidays.

Of course I agonized about the effect the divorce was going to have on the children, remembering my own experience all too vividly. I reckoned it would be better for them if I got away from the Didsbury household, rather than subjecting them to parents who had drifted apart and were starting to be sharp with each other, and hope I chose rightly. The father-son relation has never been intimate, in the Foot family, for several generations past; Richard and I have stuck, alas, to the pattern. He went from Manchester grammar school to Southampton to read chemistry, changed to philosophy, did no work (otherwise, John Roberts – by this time his vice-chancellor – told me, he would have got a first), and then vanished into the world of jazz, where his father's distaste for the genre kept him from following. He is now the leading jazz double bass player on the south coast, and composes as well, but lives several counties away, with a delightful companion (who has two teenage daughters from another failed marriage). We seldom meet.

With Sarah I have got on better. She too is an historian, though her expertise is about as far from mine as she can get without being an ancient historian: her speciality is the Anglo-Saxon church, on which she is now a leading scholar. She went up from Withington to Newnham, Cambridge, where she got a first in history, followed by a research fellowship at Caius, and is now a fully established academic, with some books under her belt, and a councillor of the Royal Historical Society. Moreover, she is a lay canon of Christ Church and a Regius professor of ecclesiastical history, so that she is professionally much my senior. Her first marriage, to a GP who had been up with her, broke up after a decade – they had drifted apart, instead of together – but has provided me with my only grandchild, Matthew, who at sixteen is already showing promise as musician, as linguist and as mathematician. We see far too little of him, but are delighted whenever we do manage to set eyes on him.

CHAPTER 7

Work and play

Mirjam and I spent our honeymoon at Concarneau in south Brittany, on which Geoffrey Rice and I had once made an outline plan for a commando raid (before we took in that SIS forbade Combined Ops to work on that coast). We had been inspired to do so by a chance set of low level oblique air photographs, which gave us magnificent cover of ninety-five per cent of the beach. In the five per cent that sortie had not covered, I now found the ruins of an 88mm gun emplacement which had commanded the whole of our proposed landing area. Just as well C had forbidden it.

We lived at first in a small flat in a delightful early nineteenth-century square, Chalcot Square near Primrose Hill. I spent about half the week there, working on Mr Gladstone, and half the week in Manchester, where I lived in a hall of residence, teaching and helping to run the department. It became my turn to head it; I had a lot of work to do which would have been done much better by a competent clerk, work that helped to impel me to leave before long.

The Gladstone task was almost cripplingly large; I used to wake sometimes in the night, and wonder however I was going to manage to index it, once I had brought it to an end. Suddenly, in December 1972 on one of my routine visits to Oxford, I was told by Colin Roberts, the secretary to my managing committee, that I had resigned. In fact I did not resign, I was sacked. The committee, which did not tell me so to my face, preferred someone in Oxford to a distant editor in Manchester. I was to hand over the manuscript and all my notes to my new research assistant, Colin Matthew, who like Mr G had been at Christ Church and who, in the end, brought the work to a triumphant conclusion. He then went on, being a workaholic, to edit the new Dictionary of National Biography, and fell down dead at the age of fifty-eight: a charming man and a great loss to scholarship.

Turned off Gladstone studies, I resumed working on resistance to Hitler, my long suits remaining sabotage and escape, rather than the study of intelligence or security. I have tried to stick to Scaliger's motto, *nulla dies sine linea*, and can hardly remember when a day passed on which I did not write a line or two at least.

Soon after we were married, we went for a short holiday to a cottage on Skye. At sundown the first evening we walked down to the beach. There was a magical view across the bay to the Cuillins. We heard, but ignored, a vehicle that stopped in the lane behind us. From it a voice I knew said, 'Surely that's Foot?' Charles Burney, one of my nicest and most distinguished Manchester colleagues, historian of Persia, turned out to have a house on Skye. We were extra glad that he did one evening when we came back from a walk, soaked right through to the skin by a Scotch mist that had waylaid us; the Burneys produced some Talisker, that had travelled perhaps three miles in its life, which even for Mirjam, who normally detests whisky, drove the gloom away. On that same holiday, we bumped into another fragment of primitive agriculture. An old man showed us a wooden ploughshare, which he used to strap onto his own chest, to plough his croft by leaning forward and thrusting – even more primitive than the Connemara winnowing by hand.

A job she had to do in the cathedral library took us both to Salisbury, where Mirjam had never been. As we stepped into the close, she cried, 'I have married into the wrong profession. Why didn't you take orders?'

Some holidays were so magical that they remain vivid in memory. On our first visit to Venice, we arrived by air in the middle of the night, and walked through the city by the light of a full moon. I had not been there for over thirty years, but was able to spring the Piazza San Marco on Mirjam, quite suddenly. Another wonderful break was at a sixteenth-century small country house near the Alpilles in Provence, turned into an hotel by the owners, whose young daughters served at table, where there was nothing to drink but their own rosé wine, which had travelled all of eighty yards. We went to Sicily, for a week, by third-class railway sleeper. Forty-eight hours of discomfort each way were well worth it for a sight of Monreale, the eighth wonder of the world, still left barely discovered by turismo, because of the Mafia's hold on the neighbourhood. Mussolini's police, dreadful in so many ways, had at least reduced the Mafia to its last gasp; it was brought round by mafiosi from New York, who had insinuated themselves into the American military government teams that administered Sicily in 1943 after HUSKY succeeded.

Dickie had settled down on the Pittwater, north of Sydney, to run a small export-import business. When he reached seventy, his colleagues invited him to retire, but he stayed on. Same again at seventy-five. Eventually he was persuaded to stop, on his seventy-seventh birthday, and was dead of boredom in a month. I resolved then never to retire, have so far outlived him by eleven years, and see no threat of boredom, with Mirjam to keep me company and so many books by me to read and re-read.

My mother had gone out to Australia, by boat, when Paddy was near her time with her second baby, and never came back. She died a few months after Dickie.

At Oxford I had got used to meeting people of like mind, if of quite different specialities, in common room; something of the same quality emerged from belonging, later in life, to clubs. In the Savile, I now and then came across memorable characters. One in particular I vividly recall. A member remarked that he had been in the Navy during the war, and had risen to command an LST(R), a Landing Ship Tank (Rocket). He had sailed her across the Channel on the night of D-1 to D day of operation NEPTUNE, had moored in precisely the spot indicated on his orders, and at the correct moment had released his 950 rockets. While they were in the air, he took a closer look at the chart, to see just what he was bombarding. They were aimed at the Grand Hotel at Cabourg, model for Proust's Grand Hotel de Balbec. Any faith he had had in human nature thereupon leaked out of the heels of his sea boots. As soon as the Navy released him, he settled down to write *Lord of the Flies*. His name was William Golding.

There was once a do for Belgian ex-resisters at Lancaster House, presided over by the Queen Mother. Several hundred Belgians appeared, most of them glowing with gold braid on half their coats. The most interesting of them, with no gold braid, simply wore a DSO preceded by a George Cross: this was 'Pat' Guérisse, who was captured after running one of the best of the escape lines, and ended the war against Hitler by handing over the concentration camp of Dachau to the American army, replacing the SS guards who had run away.

There was an admirable arrangement at Manchester, founded by Elie Auguste Bretey, a cotton merchant of Huguenot origin who died early last century. He left the university money enough to bring over a savant from France to lecture – in French, of course – on some aspect of French culture or history. The French and history departments took it in turns. It twice fell to me to invite the lecturer. First time, I tried in turn Renouvin and Baumont, the most eminent historians in the modern field. Each replied, in a charming letter, how sorry he was that his health no longer allowed him to leave Paris. So I asked my friend Henri Michel, who gave a scintillating talk on the political aspects of French resistance to Hitler. Two years later several colleagues pressed on me the necessity of inviting Soboul, the great marxist historian of the French revolution, which I did.

He turned up in my office – which was about twelve feet by fourteen – and remarked how spacious it was. I said, surely this was nothing to what he had in the Sorbonne? But he had no room in the Sorbonne; if students there wanted to talk to him, they had to chat in the corridors. This threw a strong retrospective light for me on the *évènements* of 1968–9. We went over to a lecture hall, over-full (an audience of perhaps 350 in a room that would comfortably hold 300). Soboul began to talk at half-past five.

At half-past six his audience was thinning out, as people had trains to catch, but he continued to talk – exquisite French, and a thoroughly interesting view of the revolution. At half-past seven he was still in full flow, but hardly any audience was left except those who were to dine with him. At ten to eight I had to put a note in front of him – in French – to say that if he did not stop at once, we would get no dinner. That brought him to a pause; a fleet of taxis took us up to the Midland Hotel. As we went in, the Vice-Chancellor's wife took my arm – 'I've had enough of that man, change your seating plan.' So I put Mirjam beside him instead; and she pushed out, as a conversational pawn, the fact that she had an ancestor – Gilbert Romme – who had designed the French revolutionary calendar. Soboul had been working on a life of him, and she received a further hour's lecture on her ancestor all through dinner.

It proved a mistake ever to take up the job the Foreign Office offered me when I had been five years at Manchester. As a side result of the Heath-Pompidou talks, that ensured British entry into the Common Market, the FO agreed to set up a discussion centre on the affairs of Europe, which I agreed to help run, as deputy warden under the direction of Heinz Koeppler the warden, beside an existing discussion centre called Wilton Park, located at Wiston House near Steyning in Sussex. They wanted me to start in January 1973, though I persuaded them that I had to stay on in Manchester, teaching, until the spring.

We gave up the Chalcot Square flat for a cottage at Thakeham near Pulborough, about midway between Pulborough main line station and Steyning. The core of Thakeham was a genetic curiosity. Apart from us and our next-door neighbour (a woman who worked in a Billingshurst antique shop), and the vicar and his wife, and Lady Reading – daughter-in-law of Lindsey's former boss – the entire village was surnamed Singleton or Skinner. They were all cousins. We had a distant view of Chanctonbury Ring, and close behind our cottage there was a wood in which the ground turned blue every spring with bluebells.

Before I was appointed to this new job, I made it clear that I was neither interested in, nor good at, administration. Reassuring noises were made, a man appointed with me – Alan Hughes, a good man and a sound linguist who had a charming Dutch wife – was to do all the administrative work. Unluckily, he was ill for the first six months, and I had to do all his work as well as my own. Moreover my boss, Heinz Koeppler, turned out to be (all things considered) the nastiest thing I have ever met on two feet. He fawned on his superiors and bullied his staff. The job had been advertised as an academic post, but was nothing of the sort. I stood it for eighteen months, and at the first opportunity resigned.

Wilton Park was named after the house at Beaconsfield from which Crockatt had run MI 9 during the war, where it had started up (on a bright idea of Koeppler's) just after the war's end. It began as a discussion centre to explain to young German prisoners of war that there were other ways of organizing the world than Doctor Goebbels's illusions, on which they had all been brought up. It grew, became international, and moved down to a Sussex country house, Wiston House. At the Norman conquest, the conqueror had given a friend a chunk of Sussex, some twenty-five miles square; it had been part of Harold Godwinsson's estates. The chunk had not changed families until, at the end of the sixteenth century, the current holder bankrupted himself, making too much of a display as Elizabeth I's ambassador extraordinary to Persia. The Gorings, owners by the late eighteenth century, had built Littlehampton, and Goring-by-Sea, and remained ground landlords of them both. They also owned Chanctonbury Ring, which is over two hundred metres high. Looking at the European Union's agricultural policy, they discovered that hill farmers who work land over two hundred metres high can draw a subsidy, which they duly draw, for every hectare they own.

Work consisted in part of organizing conferences, and in part of chairing informal discussions – most of the participants deep in armchairs, some deep in the arms of Morpheus as well – which might be in English, in French or in German. Mirjam did not much enjoy having a long commute from Thakeham through Pulborough to the British Museum library, and back, every weekday, at a time when railway strikes were endemic. The obstinate chairman of ASLEF, the engine drivers' union, turned up for a Wilton Park conference; he and she were not far off coming to blows. She had thought it a mistake for me to take the job, and was quite right.

An alleviation was that, while working for the BM, she was for a time Henry Davis's librarian. Indeed she went back to the museum with a magnificent gift of bookbindings he made to it, of which she is still preparing a definitive catalogue in several volumes. Davis (who had made a wartime fortune in telephone cable) was also a great benefactor of Glyndebourne, and once at least a year invited us to a performance there. Besides several spectacular Mozarts, I recall Janacek's 'Cunning little vixen', after hearing which we met a young vixen on the road beneath the South Downs as we were driving home.

We moved back to London, rescuing Mirjam from long daily grinds in the train; for a few months back to Chalcot Square, then to a matchbox of a house in East Finchley, all we could afford. While we were house-hunting, we had an experience so odd that it needs setting down. We went to look at a flat, likely to be large enough for us, at a rent we could think of paying, close to one of the bus routes that ran to the British Museum. We saw it together, and neither of us had been inside it ten seconds before it struck us that it would be uninhabitable. Something frightful had happened there, and the fright still lay in swathes, all over the flat. We made our excuses and got out as soon as we decently could.

I turned full-time author, with a book called *Resistance* that is now obsolescent, though I have not yet found time to revise it. As one reviewer was good enough to notice, it was pretty closely argued; indeed, I had numbered and sub-numbered every paragraph in it, to make a self-consistent whole, and had to be persuaded by the publisher to cut the numberings out of the published text. A spin-off from it was a book called *Six Faces of Courage* (republished by Pen and Sword Books, Selwyn Jepson provided the title), brief essays on six eminent resisters to whom I felt I had not done justice enough in the previous work. Preparing this, I got an odd literary shock. I sent off my typescript, and got it back in proof after it had been copy-edited. The copy editor (whom I never met) had been through it with great care; and whenever I had used a phrase in the slightest degree out of the ordinary, had banalised it. There was nothing to do but take the book away from that publisher, repay the advance, and re-submit it to another one – who published my original text virtually unchanged.

The *Six Faces* book led, in turn, to a book Jimmy Langley and I wrote together, about MI 9, the wartime escape service, in which Jimmy had served after a remarkable escape of his own. In 1940 he was badly wounded near Dunkirk, as a Coldstream subaltern. His platoon got him as far as the beach, on a stretcher, where he had to be left and was captured. In hospital, a British army doctor amputated his wounded arm, and he was told he had given his parole not to escape. Happening to have plenty of cash with him, he promptly withdrew his parole, got away through a lodge window, and after a series of adventures reached Marseilles, whence with a friendly doctor's aid he was repatriated. He thought he ought to call on his colonel, did so, in the clothes he had escaped in, and was told to return next morning properly dressed. When he did, the colonel said, 'You know the Regiment has the right of appeal to the Crown.' 'Sir.' 'In your case, I don't think it will do any good.' 'Sir', again – what else could he say? But his thought was, which one has he found out about? 'You will report, in plain clothes, to the ante-room of the Savoy Grill at 12.45 tomorrow. You will see a short man there, balding, in a blue pin-stripe suit with the Times crossword puzzle upside down on his knee. You will make yourself known to him. I'm afraid it's the secret service. Good-bye.' That was how Langley was introduced to Dansey of SIS (MI 6), which ran MI 9, in which he was to work. We found some of MI 9's archives, which I had been assured by Boxshall had been destroyed. Langley managed to get them transferred to the public record office, where they have now been joined by a lot more. I discovered that, withheld from us, there were thick files of escapers' reports, all carefully laundered to remove helpers' names and escapers' indiscretions, which had been issued down to squadron intelligence officers in the USAAF. They were to be seen at its record base near Montgomery, Alabama, where I went through them. Copies of them are now, thanks to the Waldegrave initiative, available at Kew in the wastes of WO 208.

When the book eventually came out, the publisher dispensed with almost all the footnotes (thus costing me a place in the British Academy, which held I had thus ceased to be a scholar). The Imperial War Museum now holds the typescript, which has masses of notes; every now and then I get an inquiry from some former escaper's relative, whom I can confidently refer to the IWM. Arthur Crook, who had moved from editing *The Times Literary Supplement* to The Bodley Head, published it. We had a good launch party for it, in the SAS mess at the Duke of York's headquarters near Sloane Square. After the party, we took Jimmy and his wife (who had run the 'Comet' line in her teens) out to dine with Arthur Crook and Juliet Wrightson at Rules. As Jimmy and I lurched down the steep SAS stairs after the party, he stumbled against me, and murmured, 'Pity, isn't it, I couldn't tell you what we were really doing?' I have never known whether he was pulling my leg, or meant it.

Through Selwyn Jepson, I went to see Robert Graves the poet, who was in St Thomas's hospital, bringing him some Vichy water, which he needed. He claimed that, as a child, he had been patted on the head by Swinburne, who as a child had been patted on the head by Wordsworth, who had shaken hands with Southey; and so on back, by actual physical contact, to Chaucer. He called it 'the apostolical succession of the English poets', and handed it on to me with a formal handshake. I have passed it on to a few other people who seemed to me to deserve it.

One of Mirjam's preoccupations was that she became secretary of the Bibliographical Society, a learned society which took up a lot of her time. I often got invited, thus extending my acquaintance among scholars, and met again a few old friends. One of these was Walter Oakeshott, who, when he was president, rang Mirjam up to ask whether the officers of the society would care to look through the Winchester Bible with him. She was to bring me too. We arranged to meet him at noon at the west door of Winchester cathedral. Lucky with traffic, we arrived a quarter of an hour early. I went to pay my respects to the Founder's tomb, and then crossed the nave to pay them to Miss Austen's. On Jane Austen's grave slab there was a bunch of fresh flowers, put there by a girl's school at Camberley that had been set *Emma* for an exam, and wanted to express its appreciation. This showed me what real literary fame is.

While we lived at Thakeham, we got to know Selwyn Jepson well. He had built a house for himself near Liss on the Hampshire-Sussex border, on ten acres he bought for a song in the depth of the great slump. We took to spending weekends in the cottage at the top of his garden, which made a refreshing break in London weeks of work. It was thoroughly rural, nothing man-made to be seen from its windows at all, except for a mown lawn in the foreground; though by now the Petersfield bypass roars across the distant view, and there was already then often a distant hum from the old A3 road, away to the east. He kept saying he would add a codicil to his will, and leave the cottage to us, but forgot to do so. When he died aged ninety that bolt-hole was closed.

We found another at the west end of Suffolk, at Coltsfoot Green, Wickhambrook: half a thatched cottage that had been put up in the post-war building boom that followed the defeat of the Armada. Mirjam bought it with money from her father. It was tiny – two rooms up, two down, with a huge open fireplace, a few yards from open country. The old lady who had lived in the other half of the cottage with her sister did nothing to it at all, beyond dusting it, after her sister died, many years before we arrived. We dreamed of buying it when she too passed on, but on reflection took in that it would be no good thinking of retiring to it, because it was incommutable. There were no good railway stations anywhere near by, and the drive out from London took ninety minutes, even quite late at night.

Having become by the late 1970s a recognised minor authority on clandestine warfare, I now and then got invited abroad to lecture. My first trip behind the iron curtain was to Prague, for which I asked in advance to see any papers they had on the Hussite movement, 1418–1420, which I wanted to consult for an impending book (that never got written) on revolutionary war. This visit was a spin-off from the recently concluded Helsinki agreements for more cultural exchange across the curtain.

As I stepped down from the aircraft, I was greeted by a man from the British Council, who only had time to say, 'Do take care – they are professionals', before he introduced me to my two interpreters, a man and a woman, each aged about forty. I could see at a glance what their profession was: police. They were both married, not to each other. One or other was at my elbow all day of every day, till about seven in the evening, when they went home, leaving me at the Czech Academy villa opposite the gates of the Ministry of the Interior. I was followed (not very skilfully) whenever I went out by myself. I went first to the state record office, one of two or three readers there that day, in a room that would have held fifty in comfort. They produced for me a batch of files on the events of 1618–20. When I pointed out that these were two centuries too late, the clerks' faces fell: it would take four weeks to get hold of the others, and by then I would have left. I took this as a sign that the current regime did not want anybody to look too closely at those sturdy protesters the Hussites.

I was at least allowed to visit Tabor, where I saw the actual black stone altar on which Huss celebrated communion in both kinds for his followers; a passing schoolboy rested his shoe on it while he retied a lace. On that same journey, I was shown the battlefield of Austerlitz, on which I had written an essay for Walter Cowland at Winchester; to see the actual ground reinforced my understanding of long familiar feats of arms. On top of the heights of Pratzen was an obelisk in memory of those who had fallen near by, inscribed in French, in German and in Russian. On the fourth side were a few words in Czech, on the value of bravery, initialled T.G.M.: the only reference in writing I saw, all the time I was in the country, to Thomas Garrigue Masaryk who had founded it, with R.W. Seton-Watson as his impresario. As Seton-Watson's pupil, I thought at least I should call on the widow of Jan Masaryk; unluckily she was out of town. My male bear-leader showed me the window from which her husband had been defenestrated, an old Prague habit.

One evening, bear-leader advised me to put on a suit next morning, as we were going first thing to the national army museum, where the director was to show me round. As we walked across, I remarked how interested I was going to be in what the museum would tell us about the Czechoslovak anabasis across Siberia in 1917–19, that had been fatal to Admiral Kolchak. He said that he would be interested too, because his grandfather had been on it. When we arrived, he went over to the entrance guichet, but returned looking crestfallen. The director had not received clearance from the general staff to show me round, therefore we could not go in, and he had had nothing else in mind for me that morning at all. I replied, come on, it's a public museum – notice there says entry 1kr 50, here are three kroner, let's try. So in we went. The anabasis, perhaps the most interesting event in Czechoslovak military history, left no record in the museum at all: it had become an unevent.

I was shown plenty of sights and museums in Prague, and my appreciation of Bohemian culture deepened. I was moved on into Slovakia, and saw more cultural treasures there, besides being taken stolidly through the local account of the Slovak national rising of August 1944, at the same time as the much better known second Warsaw rising, and similarly unsuccessful. At the museum in Kosice (Kaschau), I was shown in a glass case the kit of a Czechoslovak soldier serving with the British army in the African desert campaign – shoddy battledress, filthy webbing, a broken Short Model Lee-Enfield rifle, and a rusty British steel helmet with a bullet hole clean through it. In the case beside it stood the kit of a Czechoslovak soldier who had joined the Red Army: polished boots, smart tunic and breeches, clean sub-machine gun, intact helmet. The director had the decency to apologise to me: this was a piece of propaganda intended for the peasantry, not for visiting intelligentsia.

So backward had Czechoslovakia become under communism that I encountered just one night in the three weeks I spent there on which my bath had both hot water, and cold water, and a plug.

My journey ended at Bratislava, often referred to as Pressburg by locals talking to me or to each other in German; nobody used its third name, in Magyar, Poszony. Its museum director received me affably in front of a fine sixteenth-century tapestry in his office, boldly inscribed at the top CIVITAS POSZONIAE. Next morning both my bear-leaders saw me onto a bus, which was then locked, and turned away looking satisfied – nothing had happened to disgrace them. But I was not quite clear of Czechoslovakia. The bus driver announced that he wanted his fare in Czech kroner, and would accept nothing else. I had had to surrender all my remaining kroner before boarding the bus. He refused the Bank of England five-pound note I offered him. Luckily for me, an English stranger from Fison's fertilisers was sitting near me, and changed my fiver for kroner; otherwise, it would have been a fix, out of which I had no idea how to climb.

Next year, I went to Warsaw to give a talk to a seminar in Warsaw university, in the rebuilt city centre, about the principles of irregular warfare – with General Bor-Komorowski's chief of staff during the second Warsaw rising sitting beside me. I do not think I have ever felt stronger academic embarrassment, but the afternoon passed off perfectly amicably. Again, I had an interpreter allotted to me, who was obviously a policeman, with whom I got on quite well. He took me to see Copernicus's Torun, stopping on the way at Lowicz, where there was a crowd round the cathedral so dense – it was the main local feast day – that not even a secret policeman could get me through the crowd and into the actual building. I have never, ever, anywhere, seen crowds in and round churches as dense as I saw them then in Poland; not even in Baptist Alabama.

On one afternoon, my interpreter asked me if there was anything I particularly wanted to see. Yes, I would like to have a look at central Warsaw from the eastern side of the river. As we walked across the bridge, a little shorter than Westminster bridge, quite by ourselves, I made some comment on how odd it was that the Red Army had not been able to bridge it in August 1944. He replied that the Poles brought all their young army engineers under training to this spot, and told them that this was a river that the Red Army had been unable to bridge; they were going to prove themselves more capable. This, from a secret policeman, was a further sign that the Poles were not wholly happy with their satellite status. Not long afterwards, the Solidarity movement started the final rot.

I also had the good fortune to meet Kozaczuk, the historian who had first unveiled the secret that the wartime allies had been reading the Germans'

Enigma codes (in a book in Polish in 1967). He took me to see his friend Marian Rejewski, who told me how he had himself first broken the Enigma machine. He had got an excellent degree in mathematics at Cracow, and a further degree at Göttingen, and had then been taken on, in deadly secrecy, by Polish decipher. They poured over him the original advertisement for the machine, with its statement that ninety noughts followed any possibility. He said, 'Wait a moment – how many letters are there in the German alphabet? Twenty-six? Forget your ninety noughts', and solved it, on probability theory, at Christmas 1932, with the help of a crib. One ship in the German navy was fool enough to wish another, by Enigma, *EINE FRÖHLICHE WEIHNACHTSZEIT*, which was a help.

I was able to visit Cracow, where again I read a paper to a seminar – rather less intimidating than in Warsaw – and saw Pilsudski's tomb in the cathedral. I was taken on to see Auschwitz and Birkenau, neither of which have I ever been able quite to put out of my mind since. My sleep pattern took about a year to recover. Much of the Birkenau camp had by then already vanished, but the perimeter fence was still there, enclosing an area rather larger than Hyde Park. The Germans' pretence that they knew nothing of these camps rang all the more hollow; the brush-up with Curtius at Bonn had given me forewarning. The great piles of mixed shoes, of shorn hair and of empty suitcases haunt me yet, quite apart from the shower rooms and the crematoria. Walter Pforzheimer told me once that he had seen in 1944 an air photograph of Auschwitz, that included a long queue of people now known to have been waiting their turn for a douche – that was the cover; in fact, waiting their turn to be gassed to death. The Americans took for granted that it was a chow line, waiting to be fed.

Occasionally I went over to America to lecture, or even to research, on history. That was how I met Pforzheimer, in his celebrated flat in Watergate, which housed a remarkable collection of books on intelligence which he left, in the end, to Yale. Chance took me, at Toby Graham's invitation, to lecture at the University of New Brunswick, so deep in the winter that from my hotel window I could watch a three-ton lorry drive across the large river below it. Gordon Lee passed over to me a request from Bartlett Watt, whom I had never met: he ran a discussion group in Toronto, Caspar Weinberger had suddenly let him down, would I mind coming to give them a talk (I had six weeks' notice) on some subject to do with Churchill and secret service? His group turned out a formidable audience, a black tie occasion, about a third of the large company ex-RCAF officers, most of them wearing DFCs preceded by DSOs. They called themselves the Toronto Society for Parliamentary Democracy but were in fact a body of Churchillolaters, reluctant to hear a syllable against that great man.

As a result, I made friends with Stephen E. Ambrose, a much more copious and more successful military historian than myself. He invited me to visit Madison, Wisconsin, and talk to another body of Churchillolaters, the Other Other club. Black tie again, and we were piped in to dinner, where I was sat next to the state governor: another formidable occasion. Next day I was taken by my hosts to watch a football game they thought important. Standing in line for an elevator to get up to our seats in the grandstand, I noticed the governor standing several places behind us, in the same line, and tried to think of Margaret Thatcher, then our prime minister, standing in a queue for a lift at Wembley. It was unthinkable. The sidelight on American democracy impressed me.

Steve eked out his salary as professor of history at New Orleans by taking parties of rich Americans round General Eisenhower's footsteps in north-west Europe, spending a few days in London, crossing from Southampton to Caen on the night of 5/6 June, visiting the Normandy beaches, and in a good year going right through to Berlin. The programme came for some years to include a dinner at the Savile, for which I was the nominal host, though Steve's tour operator footed the bill. One year (now twenty years ago) we persuaded Hugh Trevor-Roper, who was much my senior at the Savile (and whom Steve admired but had never met), to turn up at this dinner, and even got him to speak. He began by saying that we all wanted him to talk about the Hitler diaries, over which he had just made such a fool of himself. He referred us to his retraction in the previous Saturday's *Times*, and would say no more about them. But he could give us some idea of what the club had been like in wartime. He had never forgotten dining in it late in February 1942, at about the trough of our wartime fortunes. Though the Americans had at last come in on our side, they were weak as water, and the Germans knew it, while we had just lost, in circumstances of the utmost humiliation, Singapore on top of Hong Kong. Only two other members were dining, both much older than himself. At this crisis in the Empire's fortunes, what were they discussing? How you ought to poach salmon; they agreed it was no use using water, you had to have Chablis.

Another year, I went over to France with Steve's tour, and split from them for a few hours over the night of 5/6 June, to take part in a telecast in Paris to celebrate the fortieth anniversary of Normandy D-Day. There was expected to be a confrontation between Passy and Buckmaster, the heads of two supposedly rival groupings working into France; in fact they got on perfectly peaceably, as they had done at the time – the inter-section rivalry was largely a media myth. There were nine ex-clandestines on the panel, and several historians, and myself with a hoof in each camp. After the programme, we walked round to the Brasserie Lipp where Hemingway had liked the beer, and a table had been reserved for us to dine. When I got there, there were seven ex-clandestines sitting in a row, with their backs to the wall. I sat down beside the last one, and had hardly done so before another, with the utmost grace, moved me across to the other side of the table so that he could talk to my neighbour. The ninth ex-clandestine was teased by the rest for having to sit with his back to the room. He assured them all that he had a better command of the room than they had, because there was a vast pier-glass behind them; he moreover had been to check the back way out through the kitchens, which none of them had bothered to do. This telecast brought me back into touch with Leo Spanin, who saw it. He had been invited by the Russians to come back after the war, had stayed in France instead, and earned his living by teaching German in French universities. So bright was he that he had passed the *concours de l'agrégation* at the first attempt, an unusual feat. Currently in Paris, he had seen the programme, and called soon after at my hotel; it was a great delight to meet him again.

On another occasion, in New Orleans, Steve got hold of Keller, another fellow escaper from St Nazaire, who also lived in the South and brought him over to dinner, where he was sat next to me. It was an embarrassing evening both for Keller and for me, as we turned out to have absolutely nothing to say to each other, except that we were both glad to be alive. It was more interesting to be introduced to Hans von Luck, who had been close to Rommel in the western desert, and had risen to command the tank brigade of 21st Panzer Division, stationed just outside Caen in June 1944. By midnight on 5/6 June he had all his tanks ready to move, with their engines running, but was forbidden to stir without the Führer's order, and that night Hitler had for once gone to bed early, and slept in next morning. Von Luck did not get his order till noon on D+1, by then too late.

By the time Mirjam's father died, aged eighty-four, he had distributed most of his wealth round his children, staking us, for example, to Wickhambrook. From his final settlement she got just enough to buy some of her mentor Howard Nixon's books on bookbinding, and to cover a trip for the two of us to Australia, which we took to meet Paddy and Jim, whom she had never seen. Twenty-six hours in an aeroplane, each way, made for tiring journeys, but on several grounds, personal and cultural, it was well worth it. Mirjam and Paddy got on, to my great relief and pleasure, like a house on fire; they bonded as sisters immediately. Paddy's husband Jim, whom I hardly knew, was tougher going, but fun. He had not been a prisoner of war for five years without picking up a trick or two. When his next-door neighbour, the local game warden, reminded him that he was not to sell crab from the local lake that weighed less than a pound, Jim took him out shooting, photographed him shooting a bird out of season, and gave him a print, remarking that he had kept the negative. He had no more trouble. He took us crab fishing, too, showed us some sea eagles, and took us into a mangrove swamp, which gave me new insights into some corners of the Pacific war. Their son Michael, then in his full glory as a beach guard, we hardly saw; and their daughter Jane was just in the process of having to leave her first husband. It was odd to see a whole country entirely unlike the European countryside in which I had been brought up. The main background colour was dun, not green, and the fauna and flora were quite new. They were newest of all on the Great Barrier Reef, where we spent a night or two on Heron Island, right on the tropic: wholly spectacular, as memorable as Lascaux.

Paddy told me that in the hottest summer weather, the last thing she did at night before she went to bed was to prop the front door open, to keep the house cool. I envied her life in so wholly civilised a society, but gather that the spread of tourists on to the Gold Coast of Queensland where she lives has now made her change her habits.

Under Elaine's guidance we went through Sydney's Museum of Modern Art. Of every recent picture she knew both the artist and the precise circumstances in which the picture had been painted. We saw enough aboriginal art to be greatly taken by it, and remain ashamed of what happened in the early days of settlement to the aborigines. Staying with Elaine was at once a delight and a series of frights. There had been no rain at all for some years; she smoked a great deal, and did not take much trouble about putting out her stubs. Her father had been a dealer in antique porcelain; we used to eat our supper off priceless seventeenth-century dishes, which it was then our task to wash up without chipping them. Every morning we woke at dawn to the screech of several score parakeets at our bedroom window.

She showed us, and promised us we would eventually have, an interesting legacy to her from Dickie: the remains of the tea and china set that Bligh of the *Bounty* had ordered, on being promoted rear-admiral and sent out to govern New South Wales. Bligh had left it to his eldest daughter, whose grand-daughter, who inherited it, had married my great-uncle Cunningham, who in turn left it to Lindsey, from whom it reached Dickie, who did not get on with Paddy. Several years afterwards, Paddy rang us up from Queensland to say that she had seen in the newspaper that the Bligh china was coming up for sale. We rang up Elaine to protest. She said she had got tired of looking after it, after forty years; a plausible young man had persuaded her there was money to be made out of it. We over-persuaded her to let us have it instead. Pitt & Scott, who handled delicate removals for great museums, moved it for us. I had a momentary tussle with customs, who wanted to charge me duty on it, but assured them I had seen proof in my father's hand that it was over a century old. Mirjam found the proof inside the coffee-pot when she washed it up on arrival.

On our Australian journey, we went on to stay with friends of Dickie and Elaine in Tasmania called Alcorso, who had built themselves a most beautiful house, Roman-courtyard style, at Moorilla just outside Hobart where they were settling down to make the perfect white wine. (They were getting quite close.) From there we went on to Melbourne, where Mirjam had a paper to read to the Australian and New Zealand Bibliographical Society, which had invited her to speak on hearing she was visiting the continent. In Melbourne we met a New College man who had bought, out-bidding the British Museum, Charles I's travelling library, a great rarity which it was a delight to see. There is also a wonderful art gallery there, including one example of every famous impressionist and post-impressionist painter, recognisable at a glance, but never exhibited outside Melbourne, as no one can afford the insurance premiums to move them.

In the mid-1980s we moved to a house in northern Kentish Town, with more room for books. A.J.P. Taylor and his third wife, Eva Harasti, turned out to live just over the hill, and we saw a little of them. We made indeed a social floater: we invited them to meet two other friends of ours, Laszlo and Laura Veress, forgetting that Eva, like them a Hungarian, had been brought up a bolshevik, and had nothing in common with an ex-diplomat and a connection of King Louis Philippe. It was not a comfortable evening. Soon after, Parkinson's disease started to bite on Alan Taylor, and Eva had to move him into an old peoples' home in north Finchley. I used to go round one afternoon a week to give Eva an afternoon off. By this time, the gearing between thought and speech had gone – he could still think, but alas could no longer find words to fit the ideas. A heart attack then carried him off.

One of my books had an origin odd enough to be worth setting down. I was at a party in the Imperial War Museum, and met there my agent, Michael Sissons, who had been in College some time after me. He remarked on the excellence of the pictures on the walls, and asked the director, Alan Borg, whether they had been written up. Borg replied that though several people had tried, all had failed. Michael suggested I might try too. I did, had an interesting time going through the hundreds of pictures stored in the basement, as well as the ones on the office walls and on show, and produced *Art and War*, an attempt to put some of the pictures into their historical context, as eyewitness accounts of warfare. Lavishly illustrated, the book did not sell very well – for reasons always obscure to me, the museum hardly pushed it in its own shop, but it became a set book in the history of art course at Oxford, which I felt was compliment enough.

I got a letter, rather grudgingly worded, from Sir Robert Armstrong, then Secretary to the Cabinet. It would have after all to be me who was invited to write the history of SOE in the low countries; did I want to take it on? I accepted by return of post. A few days later I got a chit from one of Armstrong's underlings, enclosing a form for the renewal of my security clearance – which I sent back, as I had never been cleared at all. Would I mind, Armstrong promptly replied, going through with this? It would only take about a year, after which I could start work. During the year, I happened to run into a previous Cabinet Secretary, Burke Trend, shortly before he died, and mentioned this contretemps to him. He replied that he well remembered that, when they proposed to take me on to work on SOE in France, MI 6 held all SOE's papers, but MI 5 did all the clearances, and 6 did not care to let 5 know that anyone was starting to paddle in this pool. 'So we asked Jack Wheeler-Bennett, and he said he thought you were all right.'

The French book had taken two years to write, and four to clear. The Dutch and Belgian book took ten years to write, but only two to clear, as more time had passed, and government had got less nervous. The first book, a best seller, was greeted with several libel actions. The second has made much less of a sensation, indeed the Belgians seem to have taken no notice of it at all, and so far (March 2008) nobody has sued.

Ian Dear was invited by the Oxford University Press to prepare them an Oxford companion to the world war of 1939–45, and chose me as his main historical adviser; in the end, both our names appeared on the title page. Dear had the bulk of the work to do. I had the more interesting task of establishing who was (and who was not) to be asked to write about what. We assembled a thoroughly international team, including leading scholars from both sides in the war, and took extra care to insert cover of intelligence, decipher, escape, sabotage and resistance, as well as looking after all the expected items of battle and battle equipment. When the book finally came out, in 1995, we had some splendid reviews, and I hope it has remained a useful teaching tool the world over. Eleven years on, a revised paperback version of it sold so well that OUP, for its own inscrutable reasons, has let it go out of print and intends to put it on line. I trust the editors' interest in it will not be entirely forgotten. It is now called *The Oxford Companion to World War II*. I have failed to convince anybody that it is conceited of the twentieth century to call its world wars the first and second, because there had been several before. Sir George Clark wrote of six world wars between 1588 and 1715. George III was once heard discussing with Lord North sending reinforcements to the Mississippi and the Ganges – or did he mean the Brahmaputra? Thucydides even fancied he had fought in a world war in the fifth century before Christ.

CHAPTER 8

Reflections on SOE

L et me spend a few pages reflecting on our wartime secret services, particularly on SOE, the Special Operations Executive, to which I never belonged, though I attended its parachute school and have done a lot of work on it. All were wrapped at the time in more or less dense cloaks of secrecy. With a few of them I brushed shoulders while the war went on; of a few more I never heard at all till well on into peace time. There were I believe nine of them. Conceivably one or two more may lie hidden beneath Whitehall's habitual cloak of secrecy. Many myths and rumours have grown up round them, especially round SOE. Let me try at least to explain how they stood in relation to each other.

As is usual among countries that have several such bodies, there was a pecking order among them. About this there is nothing odd, though sensation-mongers have made many attempts to blow British inter-secret-service quarrels up into world-shaking events, which they never were. Even among civilian departments, some are grander than others, and do not mind the others being made aware of it. Some of SOE's members thought it ought to have been at the top of the pecking order, as the most important secret service, but in fact it came about half-way down, while the most important was the smallest and the last formed.

This – the name was deliberately meaningless – was the London Controlling Section (LCS: the reader will have to forgive the acronyms in this chapter). The service grew out of one of the bright ideas of Jo Holland, a sapper major who spent 1938–40 at the War Office, working on means of irregular warfare. I only heard of him through meeting his former typist, Joan Astley, whose brilliant *The Inner Circle* of 1971 is at last reprinted. He invented the commandos and the escape service, as well as providing one of the three cores of SOE; and also threw off the Inter-Services Security Board, which started by allotting codenames to future operations, and grew into the LCS. It worked out of the basement of Great George Street, next door to the innermost offices of the chiefs of staff; under ground, out of sight, and unknown at the time to Parliament or to the news media. Its task was to deceive the enemy. To the few who knew of its existence, the LCS had top priority; it was thus able, for instance, to secure readily enough a submarine to float a body ashore on the coast of Spain, to sustain operation MINCEMEAT – as described by Ewen Montagu in *The Man Who Never Was*. This baffled the Germans, in midsummer 1943 after the fall of Tunis, about where our next landing in the Mediterranean was going to be. Any bright child with a school atlas could foretell Sicily, but MINCEMEAT persuaded the enemy we were going for Sardinia or – helped by another deception operation, called ANIMALS – Greece instead. The Germans reinforced both, and did not reinforce Sicily – where we landed in July 1943.

At the time, I had no idea that there was such a body as the LCS, though (as I have mentioned) I did a fragment of work for it over operation TITANIC on the first night of the Normandy landings. Long after the war, when its past existence had become public knowledge, I was able to ask Colonel Bevan, who had run it, what use he had made of SOE. As little as possible, he replied, for he did not think SOE anything like a secure enough body to be trusted with his secrets. He had been forced to use it for a corner of operation STARKEY, run in too much of a hurry in 1943, which failed to convince the Germans that we were about to invade France, thus taking some weight off the Russians. Otherwise he had only used it twice: for operation ANIMALS, mentioned just now, and for a single stroke in Belgium on 8 June 1944 which added strength to his masterpiece, FORTITUDE. The Belgian stroke I was able to recount in my *SOE in the Low Countries*. It sent messages to many groups of resisters there with whom SOE was in touch, in ciphers the Germans were known to be able to break, calling all of them into action two days after the landings in Normandy. This alarmed the Germans further about the security of the hinterland of Calais and Boulogne.

FORTITUDE convinced the Germans that Eisenhower's landing in Normandy was only a feint, before the real blow went in on the beaches south of Boulogne, so that hardly a German soldier was sent from there to the west of the Seine, until Eisenhower's beachhead was secure. R.F. Hesketh who commanded it in detail once consulted me about whether he could publish a short summary of the operation, in about a dozen closely printed pages. I advised against, because while this would have attracted a small fascinated readership of experts, it would not have sold in any quantity. He never showed me his long account, simply entitled Fortitude, written close to the time, and published to general acclaim in 1999, twelve years after his death.

Next in importance to deception came decipher, which worked at the start of the war under the cover name of the Government Code and Cipher School (GC&CS), but did no teaching. Decipher claims continuous existence at least from the downfall of Mary, Queen of Scots, which it helped to organize, though officially the tiny decipher office that had been kept in being after Waterloo was wound up in 1844, after a row over the interception of Mazzini's letters when that hero was trying from London to set up the liberation of Italy. Something must have been kept in being, quietly, behind the scenes. In 1914 it developed into Room 40, Old Buildings at the Admiralty, and played a useful part in the naval war against the Kaiser's Germany (as described in Patrick Beesly's fine book in 1982). It then proved too useful to be dropped, and all three armed forces as well as the Foreign Office kept decipher teams going during the 1920s and '30s. In 1939–40, the best of them were amalgamated at Bletchley Park, across which my grandfather had hunted the fox with the Whaddon, now a suburb of Milton Keynes; and in 1940 GC&CS began serious inroads into the German cipher machine, Enigma.

As I have remarked already, the Poles had been reading the German navy's Enigma traffic from 1932 to 1938. In the course of the war against the Axis, about twenty thousand people on both sides of the Atlantic were involved in deciphering not only Enigma, but the still more intricate *Geheimschreiber* and other cipher machines. All twenty thousand kept entirely silent about it for nearly thirty years. Their ultra-secret product was hardly ever distributed raw below army headquarters; exceptional measures were quite rightly taken to keep so important a coup away from enemy knowledge. For a great many years, also, nothing was revealed about which of our friends' and enemies' diplomatic codes decipher had managed to unravel during the war.

There can be no doubt that the ULTRA secret really was a world-shaking intelligence coup. It meant that the Allied high command could see right into the mind of its principal opponent, Hitler, thus securing an unprecedented secret advantage – so long as it remained secret. An inordinate amount of trouble was taken to make sure that nobody blabbed; quite right too. Men were said to have been indoctrinated into this task by a large unsmiling major, who explained to them that if they ever spoke about it outside the office, not only would they be cashiered and imprisoned, but, picking up a loaded Colt revolver and pointing it appropriately, 'I will come and blow your balls off with this.' Coarse but effective.

By a deft political stroke, C, the head of the secret intelligence service (SIS), who was nominally in charge of decipher – the tail that wagged the dog – arranged that it was he himself who handed the material from GC&CS over to Churchill personally, in those now famous interviews *tête-à-tête* from which even the chiefs of staff, even the King, even Mrs Churchill were excluded. If C could not come himself, the material was sent in elderly buff dispatch boxes, marked VRI for Victoria Regina Imperatrix, to which even Desmond Morton who handled Churchill's relations with the secret services did not have a key. C thus earned innumerable brownie points, based on the work of men and women far more intelligent than himself.

The ULTRA secret first started to go public, in Polish, in 1967. I first read of it in a bad book in French, in 1968, and could hardly believe what was before my eyes. When it became generally known in England in the winter of 1973–4, I called on General Gubbins and asked him who in SOE had known about it. He told me that Boyle, his head of intelligence, formerly director of air intelligence, had read some of it before he joined SOE; so had Mockler-Ferryman while chief intelligence officer to Eisenhower during operation TORCH, the Anglo-American landings in north-west Africa late in 1942; so had Keble, SOE's brigadier in Cairo. He did not say which of them remained privy to ULTRA once in SOE, and I forbore to ask: the whole subject was clearly still what was then called 'delicate', and I had been brought up not to inquire into more delicate questions than I had to. Nicholls, his chief of signals might, Gubbins thought, have been aware of it, but certainly did not read it. (Leo Marks, SOE's coding expert, often said to me that Nicholls was superb as a signals officer, but neither knew nor cared at all about cipher. Not even Marks claimed to have read ULTRA himself at the time.)

Gubbins told me that on becoming executive head of SOE, in September 1943, he made an arrangement with Ismay, Churchill's chief military assistant. Ismay kept a folder on his desk, locked up whenever he left the room, into which he put any ULTRA secret telegrams that had come his way which he thought might interest SOE. Once a week Gubbins called on him, read the folder, and took no notes; if he was out of London, Barry or Sporborg his deputies called instead. A very few very senior people in SOE thus had glimpses into ULTRA traffic. There was no need to mention this to C, who did not need to know. The bulk of the Germans' counter-espionage work was done via teleprinter or telephone, neither of which we tapped, so there was not much ULTRA traffic that bore on SOE at all. SOE thus provides an interesting example of a significant war-making body that (like half the war cabinet) was outside the ULTRA loop, and hardly the worse for it. I once tried, while an official historian, to see the Prime Minister's list of those cleared for ULTRA, but was told it could no longer be found. Perhaps this only meant that it would never be open to me.

Next below GC&CS in the pecking order came, side by side, SIS, the secret intelligence service known to the media as MI 6, and the security service, known as MI 5. Though they had both been set up formally by a cabinet decision in 1909, they no doubt had older roots. Each, privately, indicated that it was really the senior of the two; precedence between them did not matter.

SOE's relations with SIS were often frankly bad, partly for a sound professional reason, partly for more ignoble personal ones. The professional point was this: if SOE's agents did their jobs properly, they were bound to attract formidable enemy police investigations, the last thing that any SIS agent at work in the same area wanted. A competent spy does not want to be bothered with house-to-house searches, telephone taps, random arrests in the street, a paraphernalia of papers without which one cannot stir out of doors – all of them difficulties a busy SOE circuit would be likely to provoke. There were, moreover, a lot of trivial difficulties between rival staff officers from each service, trying to work into the same area from London, who did not get on well together. Still more awkwardly, SIS's official liaison officer with SOE – he had a desk in SOE's Baker Street headquarters, and access to all SOE's W/T traffic – was the notoriously abrasive Claude Dansey. Worse still, Stewart Menzies, who became C in November 1939, and Colin Gubbins, who became SOE's lynchpin a year later, could not stand each other.

Menzies was noted for his charm, first honed when he was president of Pop at Eton. He was well connected – his parents had belonged to the 'Prince of Wales's set' in the 1890s, and he took care never to deny the rumour (it was only a rumour) that his mother had known the prince intimately. He had served in the Household Brigade and was thus *bien vu* at court. Gubbins had plenty of Highland charm as well; but they rubbed each other up the wrong way. Moreover SOE had been founded, in a tearing hurry, in July 1940 by taking a whole section away from SIS to form one of the newer body's cores, and everyone was so busy that three weeks passed before Menzies received any formal notification that he had lost control of his section D, a bureaucratic slight he never forgave. I have found archive traces of him dated as late as September 1944 laying mines in SOE's path, during discussions with one of the London governments in exile. We have Richard Aldrich's word for it – echoing, I believe, what was widely thought in senior service circles during the war – that 'C was a dud'; not of course a phrase usable in an official history. C did secure, from the chiefs of staff, a ruling that if ever there was a shortage of aircraft for clandestine drops, SIS was automatically to have priority over SOE. The shortage of aircraft was a perpetual source of complaint by SOE, which keenly resented the ruling, though it was hardly ever invoked.

Relations between SOE and MI 5 were much smoother. There were no clashes of personality, indeed some members of SOE's very secure security branch came in from MI 5, and remained on friendly terms with its much increased wartime staff. Naturally enough, SOE raised several security problems for MI 5 to ponder. All were amicably resolved by discussion, or turned out irresolvable. MI 5, for example, soon saw through the Germans' attempt to play back the W/T set of 'Bishop', an F section agent captured in southern France in April 1943, but were baffled by their only too successful coups in Holland and Belgium in 1941–2 and in France in the winter of 1943–4. Country sections were always inclined to claim that they knew the W/T operators, personally, far too well to believe that they could ever be co-operating with their captors, even after capture and perhaps torture. They were too often wrong.

Nobody on SOE's security staff would ever talk to me, however eminent the introduction to them I sought, with two exceptions. Norman Mott would only talk inside a guarded building, on the understanding that he was never to be quoted. Peter Murray Lee became a family friend, but by the time we knew him well had nothing more to put forward than anecdotage. One of his anecdotes bears repeating. He claimed that it was he who had originated one of SOE's best-known covers. This was often used when writing to agents' relatives, on War Office paper, sub-headed 'M. O. 1. (S. P.)', presumed by the innocent to mean a special projects sub-section of the military operations branch. Peter said it stood for Mysterious Operations In Secret Places. Here, junior to 5 and 6, was about where SOE stood in the order of priority among the secret services.

Both 5 and 6, with their small pre-war professional cores, liked to deride SOE as 'amateur', a gibe still often met with in the news media – forgetting how amateur the two older services had themselves become, under the pressure of wartime recruiting. Nor were the professionals always impeccable. There was one man, recruited from the Indian army into SIS (and therefore assumed to be proof against anything), who went to a rendezvous on a German frontier with a supposed defector from the Nazis, and on his way there jotted down and put into his pocket a list in clear of his most valuable local agents. Carrying this, he fell into SS hands a few minutes later – at Venlo in November 1939 – and gave away anything he was asked under interrogation. Mercifully, he knew nothing of decipher.

There were a few other secret services as well. Before the war began, MI 5 and the post office between them put together a small efficient extra body, the Radio Security Service, control over which passed peaceably from MI 5 to MI 6 in 1941. The task of RSS was to locate where unlicensed wireless transmissions came from; at first, within the United Kingdom, later from anywhere within detection range, which might be almost world-wide. Many physical cripples had taken to private wireless telegraphy as a hobby – they were called radio hams – and had registered with the police. As they were physically disabled, they were unfit for any of the armed services, but scores of them performed invaluable work for RSS, never acknowledged in public. I have seen nothing about this in published print, and any attempts I made to reach RSS's wartime papers – if any survive – were gently ignored. Again, from talks with Leo Marks I gathered that if SOE's signals branch needed to know whence someone was operating an SOE transmitter, RSS would be able to explain; that was all SOE needed to know. I never knew whether my sister Paddy worked for RSS directly or for a naval Y (interception) service, quasi-independent of it. Nor, I think, did she.

Just after the war, several dons who had served with RSS returned to Oxford, and were prepared over the port to swap anecdotes about what they had been up to, till quite suddenly word came down from Somewhere, and they all fell silent. I now wish I had listened more carefully while they were still being indiscreet. The service no doubt remains in being, and it is quite proper that it should remain under wraps. It is one of the devices on which the nation's safety continues to depend, and there is no point in letting the media in to inform our enemies.

In the first autumn of the war, the chief security officer of the British Expeditionary Force in France was Gerald Templer, much later eminent in Malaya, who had served under Jo Holland in MI R. No doubt inspired by Holland, he put up to the War Office the idea that something should be done to get military intelligence back from any prisoners that might be taken from the BEF, out of their prisoner of war camps. This led to the foundation in December 1939 of MI 9, the escape service, which worked under the wing of MI 6. It proliferated, most of the world over, and has helped provide material for some of the war's best adventure stories. Whether it also provided much actual intelligence still remains a secret, which I have never been able to penetrate. We may perhaps find out when Keith Jeffrey publishes his official history of MI 6 in 2010.

SOE had its own escape section, DF, of which Leslie Humphreys its head once boasted to me that it had never lost a passenger. It worked, fast and efficiently, over most of north-west Europe. SOE's relations with MI 9 were perfectly amicable. Indeed from Victor Gerson, who ran one of Humphreys' best lines, I gathered that 'in the field' there had been a certain amount of quiet exchange of passengers between DF lines and the less deadly secret escape lines run by 9, with which nobody needed to bother London.

There were also the Auxiliary Units – another nice meaningless phrase – which never went into action. They long kept themselves to themselves, as a distinct and separate secret body. SIS's section D was tasked to form them, in a hurry, in the summer of 1940 when invasion seemed imminent. Section D made a hash of it, then MI R took over, and made sense instead. The task of the AUs would have been to disrupt the communications and the petrol supplies of the invading Wehrmacht, which thanks to the combined efforts of the Royal Navy and the RAF never got ashore in England after all. Gamekeepers and poachers, working side by side, provided most of their strength; men who knew their own patch of countryside, bush by bush, and could move across it without attracting notice. 'We might', one of the best of them said to me once, 'have lasted forty-eight hours in any given area before the Germans rumbled us, but we might in that time have done them quite a lot of harm.' Their commander was one of the few soldiers to return from Norway with his military reputation enhanced: Colin Gubbins, who went on into SOE next November. He took with him from the AUs into SOE several of their most promising officers and men. The rest absorbed themselves quietly into the Home Guard, and continued to lie low and to think about what they might do, if the tide of war suddenly turned against us. Their wives resigned themselves to long unexplained absences. None of them noticed or cared that Gubbins had put up a black in Norway by dismissing a Guards battalion commander for incompetence in the face of the enemy, which made him enemies at court. Guards battalion commanders are supposed to be like Rolls Royce axles, unbreakable.

The AUs were wrapped in an extra dense blanket of secrecy, and have still (so far as I know) received no published official history, but a few old stalwarts survive. They call themselves 'auxiliers', a back formation I suppose from my grandfather's fusiliers, have a museum at Parham in east Anglia and a busy website, and nowadays appear with other veterans on war memorial parades, which they were long forbidden to do.

One other service remained, at the bottom of the pile: the political warfare executive, PWE, which ran propaganda, both white (admissible by government) and black (more powerful, and inadmissible). After thirteen months' bitter inter-departmental warfare in Whitehall, it was formed out of SOE, by taking away from it the semi-secret propaganda sub-branch originally brought in from the Foreign Office. SOE continued to regard it as a sort of younger sister, and got on quite smoothly with it, often acting as its taxidriver. (Compare and contrast David Stafford's admirable simile, that SOE and SIS often behaved like an ex-couple in a savagely hostile divorce case.) Several agents worked well in the field for both PWE and SOE – the names of Pertschuk, Menesson and Chalmers Wright stay with me. Chalmers Wright I met and liked after the war; the other two fell into German hands and were murdered.

David Garnett, the novelist, who had himself been in PWE, wrote its official history at the end of the war, just as Mackenzie wrote SOE's; his book, like Mackenzie's, was put away in a locked cupboard in Whitehall, and – again like Mackenzie's – was let out into published print recently (edited by Andrew Roberts in 2002). In it Garnett mentions that PWE used for one of its covers PID, the political intelligence department of the Foreign Office, and even sometimes used its writing paper. This will prove an endless source of confusion for historians. Now that all the important witnesses are dead, who is ever going to be able to detect which letters written with a PID letter-head were really PID's, and which were PWE's acting under cover?

It was an advantage to PWE that back in 1934 a British firm, Monotype, won an international competition for a set of new gothic types for every ministry (including the secret police) in Nazi Germany, and kept a set of the types. In 1941 a Monotype director showed the set, as a curiosity, to Ellic Howe the bibliographer, who was then a company sergeant-major clerk at anti-aircraft command headquarters. Howe put up a paper about what might be done with these types, and spent the rest of the war forging various types of black propaganda with them, as described in his admirable *Black Game*. Sefton Delmer, who ran black broadcasting, also wrote a good book on it, *Black Boomerang*, and Donald McLachlan who worked with him weighed in with *Room 39*, a more general study of the wartime intelligence field, crammed with asterisks. He put in an asterisk whenever he would have been able to say more, had not the ULTRA secret remained secret; his book came out in 1968, when it was still in this country firmly banned.

The one feature all these services had in common was secrecy, which is now going out of fashion. Some reporters from the news media seem hardly to have heard of it, but you cannot run any secret service without it. Secret agents overseas had to get used to living a life of incessant deceit, never relaxing their guard, never off duty, never forgetting that they were not what they purported to be. Even staff in England, of all ranks, had to remember never to let on – even to their nearest and dearest – what they were actually doing. This called for qualities of character quite a long way out of the ordinary; but without it, nothing could get done at all. I understand that it remains a dictum in the secret world, 'If it's really secret, old boy, don't write it down.'

Disputes will long rage about how much actual good SOE, or indeed any other of the secret services, 'really' did. By now it is clear that both LCS and GC&CS affected the course of the war, substantially, probable that SIS did as much, and certain too that MI 5 kept the state secure through all manner of dangers. One potentate, Lord Moyne, fell to a single group of assassins (one of whom, Menachem Begin, lived on to be Prime Minister of Israel and to win a Nobel peace prize, but that is another story). Beyond that, there were no important subversive coups against us, apart from the still publicly unassessed penetrations made by the (supposedly allied) Russian secret service. We lost the king's younger brother Kent, in a flying accident; his eldest brother Windsor, target of the Nazis in 1940, was posted out of their reach. Churchill's frequent long voyages overseas were untroubled by enemy action. From one of his short journeys, to France, he only survived because some German fighter pilots looked down, and shot up a fishing boat, instead of looking up, and shooting down his airliner: an instance of providence at work. MI 9 and its sister American organization MIS-X between them helped over thirty thousand prisoners of war to escape back to active duty.

SOE's record can stand alongside those. To have blocked Hitler's and Heisenberg's approach to an atomic bomb, as nine Norwegian SOE agents did; to have helped persuade United States opinion that it was sounder to be anti-Nazi than to be isolationist; to have given back – through arming their resisters – their self-respect to several nations that forfeited it on being overrun by the Nazis in 1939–41; these were not mean achievements. Numerous satellite regimes set up by the Nazis, such as Quisling's and Pétain's, were overturned, with the help of more formal armed forces. Tito was brought to power in Yugoslavia, because GC&CS's work proved that the Germans were afraid of him, and SOE (not privy to ULTRA) was therefore ordered to back him. There was moreover a whole series of successful sabotage coups, not to speak of the killing of Heydrich, or the various triumphs in Burma, or the smuggling of special steels out of Sweden, or the astonishing financial feat of extracting £77m in cash (now worth about a billion pounds), legitimately, from China. I know of no other secret service that has ever wound up a campaign with its accounts in the black.

It is comparatively easy to write articles, or even books, pillorying SOE for some of its myriad of faults. The balance of serious history is now starting to swing the other way; we can see that the triumphs far outweigh the disasters. For example, SOE's catastrophe in Holland used to be an Awful Warning in the world's spy schools, as an example of what not to do, till it turned out that what the Germans had done to the British in Holland for eighteen months the British had done to the Germans in Britain for six years, with much greater strategic results.

In this shift of emphasis I can claim to have taken part; indeed was in close to the start, following on Bickham Sweet-Escott's splendid *Baker Street Irregular* which he wrote in 1954, but was forbidden to publish until 1965. It gave us our first picture of SOE's high command from inside. He only got leave to bring his book out when the future appearance of mine was announced in Parliament. Luckily, I could make some use of his in the closing stages of sending mine to press.

My *SOE in France*, published in April 1966, was something of a ground-breaker. It was the first history of any secret service ever officially published by HM government, and triggered off the serious interest in intelligence-related history that has led, many years later, to a flourishing academic sub-industry in several universities. The credit for this belongs not to me, but mainly to Christopher Andrew, now the official historian of MI 5 (to publish in 2009), and to David Dilks, who put into circulation a remark of Sir Alexander Cadogan's that David unearthed while editing his diaries, about 'the missing dimension' of history as normally written by diplomatic and military historians. This was a dimension that Ian Dear and I took trouble to make sure that we inserted in our *Oxford Companion*.

It was worth rescuing SOE from the mere sensation-mongers, of whom there have been too many, not all of them yet dead. At first I suspected government might be playing a variant on a game common in the nurseries of my childhood, called 'Wolf'. All the children present suppose themselves in a sledge, pursued by wolves, and vote for which one is to be thrown out in turn, so that the rest have a better chance of getting away. If SOE, now safely dead, was sacrificed to the media, might they not leave the still current services alone? It did not work out like that. Various revelations about the Allied solution of the Enigma machine, beginning in Warsaw in 1967, led government to sanction Harry Hinsley's masterly series of official histories of British intelligence in the war against Hitler (six volumes in seven, 1979–93), covering decipher, security and deception. Of decipher method he said nothing; why should he? Some of Bletchley's mathematicians, and a biographer of Alan Turing, have been less discreet, but not under official auspices. The Waldegrave initiative then led to the release of vast quantities of once highly secret written material to the National Archive, where almost all of SOE's surviving paperfall has joined them. There is now plenty of original material at Kew on which research students can beaver away, seeking to prove the official historians wrong. Nothing has come out officially at all about interception – quite right too; we still need that service to remain secret.

So far as SOE is concerned, there have been several more official histories, one of them by me (on the Low Countries, 2001), with some more in progress. Mackenzie's official history of the whole show, written in the late 1940s, was at last cleared (2000) for the public to read too – I had the delight of editing it. (I cannot resist throwing in Mackenzie's comment in his own brief autobiographical notes, that he had found nothing in SOE's papers for which Thucydides had not prepared him; so much for many SOE agents' belief, that nothing like this had ever been done before.) Something has I hope been done to rescue SOE from the despite in which it was long held by old-fashioned senior officers and by military theorists, who were content to follow Clausewitz and Wellington, neither of whom would have approved; any more than did its rivals in SIS, not all of whom have been silent in talks to friends.

Now that the cold war is over, and no great power threatens the day-to-day existence of Great Britain, it is possible to relax the rules about what can be published from the past secret world. Former agents of SOE, like all its official historians, took care not to say too much about training methods and weaponry, but books are now starting to come out about some of SOE's schools and factories, whole catalogues of its weapons have been released, and so have the lecture notes from its school near Toronto, supposed identic with what was said at its main school at Beaulieu. The Imperial War Museum now runs a 'secret war' gallery, paid for by Sir Paul Getty, Jr, which displays items used by MI 5, MI 6, SOE and SAS for adults and schoolchildren to marvel over.

Ever since hearing Wavell's lecture at Winchester early in 1937, I have remained fascinated by the concept that a deft stroke or two far behind the fighting lines can affect the course of a battle or even of a war. I remember Paddy Mayne (SAS, of course, not SOE), who in one night destroyed with his own hands more enemy aircraft than any pilot in fighter command shot down all through the war. I remember the two French schoolgirls, equipped by Tony Brooks (my best man when I married Mirjam): they helped delay the move of an SS Panzer division from southern France to Normandy in June 1944, making a killing on the black market with the sump oil they stole from the division's tank transporters and replaced by abrasive grease. I remember the Belgian graduate electrical engineer who organized a single power stoppage that cost the German armaments industry fifteen million man-hours of work. I recall the Karenni rising in the hills of Burma, armed by SOE, that cost the Japanese army ten thousand dead as the war drew to an end.

There were awful SOE catastrophes both in Belgium and in Holland: over forty agents parachuted into Holland were arrested in turn on their dropping zones, and all eight of the wireless operators working out of Belgium to SOE at the end of 1942 were being worked back by the Germans, unspotted by London. Both disasters were retrieved, and both resulted simply from incompetence and over-confidence in London, by SOE's staff and among the governments in exile. Neither was a deep-laid deception plot by the wily British, as has only too often been believed at the victims' end. Equally the disaster to the 'PROSPER' group in Paris, which led in the summer of 1943 to several hundred arrests and a sharp check to SOE's plans, was due to incompetence and bad luck, not to deceit. What purpose such deceit could have served remains obscure.

Mackenzie remarked once that SOE could do nothing without political implications. On the political side, it had plenty to show. All over Europe, west of the iron curtain, leading post-war figures owed their prominence to the work they had done alongside SOE during the war – as, farther east, did Tito. Charles de Gaulle, who deeply disapproved of SOE but could never have reached power without it, was only the most eminent of them. Douglas Dodds-Parker, a leading personality in SOE in the Abyssinian venture and later in the Mediterranean, later still served in the European parliament at Strasbourg and was fascinated to find there a bloc of former SOE adherents, who shared much common ground. The Foreign Office, guided by C (who was nominally the Foreign Secretary's subordinate), could never bring itself to like SOE, which had created endless awkwardnesses for it. The FO did nothing to cash in on the huge funds of pro-British enthusiasm built up by SOE's agents in Nazi-occupied Europe. Probably this could not be helped, but it was a pity. A very few of SOE's most promising characters were even absorbed into the diplomatic and secret services after the war, where one or two rose high.

There remains a lot more for historians to do, following up what has now been revealed. Nearly thirty years ago Ronald Lewin remarked that the whole east African campaign of 1940–1 would need re-writing in the knowledge that a few British senior commanders were reading much Italian wireless traffic, a challenge nobody has yet I think taken up. Twenty years ago, I remarked to a conference of Chris Andrew's that a great deal more remains to be done, out of the files available to the researcher who is both careful and lucky in the public record office, towards defining SOE's real contributions both to strategy and to politics. Similarly, the wartime story of British relations with Scandinavia needs revision in the light of SOE's successes and failures there. SOE's important role in the Italian campaign awaits an official history, not yet complete; the Greek official history, like the Yugoslav, seems to have got stuck; the Poles continue to grumble that the British do not give them as much credit as they deserve for the secret role they played on the eastern front; and so on. Stalin's propaganda teams had the effrontery to denounce the Polish Home Army as 'fascist', in the teeth of the evidence that it had destroyed thousands of German locomotives pulling supplies to the eastern front; only since the fall of the USSR have the Poles in Poland been able to learn their own real wartime history.

On the military side, some of SOE's tasks seem to have been taken over by SAS. When I read, early in the first Gulf War, that Peter de la Billière was to command the British contingent, I said to myself – remembering his SAS past – that he would know how to cut out Saddam Hussein, but forgot that the regiment had omitted to marry into Saddam's family, and thus could not reach him. Presumably SIS includes a branch that can cope with the rest of SOE's tasks; this is not the sort of point that is fit to be aired in public. Naturally, the histories of SOE have been of some use to more recent commanders and their staffs, and to more recent subversives, of many nationalities, not to speak of the criminal classes, who are out to make trouble for governments. The exploits of 161 Squadron RAF, for instance, are bound to be of interest to those seeking to smuggle drugs or people by air, and to the police forces that wish to check them. A great many agents and sub-agents in SOE (as in SIS) during the war did not know the title of the body for which they worked, and described themselves simply as working for 'the firm'. Those two words translate into Arabic as 'al Qaeda'. Al Qaeda's world-wide notoriety is thus a sort of back-handed compliment to SOE.

Al Qaeda has introduced the suicide bomber into the security equation, making it a lot harder to solve. Macaulay reminded us long ago that prophecy in politics is the most foolish occupation open to man, so I shall go no farther than to remark how glad I am that I am now too old to bear much responsibility for clearing up this mess.

Chapter 9

Peace by the Quin

In the middle '90s, Mirjam broke it to me that she could stand London no longer. The Suffolk cottage, though a delight for weekends, would not do as a permanency and was too small to hold our books. I was less tied to an office chair than she, who was by then director of preservation at the British Library; could I bear to house-hunt?

We needed to reach easily the new British Library building, just west of St Pancras. We first tried the central Chilterns: enchanting villages, but catastrophic prices. Bedfordshire held out some promise, but not enough. I next tried the north-east corner of Hertfordshire. There, at Therfield, I saw a delicious seventeenth-century half-timbered house, with a For Sale board just up outside it, but was put off by the selling agent's remark that he was only considering offers over twice the amount of money we might have, only. Farther east, at Nuthampstead beyond Barkway, I stumbled on another, originally a mere group of workmen's cottages run together, but run together well. A good wood block floor, an elegantly timbered ceiling, sound thatch, all augured well. A paddock opposite went with it (on condition we never built on it). A surveyor thought it would do.

Mirjam put in an absurdly low offer, well below the asking price. (Thirty years earlier, we heard afterwards, the whole property had changed hands for less than a thousand pounds.) Her offer was accepted. We thought we had sold our London house. The sale fell through at the last minute, and we had an awkward winter owning three freeholds on incomes that would just support two, but pulled through with help from Sylvia Lewin, and found another London buyer next spring. We have lived at Nuthampstead ever since.

A timber expert assured us that the western end of Martins Cottage had been built in the 1630s, apart from a modern lean-to, called locally the outshut (out of which a pony has been seen to walk within living memory). The eastern end dates to the late 1690s, again with a modern porch added.

The deeds do not run back beyond the early nineteenth century. The couple who sold it to us had had two Jaguars, with a double garage for each. One of these garages we converted into a bookstore. By good luck, we had met Bob Cannon, a local builder sound on old houses. Mirjam mentioned we wanted a garage converted to hold books. He began what the army would have called a lecturette. She let him run on for a minute or two, and then said, 'Mr Cannon, I think I ought to let you know that I am involved in writing an international standard for the storage of books and archives.'

Nuthampstead has perhaps a hundred and twenty souls living in it. In the winter of 1944–5, about seven thousand people lived here, for there was an American air base holding four squadrons of B-17 Flying Fortresses that flew off the open ground to the east of the village, beyond the inn. There are now two public buildings, the Woodman inn and a telephone box. Outside the Woodman stand two memorials, one to the 43 fighter and one to the 293 American bomber aircrew who flew out of Nuthampstead and never came back. The bomber aircrew also now have a memorial window in Anstey church, the next village to the south. When it was dedicated, a dozen survivors sang at the service: a moving moment. The bomber group set off, with several others, to stoke up the fires started the night before by the RAF in Dresden in February 1945. Something went wrong with their radar, and they got lost in cloud. When their clocks told them they were nearing their target, a gap in the clouds opened, revealing a sizeable city with an ancient core, and a river running ESE-WNW through it, so they bombed that. It was not Dresden but Prague.

We visited Anstey soon after we arrived, reading in Pevsner that it has a Norman font – indeed it has, a lovely one. Against it leaned a notice inviting visitors not to deface it, initialled by the churchwarden, RWH du B. Those initials I recognised: Roger Houssemayne du Boulay, two years my junior in College, who had gone on to a knighthood and the post of chief of protocol in the Foreign Office. He and his wife, Pile's step-daughter, were pillars of helpfulness to us when we arrived. At the dedication of the memorial window, he remarked that Anstey castle had continued into modern times its medieval role of protecting the church, for when one of the B-17s that had just taken off from Nuthampstead developed immediate engine trouble and crash-landed, heading for the church, it fell on to the ruins of the castle beside it instead.

The neighbourhood, on the easternmost part of the Chiltern ridge, is quietly beautiful, untroubled by tourism. In Nuthampstead three or four little streams start up, and grow into the River Quin, that joins the River Rib a few miles away, which flows in turn into the Lea, and so into the Thames and away to sea. The soil is heavy clay, with chalk not far below – hence oak and beech woods and good crops of wheat. One of the beech woods, Earl's Wood, is said by the Victoria County History to be named after Earl Hugo de Bohun, to whom the Conqueror gave this part of England; local opinion has it that it was planted by one of Alfred's earls. The pace of life is reasonably slow. A little light industry, out of our earshot, stops in the late afternoon. I can sit at my computer and watch the wild deer go by. Our paddock, once the site of the airfield's PX hut, is now leased to a Barkway neighbour, who keeps ponies on it, at which we can look in the intervals of work. Beyond the paddock lie cornfields up to a wooded crest, beyond which there is little between us and the Arctic ice-cap, so north winds can be chill. In the spring the ditches are full of cowslips and primroses, the bluebells are as thick as in Sussex, pheasants stroll about as if the place belonged to them. And all this lies within forty miles of Charing Cross.

We have many more friendly acquaintances here than we did further south – partly perhaps because we are here more constantly. The nearest decent bookshop is in Saffron Walden, across the Essex border; the nearest first-rate museum is the Fitzwilliam in Cambridge, half an hour's drive away, with its occasional matchless exhibitions and a good standing show of pictures, armour and furniture. In Cambridge there are concerts worth attending, as well as a great university with a copyright library, so leaving London has not cut us off from culture. There are several great houses not too far away – Audley End by Saffron Walden, Hatfield, Wimpole, Hinchinbrooke, Knebworth; and the odd ruined castle here and there. Henry Moore's sculptures at Much Hadham are wonderful to see in their field setting (one was stolen the other day by an ignoramus who wanted to flog its copper content). There is Cromwell's birthplace at Huntingdon. Nearer still, at Barkway, is the Barkway Pit, visited by hundreds of geologists, which has made clearer to me than anything else what the last ice age did to the English landscape. At Fowlmere, formerly Foulmire, is an RSPB bird reserve with a kingfisher; Wicken Fen is not too far away; nor is a sometimes floodlit swan-pond at Welney beyond Ely, which in turn has a fine cathedral.

To get to London we drive over six miles to Royston, park at the station if we can, and sit for forty or fifty minutes in a train for King's Cross, just a few yards from the new British Library, into which Mirjam supervised the move of some sixteen million books from eight different sites. She reckoned she could not possibly have done it without the help both of computers and of devoted colleagues. BL then told her she would do three jobs instead of two, and do them from Yorkshire. She bowed out, and was at once snapped up by University College London, which appointed her to a chair in library and archive studies, which she has just left, becoming professor emeritus.

Our nearest shop is in Barley, four miles away over the watershed. Barkway, like Barley on the old road – Pepys's road – from London to Cambridge is our nearer real village. Mirjam provides a quarter of its church choir, and has lately become a churchwarden, but though Barkway has a church, a chapel, a war memorial, a school, a pub, and three garages, it has no village shop. The Tesco superstore on the north side of Royston caters for most of us. I confess that, if I dare use a phrase more common two centuries ago than now, I hardly ever catch sight in Tesco's of a man with whom I would wish to go tiger-shooting. Someone might write a learned article about the role of the supermarket, in place of the hunting field, as the area where social classes now intermingle on terms of equality.

Royston was once prominent: James I and VI had a hunting-lodge there, to pursue boar and deer. He was there when he got news of Gunpowder Plot; it was there too that he signed Raleigh's death warrant. The town, named after an eleventh-century Lady Roysia, has been there much longer. It is at the crossing of Ermine Street, the Roman road from Londinium to Eboracum (along which Hadrian and Constantine must have travelled) and the much older Icknield Way, the drove road from Norfolk to Dorset. Sheep and cattle are no longer driven along the Icknield Way, but I have shaken hands with old Shepherd, Betty Pinney's gardener, who had driven sheep along it as a boy, as his ancestors had done for centuries uncounted. Secure though life here seems to be, it depends on a steady supply of petrol. A severe oil crisis would scupper us, and thousands like us who live in similar semi-isolation. A sturdy Volkswagen keeps us mobile. If another bad oil crisis blows up, we shall have to buy one of Anne Smalley's ponies from the paddock and get a dog-cart, or starve.

Just north of Barkway are two large houses. From one, Cokenach, came James Pigg, immortalised by Surtees as Mr Jorrocks's whip – he had been the coachman there, and was spotted by Leech the illustrator in Barkway church. Opposite Cokenach is Newsells, once owned by the Jennings family who used to share with the Dimsdales most of the local landowning. Its most famous member was Sarah, confidante of Queen Anne and first Duchess of Marlborough. I took for granted a big brown obelisk in Newsells grounds was a memorial to her, till Robert Dimsdale told me that it was put up in the 1870s by Lord Strathnairn in memory of his horse, which had carried him all through the Indian Mutiny – when he was General Sir Hugh Rose – and so earned him his peerage. By chance, Mirjam had already met Robert Dimsdale before we moved here. She was asked at a British Library do to look after the high sheriff of Hertfordshire, who that year was Robert. He chooses not to use his title, but is in fact a baron of the Romanoff peerage, allowed by the Crown to style himself so. Catherine the Great granted the title to his ancestor Thomas, in gratitude for having inoculated her against smallpox.

Our neighbours the Westons (he is a potter and a poet, she an actress) once introduced us to an English friend of theirs with a Dutch husband, called van der Weyden, a descendant of the master-painter, and a painter himself. Striking that the painterly gene should last through so many centuries.

As our twenty-fifth wedding anniversary approached, I thought I ought to buy Mirjam a piece of silver, and went to talk to Garrard's. They still made replica Hester Bateman salvers, and I arranged an inscription for a tiny one, all I could afford, with both our coats of arms impaled on it. Garrard's told me there was a hitch, and referred me to the College of Arms. What the lawyers tell you, that the memory of man runneth not back before the reign of Richard II, is not true: the memory of the College of Arms goes back to Henry II. A disquisition several pages long from a herald informed me that the Romme arms were 'unknown to English armoury'. After expounding what arms gentlemen and their wives are entitled to bear, he slipped in that all that was needed to record them was a cheque for fourteen hundred guineas made out to the Duke of Norfolk. I had the two coats engraved side by side, instead of impaled.

In the summer of 1999 I got a note with a lightly imperative edge from Hugh Verity, the former Lysander pilot, telling me that I was to lunch with him shortly at his club. I jotted '1245 lunch HBV club' in my diary, but forgot to write down whether he had invited me to the RAF Club in Piccadilly or to the Special Forces Club. I looked in at the SF Club at 1215, which left me time to get to Piccadilly if need be; no need, he was already in the bar. I joined him there, and we gossiped over a bottle of white wine. Suddenly the bar filled up with friends of mine, hardly any of them members, with Mirjam at the back of them. They broke it to me that they were preparing a Festschrift for my impending eightieth birthday, in which each of them had written a chapter. The publisher insisted on copy by midsummer, and they doubted whether they could keep the secret any longer. Would I care to lunch with them? I was bowled over with surprise and delight. Ken Robertson had done the editing of *War, Resistance and Intelligence* (published by Pen and Sword Books, 1999), carrying on a long correspondence by e-mail with Mirjam while I was away from home, researching on SOE in the Low Countries, and she was recovering from her first hip replacement and indexing the book. It was a tremendous professional compliment to me to receive essays from several eminent scholars, and the launch party in the ballroom at the Savile on my eightieth birthday was the best party I ever remember. The occasion pleased me even more than an unexpected CBE, to which I was appointed in the new year's honours list for 2001. (The queen signed the warrant in the old millennium, but the year-books all agree to date new year honours from the new year.) The actual investment was entertaining; Mirjam, Sarah and Richard were all there to watch. The show was stolen by the beefeaters, dressed exactly as in Tenniel's *Alice* cartoons, down to the pom-poms on their shoes.

I still sometimes have to go to France for work, as well as for holidays. In March 2003 I was confronted with about a hundred members of the Association des Anciennes Déportées et Internées de la Résistance, wonderful women, most of them survivors of Ravensbrueck in their eighties or nineties, who had to listen to a talk in my bad French about what SOE had been. At question time I made something of a sensation by explaining that the *Prosper* réseau (network) had collapsed because of its inner leadership's insecurity, not because it had been deliberately sacrificed (as many of the French have come to believe) to suit some dark plot hatched by British intelligence.   That September I was in St Malo, lecturing on seaborne cross-Channel support for French resistance. I had last seen St Malo on a bank holiday in 1938 when it was thronged with drunken English tourists, and I had been ashamed to be English. Luckily, this put me back in touch with Peter Minns, Odile de la Varende's husband (she is now dead), whom I had not seen for years.

Templer remarked to me once, near the end of his life, that he reckoned on going to two memorial services a week. Being much less able or well known, I have been luckier, but have to go to them now and again. At short notice, I was paraded to read a lesson (Philippians iv.4–9) at Brooks Richards's memorial service in the Guards Chapel, which was full of people a great deal more distinguished than I am. At the wake afterwards, in the Guards Museum opposite, a stranger whom I did not know from Eve strode up to me, kissed me on both cheeks, remarked, 'You read like an angel', and was swept away in the press before I could find out who she was. Months later I found out she was Brooks's daughter. I still miss Brooks, whom I never knew well but found immensely likeable: my model of the perfectly approachable man.

When his *Secret Flotillas* came out in a new edition – after his death, alas – at the same time as a fresh edition of *SOE in France*, the historical section of the Cabinet Office kindly threw a book launch for both, at the Admiralty. It was in mid-August 2004, so that there was hardly a literary critic present, but there was a fine turn-out of old resisters, including Joan Astley who had been Holland's typist in MI R when the whole clandestine-action show started up, and van Maurik who had trained the lads who disposed of Heydrich, and George Millar himself – blind, in a wheel chair, but *there*. My son Richard whom we had not seen for months turned up, straight off an aeroplane from Chicago, and I was able to introduce him to George, who died, alas again, a few months afterwards.

Opposite Barkway church live the Blounts – she, brought up at Knebworth, was cousin-in-law to Monty Woodhouse, some years my senior in College, who became head of the British secret mission to Greece in 1943. I had to give a talk for a local charity at a marquee in the Blounts' garden about the daily life of British secret agents in the war against Hitler. The audience included a former member of section D, the branch of SIS from which much of SOE grew; an expert on Bletchley; the widow of the head of SOE's Hungarian section; a parachutist from 6th Airborne Division who claimed to have gone on a deeply secret mission to France and back in May 1944; and a former member of SAS whose drop zone in the Forêt de Morvan I had helped choose; as well as the bell-ringers: not an easy body to address. I still now and then get asked to give a view on television, usually about some once secret matter I have written about in the past. This brings odd glances from people in the street, who have seen me on the box in their own sitting-rooms but cannot remember who I am.

Not all these talks are one-sided. The county airfield history group invited me to talk at Sawbridgeworth, a small town near Harlow on the Hertfordshire side of the border, about its role in the secret war. I read up the station's operational record book at Kew, and found only one trace of secrecy – a visit from Colonel Turner. Turner, well known to be a bad man to cross, organized from a corner of the Air Ministry dummy airfields and dummy factories, which between them attracted about a tenth of the bombs the Luftwaffe tried to drop on England in 1940–41 and about half what it dropped on the Normandy beach-head in 1944. Otherwise, there was nothing that I could find; but I was saved from making a fool of myself by an acquaintance who produced a local pamphlet just in time. I found that 2 Squadron RAF, which had limped back from France at the end of May 1940 after losing most of its Lysanders in action, had in fact provided the aircraft for a very early secret landing in France, a flight on 3 September 1940 by its commanding officer to a spot near Tours where he set down a spy. Even in his own log-book he called it a long-range test, and Verity left it out of his authoritative table of secret flights, but history has for once caught up with fact.

Again, I had to go over to Amsterdam – on the sixtieth anniversary of the drop into Arnhem in 1944 – to defend my Low Countries book against a Dutch lawyer who clings to the belief that the Englandspiel was a British deception. Under cross-questioning, he turned out to rely on three small double-cross operations run by SIS in 1942, which I had friends behind the scenes enough to prove, afterwards, had nothing to do with the Englandspiel at all. I sent off a piece to *Intelligence and National Security,* the leading learned quarterly on the subject, which appeared in midsummer 2005, and I hope will finally scotch the long-standing conspiracy theories; as may another piece by me in the same journal, about the death of General Sikorski, which I believe I can prove was accident, and not, as Goebbels would have it, murder. After long delays, this came out in July 2006.

Thanks to a talk years ago at Mirjam's dining-table between Gervase Cowell, then the Foreign Office's SOE adviser, and Sarah Tyacke who became head of the public record office, almost all SOE's surviving papers have now gone public, and research students can do their best to prove Foot and others wrong. Quite often they succeed; and I have just re-done my outline history of SOE as well as the big book on France. The Dies Irae was quite right: *quidquid latet apparebit,* and all sorts of secrets are now coming out, even before the day of judgement. I am often asked, 'Are there any more important secrets to come?', and can only reply that I do not know. I was not privy during the war to ULTRA secret material, and for all I know there are whole categories of secret yet to be thrown open to the credulous. Trevor-Roper was fond of another Latin tag, *vulgus vult decipi, et decipiatur.*

Mirjam and I foresee a time when the university library at Cambridge, rather than BL, will suffice for such needs as we have. Peter Fox, the librarian, is a friend. Mirjam knows most of the Cambridge college libraries well, from past work on their bindings, had position enough in the library world to be invited at once on to the committee of the friends of CUL, and soon found herself asked to deliver the Sanders lectures on bibliography, a task triumphantly performed in March 2003 and put into published print two years later.

The SAS regimental association sent me to Brittany in June 2004 to lay some wreaths in memory of a very early casualty of NEPTUNE, the assault phase of OVERLORD: a French SAS corporal, Emile Bouétard, whom I had seen emplane at Fairford. He was dropped too close to the Wehrmacht by mistake, and shot by some Georgians in German uniform shortly after midnight on 5/6 June 1944. A minister from Paris gave an admirable pep-talk on the SAS virtues of speed and courage, as they apply in the war against terrorism, and ten professional parachutists appeared, one by one, out of cloud to land in a space half the size of a tennis court. The village children then sang the 'Chant des Partisans' – not, I think, aware that Maurice Druon and Joseph Kessel had compiled it in the comfort of armchairs at the Savile, to which Druon still belongs. We were then given a splendid meal.

By a stroke of luck, I sat next to Druon at a Savile luncheon for elderly members, and mentioned to him the troubles I was having about getting *SOE in France* translated into French. (The Foreign Office banned an excellent original translation, now lost, but relented when I prepared a fresh edition.) Jean-Louis Crémieux-Brilhac, who had worked alongside Druon in London during the war after an extraordinary eastabout escape and a spell in a Russian concentration camp, had been beavering away for me for months, purely out of good will, but had not yet got far. Druon too took up the cause when he got back to France, with the extra prestige that attaches to *membres de l'Académie*, and at last I have signed a contract with Editions Tallandier. Retitled *Des Anglais dans la Résistance*, it now exists as a book, and I hope will make some impact in France.

Through Arnold Rosen, a solicitor member of the Reform, I have got involved with a society of members of that club, called Cryptos, which meets once a month or so to discuss subjects bearing on intelligence and strategy. In 2004 I gave them a talk on my own wartime experiences as an intelligence officer – I thought it rather low-grade material, but they were enchanted by it, so much so that they thereupon gave a dinner in my honour, at which I had to make an after-dinner speech, nowhere near my long suit.

Out of the blue, I was summoned to the French embassy and created a Chevalier of the Legion of Honour, in company with several other survivors of the Normandy landings of 1944. I had never thought, when I worked on Boney in the nineteen-thirties, that I would ever feel grateful to him for anything, but have now changed my mind. Proust's Swann altered his will, to provide that he should be buried with the full military ceremonial due to such a chevalier. I shall not bother my executors with any such provision, but remain proud of such distinction as it conveys.

Chris Andrew, the historian of secret service who created in Cambridge a centre for intelligence studies, Donald Cameron Watt at LSE and Kenneth Robertson at Reading joined with me in 1982 in setting up a study group on intelligence, which is still in working order, meets two or three times a year, and usually manages to produce some old hand with knowledge of some hitherto unrevealed past secret crisis, who can be paired with a young blood of intelligence analysis eager to try out some new idea. I have been able to produce for them a few stars of the secret war against Hitler, such as Tony Brooks, the railway saboteur, Jeannie de Clarens who was R.V. Jones's 'Amniarix', gave us our earliest news of the doodle-bug bomb, and survived Ravensbrück, and Baron Louis d'Aulnis who survived two years as a spy in Holland. Chris is now president of Corpus as well as professor in his university, and runs a fortnightly graduate class which I can now and then attend. This keeps me in touch with subjects I still write and review on, and introduces me to some of the up-and-coming figures in this burgeoning academic growth industry.

Uncle Jack's papers are now in Churchill College archive. A brief reconnaissance of them in summer 2002, as I finished revising *SOE in France*, indicated that they ignore our branch of his family. No wonder. All the same, they may not be useless for my next book, a politico-military history of the rise and fall of liberal England, running from Waterloo to the Somme. To assist that, I have done a little work in the royal archives at Windsor, which are kept at the top of a flight of a hundred and three steps inside Wyattville's round tower. One morning, a door at the top was open, and I stepped out on to the parapet, to find that the tower is encircled with cannon – six-pounders, I should think – bearing the cipher of Charles I. Ramrods and sponges stand in a rack near the book where visitors have to sign in. I got blank looks from the ladies on the staff when I ventured to inquire one morning, when they had invited me to coffee, on which day they did their gun drill.

Since the old stone age, old men have been complaining that the young have no respect for their elders, and that the community is going to the dogs. I try hard in my late eighties not to follow in their footsteps, but have one proof of degeneration so clear that I must record it. At Paddington station there used to be a good life-size bronze statue of Isambard Kingdom Brunel, who laid out the line from there to Bristol. Brunel has now been sent down; in his place there is a larger-than-life bronze of Paddington Bear.

As I get older, I get more decrepit: by now I wear hearing aids, have had a cataract removed from each eye, have two artificial knees, and have a fight impending with cancer. Twenty-odd years ago, a GP recommended to me "Die *with* your cancers, not *of* them", advice I shall do my best to follow, but nothing is more boring than other peoples' illnesses, so this book must now stop.

Index